The Book of the
KING 4-6-0s

John Jennison

Irwell Press Ltd.

Copyright IRWELL PRESS LIMITED

ISBN 13 978-1-911262-20-6

First published in the United Kingdom in 2018
by Irwell Press Limited, 59A, High Street, Clophill,
Bedfordshire MK45 4BE
Printed by Akcent Publishing, UK

Contents

Taken from a footbridge at Saltram Park, Peter Kerslake's picture shows Laira's 6008 KING JAMES II with the 'Cornish Riviera' crossing the River Plym at Marsh Mills, just east of Plymouth, building up speed for the forthcoming ascent of Hemerdon Bank which lies just ahead. The driver appears to have opened the regulator following the easy drop down to sea level from North Road station past Laira shed a mile or so back. P. Kerslake/www.rail-online.co.uk

4

Introduction and Acknowledgements

The Kings were the final development of the Churchward four-cylinder 4-6-0, stretched to the very limits of the loading gauge. Many people have asked why this, the premier Great Western Railway express passenger class, had not been covered in the 'Book of' series when books had been devoted to the humble pannier tanks and the 'lesser' 4-6-0 classes. The answer lies partly in the mists of time - in the previous millennium when Irwell Press published *Peto's Register* on the Kings in 1995. Although it has stood the test of time quite well, it was thought the material should be dusted down, refurbished and re-invigorated with a generous helping of new pictures to take its rightful place at the head of the GWR 'Books of'.

The Chairman of the Great Western wanted the most powerful express engines in the country, and the successors to the Castle were designed to achieve this. His publicity department, never shy of trumpeting the company to the outside world, took full advantage of its new engines and pressed its claim, both at home and to the world via a trip to the USA. They even produced a book titled *The 'King' of Railway Locomotives* and details taken from several of its chapters have been included as a fascinating contemporary account of the building of the engines.

As befits their status, the Kings attracted much attention from the enthusiast community from first to last, and many column inches have been devoted to their workings in both contemporary and historical journals and magazines. In particular, the details of pre- and post-war diagrams compiled for the *Great Western Railway Journal* have been included in the chapter on operations.

The detailed material from the Engine Registers forms the basis of the Record section, but has been both simplified and, at the same time, expanded. To do proper justice to the subject, many tens of photographs have been included. Particular thanks go to Rail-Online and Rail-Archive Stephenson for allowing me to use their pictures, to Peter Kerslake who took a number of the 1950s photographs and provided details for many of the captions, and to the two Richards, Abbey and Derry, for their help in finalising the manuscript and tables. In particular I must thank Eric Youldon for help in finalising the text and captions.

REFERENCES
In addition to examining material held at the National Archives, I have also consulted a number of magazines including *The Railway Gazette*, *SLS Journal*, *The Railway Observer*, *The Railway Magazine* and the *Great Western Railway Journal*.

Three Kings at Laira, though the photographer's notes show that there were ten on shed that day! 6004 KING GEORGE III, nearest, is probably booked for the 4.10pm to Paddington, and from the faint '605' on the smokebox door looks as though it has recently worked the 8.30am to London. In the centre, with '665' chalked on its smokebox door, is Old Oak's 6012 KING EDWARD VI ready for the 3.45pm 'North Mail' (the 12 noon from Penzance) which it will take to Bristol Temple Meads. Furthest is Laira's 6023 KING EDWARD II with the 'Cornish Riviera' headboard, which will be the first of this trio to come off shed for its non-stop run up to Paddington. P.Kerslake/www.rail-online.co.uk

The Kings were initially referred to as 'Super-Castles'. The design incorporated the salient features of the Stars and Castles, albeit enlarged to the absolute limits and therefore departing from almost every standard Swindon dimension. The GWR General Manager, Sir Felix Pole, had instructed CME Charles Collett to design a new type of express engine which, if necessary, went to the absolute limit of permitted axle-weights. In order for the new engine to have the title of the 'most powerful' locomotive, Pole apparently told Collett to ensure that the 'Super-Castle' should have a tractive effort of no less than 40,000lb. Since the preliminary design already incorporated the largest possible boiler and cylinders, the diameter of the driving wheels was reduced from the GWR standard 6ft 8½in to 6ft 6in to break the 40,000lb barrier. The bogie was of the plate-frame type, but the advanced positioning of the inside cylinders left insufficient room for overhung springs between the leading bogie wheels, and so it was necessary to use outside springs, axleboxes and frame-plates for the bogie's leading axle. The rear bogie axle, however, incorporated inside springs and bearings, features dictated by the position of the outside cylinders. Another consequence was that the bogies were fitted with 3ft diameter wheels, instead of the standard 3ft 2in.

1. 'The Super-Castles'

The Great Western Railway had been relatively unaffected by the 1923 grouping and was therefore able to perpetuate long established policies and practices. One field in which continuity was clearly seen was that of locomotive development, the company being able to follow the principles which George Jackson Churchward had established to such good effect in the early 1900s.

The GWR's said continuity of locomotive development is, perhaps, best illustrated by its four-cylinder 4-6-0s. The design of Churchward's Star class of 1907 was updated and enlarged by Charles Collett for the Castle class, which made their debut in 1923. Apart from the logical upgrading of certain components, that design was largely unaltered when the last Castle was

completed twenty-seven years later. Furthermore, the basic Castle design was itself enlarged – albeit with important alterations to many of the principal dimensions – for what became the Great Western's flagship locomotives, the King class.

In order to understand why the Kings were developed, one needs to go back to the introduction of the Castles in 1923. As had been intended, the Castles took over many of the company's principal express workings. Much was expected of them but, during the first two or three years of their existence, performances sometimes disappointed. This caused no little concern in the GWR Traffic Department, as their sights had already been set on train loadings and schedules which, to many observers, seemed rather

adventurous. Nevertheless, in the mid-1920s a degree of increase in the weights of the trains was definitely on the cards, and something more powerful than the Castles was required. To many, a Pacific seemed the logical option, but the Great Western had only recently dispensed with the less-than-successful 111 THE GREAT BEAR.

As for the problem of even heavier train weights, the need for quick action ruled out the development of a completely new type of locomotive and so the GWR's only sensible option was a more powerful 4-6-0. That, however, presented one particularly difficult problem. Such a design would inevitably necessitate an increase in axle weight, and the axle weights of the Castles were already within a hair's breadth of the 20-ton limit permitted by the Civil

A new boiler was designed for the Kings, designated Standard 12 (coded 'WA') and incorporating a standard 16-element Swindon superheater. Tapered and domeless, it was 16ft long and its outside diameters tapered from 6ft to 5ft 6¼in (1ft 2in longer than a Castle boiler, and between 3in and 4¼in larger in diameter). The boiler had a working pressure of 250lb per sq.in - the highest used on any conventional locomotive in Britain up to that time.

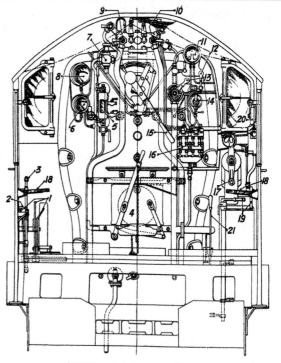

ARRANGEMENT OF FOOTPLATE FITTINGS:
G.W.R. "KING" CLASS LOCOMOTIVE.

In its issue for 15 July 1927, *The Locomotive* commented that 6000 had a '...new pattern cab with an extended roof which was '...roomy and well protected while the various fittings are very well arranged'. It was also noted (see below) that 'A novelty is the arrangement for carrying the fire irons alongside the firebox'. Oddly the vertical slot opening for the fire iron (visible on the left above) was omitted from the drawing.

1. Damper controls.
2. Coal-watering cock.
3. Exhaust injector control.
4. Firehole doors.
5. Water gauge.
6. Steam-heating pressure gauge.
7. Steam-heating valve.
8. Boiler steam-pressure gauge.
9. Exhaust injector live steam valve.
10. Right-hand injector live steam valve.
11. Vacuum gauge.
12. Ejector steam valve.
13. Ejector air valve.
14. Blower valve.
15. Regulator handle.
16. Lubricator.
17. Reversing handle.
18. Tip-up seat.
19. Sanding-gear levers.
20. Audible signalling apparatus.
21. Cylinder cock lever.

Engineer. The fact that the Castles (and their proposed successors) were well-balanced four-cylinder locomotives, with a proportionately low hammer-blow, counted for little at first.

Investigations were made by the GWR General Manager, Sir Felix Pole, and they revealed that all new bridge work had, for some time, actually provided for a maximum axle-weight of 22½ tons. Indeed, on the Paddington-West of England main line, by the end of 1926 only four bridges were still subject to the old 20-ton limit. Pole therefore ordered the upgrading of those four bridges and, simultaneously, he instructed his CME, Charles Collett, to design a new type of express engine which, if necessary, went to the absolute limit of permitted axle-weight.

The order for twenty 4-6-0s (albeit of an unspecified class) was ratified by the

Locomotive Committee on 17 December 1925, at an estimated cost of £120,000. On the same day as the order for the new 4-6-0s was placed, authorisation was given to condemn ten Atbara and ten City class 4-4-0s, valued at a total of £92,300.

The new 4-6-0s were initially referred to as 'Super-Castles'. The design incorporated the salient features of the Stars and Castles, albeit enlarged to the absolute limits and therefore departing from almost every standard Swindon dimension. The necessity to go to the limits was due partly to Sir Felix Pole's directive and resulted in high capital costs for new patterns and tools, much of which could have been avoided if the design had not been required to exceed 40,000lb tractive effort. The explanation lies, at least partly, in factors other than the strictly engineering or operational...

To many of the public, a locomotive's tractive effort was all-important. The railway companies were well aware of the public fascination with tractive effort figures and there was much prestige to be gained from a locomotive with a very high 'power' of this sort. Naturally, this was not ignored by the GWR – indeed, it was the GWR itself which, earlier in the decade, had put so much emphasis on tractive effort figures – and no little satisfaction was gained from the fact that the proposed 'Super-Castle' would have the highest tractive effort of any British passenger locomotive. Since August 1926, the Southern Railway's Lord Nelson 4-6-0s had claimed the title of Britain's 'most powerful passenger engines' (on the contentious basis of tractive effort) but their 33,510lb would be comfortably beaten by the Great Western's new

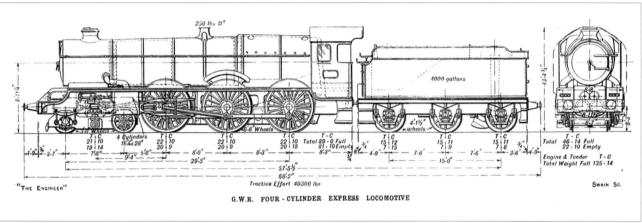

G.W.R. FOUR - CYLINDER EXPRESS LOCOMOTIVE

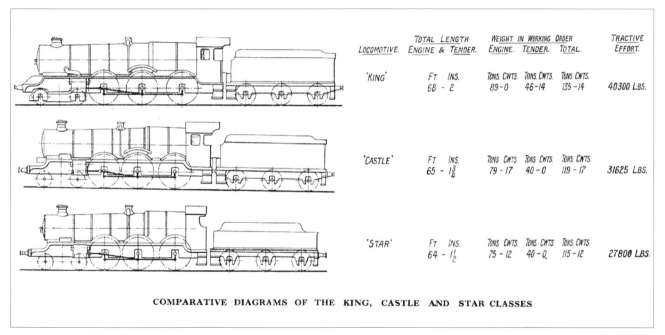

LOCOMOTIVE.	TOTAL LENGTH ENGINE & TENDER.	WEIGHT IN WORKING ORDER			TRACTIVE EFFORT.
		ENGINE.	TENDER.	TOTAL.	
'KING'	FT. INS. 68 - 2	TONS. CWTS. 89 - 0	TONS. CWTS. 46 - 14	TONS. CWTS. 135 - 14	40300 LBS.
'CASTLE'	FT. INS. 65 - 1¾	TONS. CWTS. 79 - 17	TONS. CWTS. 40 - 0	TONS. CWTS. 119 - 17	31625 LBS.
'STAR'	FT. INS. 64 - 1½	TONS. CWTS. 75 - 12	TONS. CWTS. 40 - 0	TONS. CWTS. 115 - 12	27800 LBS.

COMPARATIVE DIAGRAMS OF THE KING, CASTLE AND STAR CLASSES

Statistics do not lie – the King produced a 45% increase of tractive effort over the Star and 27% over the Castle, although the engine weight was less than 20% above that of the earlier designs.

engine. However, even before construction of the first 'Super-Castle' had begun, the obsession with the tractive effort figure would have a major influence on the design of the new engines. By late 1926 it was known that the LMS had a powerful express passenger locomotive in the planning stage, and also that Gresley was planning experiments with higher boiler pressures for LNER locomotives. Rather than see the Great Western lose out, or even be subjected to a close challenge

for the 'most powerful' title, Sir Felix Pole apparently told Collett to ensure that the 'Super-Castle' had a tractive effort of no less than 40,000lb.

Collett's preliminary design already incorporated the largest possible boiler and cylinders, and so, to break the 40,000lb barrier, the diameter of the driving wheels was reduced from the Great Western standard 6ft 8½in to 6ft 6in. In conjunction with the other principal dimensions, this resulted in a tractive effort of 40,300lb. It must be

emphasised once again that the decision to use tractive effort figures to denote power was one chosen by the railway companies themselves. The use of these figures was, at the very least, questionable, but perhaps the companies felt that it would be unkind to confuse the general public with such mysteries as drawbar brake horsepower and the like. Unsurprisingly, *The Engineer* in its issue of 1 July 1927 started off its description of the new engine, 'It is noteworthy through having the greatest

Three generations of GWR express locomotives at Old Oak Common in 1928 demonstrate how far Collett had enlarged Churchward's basic 4-6-0 design. From Left to Right, 6000 KING GEORGE V, Castle No 5010 RESTORMEL CASTLE and Star 4004 MORNING STAR. W.J. Reynolds/Rail Archive Stephenson

tractive effort of any express locomotive in Great Britain, the drawbar pull being 40,300lb at 85 per cent of the boiler pressure'. In August 1927, *The Railway Magazine* headed up its own description as the 'New 'Super-Castle' Locomotive'.

Returning to more pertinent matters, the design of the 'Super-Castle' included, of course, four cylinders, but these were 16¼in x 28in compared with the 16in x 26in of the Castles. Cylinders with 30in stroke had previously been used on two-cylinder GWR locomotives such as the Saint class 4-6-0s and the 28XX and 47XX 2-8-0s, but Collett fought shy of using

such a lengthy stroke where inside cylinders (and crank axles) were involved. According to O.S Nock in *The GWR Stars, Castles & Kings*, only the first six engines were built with cylinders bored out to 16¼in, and those on 6006 onwards were 16in which, of course, would increase when re-bored during overhaul.

A new boiler was designed, designated Standard 12 (coded 'WA') and incorporating a standard 16-element Swindon superheater. Tapered and domeless, it was 16ft long and its outside diameters tapered from 6ft to 5ft 6¼in

(1ft 2in longer than a Castle boiler, and between 3in and 4¼in larger in diameter). The boiler had a working pressure of 250lb per sq.in – the highest then used on any conventional locomotive in Britain – with a firebox 11ft 6in long. The original intention was that the 'Super-Castles' should be named after cathedrals. Indeed, it has been suggested that TRURO CATHEDRAL was earmarked for the first of the class (with subsequent names working up from the west, perhaps?) but there is no firm evidence to support that theory. Also, there were only around

10

fifteen cathedral cities in the area served by the GWR – not enough local' names for the whole class.

Whatever the case, the issue of a name theme for the 'Super-Castles' was effectively settled in 1927 when the first engine under construction was booked for a visit, in August of that year, to the United States of America. It was considered that, as the engine would act as an ambassador for British engineering, nothing could be more patriotic than naming it after the reigning monarch.

The GWR had to obtain royal permission to use the monarch's name, and the company's formal request was accompanied by an artist's impression of the engine. This drawing was, apparently, retained at Buckingham Palace, and it is alleged that a visiting representative from the Royal College of Heralds saw the picture and objected to the use of the garter emblem in the GWR's coat of arms; in heraldry, the garter was reserved for those holding the Order of Chivalry 'Knight of the Garter'. That story is uncorroborated;

however, shortly afterwards the Great Western changed its livery, this time omitting the garter.

Livery problems aside, with the name KING GEORGE V agreed on for the first engine, the class as a whole became known as 'Kings'. The subsequent plan was that they would carry the names of English kings in reverse chronological order and so ensure that generations of enthusiasts could impress their parents and teachers with their knowledge of the monarchy. In order to avoid confusion, ten of the

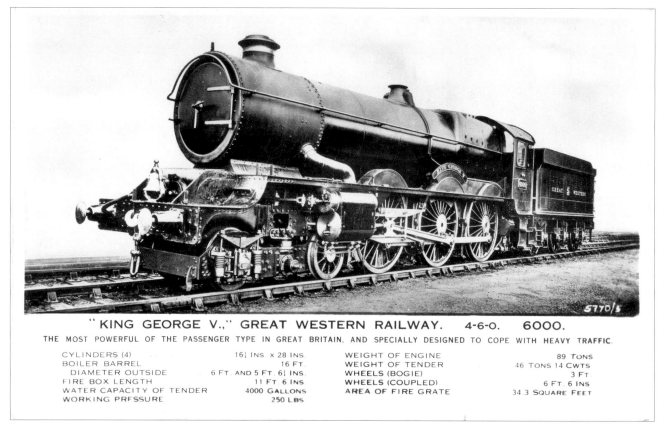

"KING GEORGE V.," GREAT WESTERN RAILWAY. 4-6-0. 6000.

THE MOST POWERFUL OF THE PASSENGER TYPE IN GREAT BRITAIN, AND SPECIALLY DESIGNED TO COPE WITH HEAVY TRAFFIC.

CYLINDERS (4)	16¼ INS. x 28 INS.	WEIGHT OF ENGINE	89 TONS
BOILER BARREL	16 FT.	WEIGHT OF TENDER	46 TONS 14 CWTS
DIAMETER OUTSIDE	6 FT. AND 5 FT. 6¼ INS.	WHEELS (BOGIE)	3 FT.
FIRE BOX LENGTH	11 FT 6 INS	WHEELS (COUPLED)	6 FT. 6 INS
WATER CAPACITY OF TENDER	4000 GALLONS	AREA OF FIRE GRATE	34.3 SQUARE FEET
WORKING PRESSURE	250 LBS		

The Great Western publicity machine went to town with the new engine. This postcard proclaims KING GEORGE V as 'The most powerful of the passenger type in Great Britain, and specially designed to cope with heavy traffic'.

Seven Kings lined up outside Swindon Running Shed on 2 July 1930, with from left to right 6005, 6008, 6017, 6020, 6022, 6023, 6024. The last three only entered traffic at the end of June and had not yet been formally allocated to their first sheds.

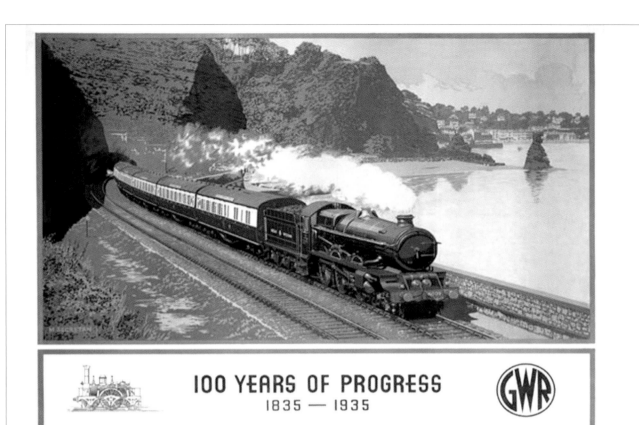

The Kings naturally featured on the GWR posters of the day. This 1935 one shows the classic sea wall setting with the train emerging from Coryton Tunnel, the second of five on the Down line between Dawlish and Teignmouth.

The size and power of the Kings is to the fore on this late 1930s travel poster for the USA market. The featured engine is 6028 KING GEORGE V1.

A brand new 6011 KING JAMES I in April 1928 showing the original design of inside valve covers and the straight top feed pipes used on 6000-19. The polished cylinder covers and driving wheel bosses continued up to the outbreak of war in 1939; thereafter they were painted black. The upper lamp iron is still on the top of the smokebox; as noted elsewhere more than once, from around 1932 these were re-sited on the smokebox doors where they were easier to reach and the lit lamps were not so vulnerable to wind eddies.

Star class, 4021-4030, had their 'King' names promptly changed to 'Monarchs'. Furthermore, in deference to the new engines, Bulldog class 4-4-0 3361 lost its name of EDWARD VII and Duke 4-4-0 3257, quite unnecessarily, lost its name of KING ARTHUR.

The first of the class, 6000 KING GEORGE V, emerged from Swindon Works in June 1927 – it was fitted with its ATC equipment (at Swindon) on 29 June. The engine's completion date had originally been scheduled for September, but the opportunity to send it to America necessitated a swifter completion than had been envisaged. The new engine cost £6,383 to construct, of which £1,699 was accounted for by the boiler. The ATC equipment is believed to have cost an additional £44. The 4,000-gallon Collett tender – 2389 of Lot A113 – was priced at £1,163,

although the tenders for the next five Kings were priced a little lower at £1,036 each. The price difference was presumably accounted for by 6000 being necessarily fitted with different braking and coupling equipment for its forthcoming American trip. The principal dimensions of the new engine compared with its predecessor Castles and Stars (both as originally built) were, *below*.

The outside cylinders drove the intermediate coupled axle and the inside cylinders drove the leading axle; the inside connecting rods had forked big-ends fitted with gibs and cotters while the outside rods had solid bushed ends. In view of the locomotive's lengthy wheelbase, the rear axle was permitted a degree of side play.

The bogie was of the plate-frame type, the earlier Churchward-style bar-frame bogies having developed an

occasional tendency to break rivets. On the Kings, the advanced positioning of the inside cylinders left insufficient room for overhung springs between the leading bogie wheels, and although the rear axle had conventional inside springs and bearings, it was necessary to use outside springs, axleboxes and frame-plates for the bogie's leading axle, a feature dictated by the position of the outside cylinders. Another consequence of the restricted clearances was that the bogies were fitted with 3ft diameter wheels, the standard Swindon bogie wheel having previously been 3ft 2in.

In its issue for 15 July 1927, *The Locomotive* magazine commented that 6000 had a '...new pattern cab with an extended roof' which was '...roomy and well protected while the various fittings are very well arranged'. It was also noted that 'A novelty is the arrangement for carrying the fire irons alongside the firebox...the damper gear, too, is of a somewhat refined type'.

Five more engines, 6001-6005, were completed in July 1927 and a further fourteen, 6006-6019, between February and July 1928. All nineteen were built under Lot 243 (as was 6000) at a cost of £6,383 each.

Another ten Kings were constructed between May and August 1930, 6020-6029, built under Lot 267 and costing £6,172 each (including £1,687 for the boiler). The tenders of 6020 and 6021 were priced at £1,014 each, those of 6022 and 6023 at £1,010, and the others at £1,003 each. Another King was nominally built in 1936, but all was not what it seemed. Following a serious accident at Shrivenham in January of that year, 6007 KING WILLIAM III was officially condemned and a replacement built under Lot 309 at a cost of £4,393. The 'new' locomotive, which entered traffic on 24 March 1936, was, however, little more than the original one repaired.

Ignoring the 'new' 6007, the total number of Kings remained at thirty. It might be asked why, as they were such

	King	Castle	Star
Cylinders (4)	16¼in x 28in	16in x 26in	14¼in x 26in
Heating surfaces			
Tubes	2007.5 sq ft	1885.62 sq ft	1988.65 sq ft
Firebox	193.5 sq ft	163.76 sq ft	154.26 sq ft
Superheater	313 sq ft	263.62 sq ft	-
Total	2,514 sq ft	2,312 sq ft	2,142 sq ft
Firebox	11ft 6in long	10ft 0in long	9ft 0in long
Grate area	34.3 sq ft	30.28 sq ft	27.07 sq ft
Boiler			
Barrel	16ft 0in	14ft 10in	14ft 10in
Diameter	5ft 6¼in to 6ft 0in	5ft 1-15/16in to 5ft 9in	4ft 10¾in to 5ft 6in
Pitch	8ft 11¼in	8ft 8½in	8ft 6in
Boiler pressure	250lb per sq in	225lb per sq in	225lb per sq in
Tractive effort (85%)	40,300lb	31,625lb	27,800lb
Driving wheels	6ft 6in	6ft 8½in	6ft 8½in
Bogie wheels	3ft 0in	3ft 2in	3ft 2in
Wheelbase (engine)	29ft 5in (7ft 8in + 5ft 6in + 8ft 0in + 8ft 3in)	27ft 3in (7ft 0in + 5ft 6in + 7ft 0in + 7ft 9in)	27ft 3in (7ft 0in + 5ft 6in + 7ft 0in + 7ft 9in)
Weight full			
Bogie	21 tons 10cwt	21 tons 10cwt	20 tons 4cwt
Leading coupled	22 tons 10cwt	19 tons 10cwt	18 tons 12cwt
Centre coupled	22 tons 10cwt	19 tons 14cwt	18 tons 10cwt
Trailing coupled	22 tons 10cwt	19 tons 13cwt	18 tons 4cwt
Total (engine)	89tons 0cwt	79tons 17cwt	75tons 12cwt
Tender	46tons 14cwt	40tons 0cwt	40tons 0cwt
Tender capacity	4,000 gallons, 6 tons	3,500 gallons, 6 tons	3,500 gallons, 6 tons

powerful engines, the class wasn't expanded. The simple answer is the 22½ ton axle weights, which restricted them to 'full strength' main lines, and thirty engines were sufficient for the heaviest trains on these routes.

Loco	Built
6000 KING GEORGE V	6/27
6001 KING EDWARD VII	7/27
6002 KING WILLIAM IV	7/27
6003 KING GEORGE IV	7/27
6004 KING GEORGE III	7/27
6005 KING GEORGE II	7/27
6006 KING GEORGE I	2/28
6007 KING WLLIAM III	3/28
6008 KING JAMES II	3/28
6009 KING CHARLES II	3/28
6010 KING CHARLES I	3/28
6011 KING JAMES I	4/28
6012 KING EDWARD VI	4/28
6013 KING HENRY VIII	4/28
6014 KING HENRY VII	5/28
6015 KING RICHARD III	6/28
6016 KING EDWARD V	6/28
6017 KING EDWARD IV	6/28
6018 KING HENRY VI	6/28
6019 KING HENRY V	7/28
6020 KING HENRY IV	5/30
6021 KING RICHARD II	6/30
6022 KING EDWARD III	6/30
6023 KING EDWARD II	6/30
6024 KING EDWARD I	6/30
6025 KING HENRY III	7/30
6026 KING JOHN	7/30
6027 KING RICHARD I	7/30
6028 KING HENRY II*	7/30
6029 KING STEPHEN*	8/30
*6028 renamed KING GEORGE VI 12 January 1937	
*6029 renamed KING EDWARD VIII 14 May 1936	

6022 KING EDWARD III at Newton Abbot in 1930 shows the changes introduced on the final ten engines. The top feed pipes are curved and the inside valve spindle casings have been modified. The smokebox door footsteps (added to each engine soon after building principally to improve access to the upper iron) were rendered largely superfluous when the upper lamp irons were re-sited on the smokebox doors, and were eventually removed. www.rail-online.co.uk

6016 KING EDWARD V at Kingswear in the early 1930s. Its straight top feed pipes have been modified to curve behind the nameplate. The Kings were originally painted in the GWR passenger livery of middle chrome green, lined on the cab, boiler bands and tender with eighth inch orange chrome, half inch green, one inch black in the centre, half inch green and eighth inch orange chrome. This was embellished with polished steel handrails and brass and copper fittings; the nameplates were the standard GWR pattern with brass letters riveted onto a steel plate 13 inches deep; the curved part carrying the letters was 6½ inch deep with tubular brass beading. www.rail-online.co.uk

The boiler suspended over the jaws of the hydraulic riveter.

2. Kings in the Making

The GWR published a book in its series 'For Boys of All Ages' to commemorate its new engines, modestly titled 'THE 'KING' OF RAILWAY LOCOMOTIVES – THE BOOK OF BRITAIN'S MIGHTIEST PASSENGER LOCOMOTIVE'. This followed the style of its earlier tome on 4073 CAERPHILLY CASTLE, and in addition to describing the evolution of its design, the 149 page book explained the building of the engines, their principal features, the visit of 6000 to the USA and a trip on the Cornish Riviera. In three chapters entitled 'Kings in the Making', the reader was taken through the stages of construction, with a quite technical description of a number of aspects of the design.

CYLINDERS

First and foremost come the cylinders in which the energy latent in the steam is converted into work. In the 'King' class, the cylinders comprise three separate castings. The two inside cylinders are combined with a saddle supporting the smokebox to form one casting, and the two outside cylinders are cast separately. The steam chests are embodied in their respective cylinder castings and passages are provided in both the outside and inside cylinders for tapping off a certain proportion of the exhaust steam for use in working the exhaust steam injector.

The cylinders are cast from a specially selected close-grained iron, as hard as can be satisfactorily worked. The castings have to be free from blowholes, porous places, and all other defects. The cupola, in which the iron is melted, is a vertical brick-lined furnace which is charged from a platform near the top, with alternate layers of coke, limestone, and a mixture of pig iron and 'scrap', the latter being obtained by breaking up old cylinders.

With the aid of a forced draught, produced by a powerful blower capable of forcing 30,000 cubic ft. of air per minute against a pressure of 20 in. of water, the combustion of the coke produces a heat sufficient to melt the iron, which trickles to the bottom of the cupola, ready to be tapped off through a small hole normally kept sealed by means of a fireclay plug. The limestone acts as a flux and unites with any impurities to form a slag which floats on the surface of the molten mass.

The iron is drawn off from the cupola into huge ladles, from which it is poured into the moulds. To make the moulds, wooden patterns of the cylinders are embedded in special sands contained in strong iron boxes, and the mould left when the pattern is withdrawn is filed with the molten metal. When pouring the metal, the bores of the cylinder, steam chest, etc., are taken up by 'cores' which have to be broken up and removed from the casting when completed. For such a casting as the combined inside cylinders and saddle, no less than twenty cores are required and the moulding box has to be built in four separate portions.

Copper firebox wrapping plate in bending rolls.

A shop at Swindon Works is set aside for the machining and fitting of cylinders. The sides have to be carefully planed, as has also the radiused face of the smokebox saddle. The steam chests are bored to receive the piston valve bushes in a special machine, which deals with all four of the inside cylinder bushes at the same time, thus effecting a considerable saving. The bores of the cylinders and piston valve bushes are brought to their finished dimensions in a large grinding machine. A battery of machines for drilling and tapping the various bolt and stud holes is also included in the equipment of the cylinder-machining shop.

MAIN FRAMES

The main frames of the engines are received from the steel makers in the form of long rectangular slabs some 41ft. 4in. in length, by 3ft. 6in. in width, and 1¼ in thick. These are first of all roughly punched* to shape and, after annealing and levelling, are assembled in lots of eight or ten and machined to the finished dimensions in a slotting machine. The frames are next 'dished' at the leading end in powerful hydraulic presses so as to provide the

Copper firebox set up on jig.

Firebox casing on jig – end view.

Underside of firebox casing.

necessary clearance for the movement of the leading wheels of the bogie. They are subsequently assembled in pairs for drilling.

*Note. A curious term applied to 1¼ in thick steel but there it is!

PISTONS
The piston head is a hollow iron casting of the 'box' type, and is secured to the piston rod by a tapered screw thread and dowel which, though difficult to separate for renewal, preserves a flat face to the front of the piston head and thus enables the cylinder cover to be of strong and simple design. Steam-tightness is secured by fitting the piston head with two piston rings which expand evenly against the cylinder walls as in a motor-cycle engine. The width of the rings is a matter of great importance as, if too wide, they are difficult to keep steam-tight; whilst, if too narrow, they wear

quickly and tend to score the cylinder. The piston rod is kept steam-tight in passing through the back cylinder cover by means of a stuffing box and gland. Three or four turns of a flexible metallic packing covered with graphite paste are pressed into the stuffing box sufficiently tightly to prevent leakage of steam without scoring the rod.

CROSSHEADS
The crossheads are steel castings in which the slippers are incorporated. The faces of the slippers are lined with ant-friction metal held in position by means of corrugations in the face of the slipper. Bronze safety strips are let in so that, should the white metal get hot and run out no damage will be done. A 50-ton press is employed to force the crosshead onto the piston rod and a special broaching machine cuts out the hole for the cotter with the two units so assembled, so securing perfect alignment.

CONNECTING AND COUPLING RODS
The connecting and coupling rods are machined from forgings of the highest quality carbon steel to an 'I' section giving maximum strength with a minimum weight of material. The holes for the bushes at the ends of the rods are ground out to the finished dimensions.

AXLE BOXES
The driving axle boxes are steel castings into which are pressed gun-metal liners with white metal cast on the bearing surfaces. Oil is supplied to the horn cheeks and to the top of the journal by means of pipes leading from oil boxes carried on the frames, and fed to the bottom of the journal by pads saturated with oil and pressed against the journal by springs.

AXLES
The crank axle, on to which the inside cylinders drive, is built up from slabs and rolled bars. The slabs are planed and bored to form the webs and are shrunk on to the bars, which are turned to form the crank pins and shaft. The other axles are straight, the crank pins for the outside cylinders being shrunk into the bosses of the intermediate driving wheels.

WHEELS
The wheel centres are of cast steel and are bored to receive the ends of the axles on to which they are forced with a hydraulic pressure of about 130 tons using a duplex press. A tyre is bored somewhat smaller than the diameter of its wheel centre, and is heated in the gas furnace by a series of gas jets until the diameter has increased to something greater than that of the centre. The tyre is then placed over the centre and allowed to shrink so that it grips tightly. A retaining ring is then hammered down between a lip on the tyre and the rim of the wheel centre in order to hold the tyre in the remote possibility of it ever becoming loose.

The wheels and axle are now taken to a wheel lathe and, after the tyre has been turned to the correct profile, the holes which receive the crank or coupling-rod pins are bored out in a quartering machine. This machine has two heads arranged at right angles so that both wheels can be bored simultaneously and at the correct angle. The wheels and axle finally go to a specially designed machine in which they are correctly balanced at speeds representing 60 miles per hour on the rail.

VALVE GEAR
The piston valves for the inside cylinders are driven directly by Walschaerts' valve gear, which gives a motion compounded of two distinct movements. The principal movement is derived from an eccentric keyed to the axle, and the other movement from a connection taken from the crosshead. These two movements are conveyed one to each end of a combining lever from some intermediate point along which the valve derives its ultimate motion. This gear is adopted because of the relative lightness of

18

Our friend from page 16 spots another photographic opportunity

The completed boiler being moved from the Boiler Shop. The two safety valves are situated on top of the barrel.

Main frames being marked out.

Main frames on trestles for marking out.

Two Kings under construction – the one on the right has the inside cylinders in position and the one on the left has the outside cylinders fitted.

The boiler being lowered on the frames by the 100 ton cranes.

The boiler in position ready for fixing to the cylinder saddle and frames.

Kings in line in various stages of construction.

A King with boiler in its 'suit' of insulating material which prevents loss of heat by radiation. This coating is subsequently covered by thin steel sheets which are finally painted in the Company's familiar green livery. In the foreground of this picture can be seen the frame of another locomotive in course of erection, the cylinders having been already bolted in position, as shown to the right.

its moving parts and its special suitability for high speeds. The motion for the valves of the outside cylinders is derived from that of the inside by means of levers fulcrumed about pivots carried on the engine frames.

LUBRICATORS

The Swindon improved triple sight-feed lubricator distributes oil to the regulator and to the cylinders. The oil contained in the lubricator is displaced through the sight-feed glasses by steam from the boiler, condensing in pipes. The feed to the cylinders is taken through to a combining valve; here the oil is mixed with steam from the boiler and is carried along a pipe to the steam pipes in the smokebox and thence to the cylinders. A valve, operated by moving the regulator handle, is so arranged that oil is fed to the cylinders when the engine is drifting (or 'coasting') and the regulator valve is shut.

THE BOILER

The characteristic feature of the G.W.R. standard boiler is the coning of the barrel. Introduced in 1903 the coning was first restricted to the back barrel plate, but was later extended to the whole length of the barrel in order still further to improve the circulation of the water in the boiler. The tapering of the barrel enables the fullest use to be made of the intense heat in the neighbourhood of the firebox end, and it

minimises the danger of uncovering the firebox crown plates. Steam is collected by means of an internal pipe with upturned mouths situated above the top of the front end of the firebox this ensuring that dry steam only is taken to the regulator or main steam valve. This construction enables the latter to be placed in the smokebox, where it is readily accessible and obviates the need for a steam dome.

FIREBOX

The firebox consists of an inner box surrounded by an outer casing or shell, the two being connected at the bottom by the foundation ring. The inner box is built up from three plates riveted together, the front or tube plate, the back plate, and the wrapper plate. In English locomotive practice copper is invariably used on account of the greater resilience which it offers to the corrosive action of the fire, and its ability to withstand the distortion set up by the high temperatures developed in the firebox. The outer firebox casing is of mild steel and consists of a throat plate, into which one end of the barrel is fitted; a back plate, flanged with the copper back plate to form the Firehole; and a wrapper plate, which is usually in three portions, one crown and two side sheets, riveted together with butt strips.

BARREL

The barrel is built up from two mild steel plates rolled into butt-jointed circular rings riveted together with a circumferential lap joint. The front end is closed by a steel tube plate drilled to receive a large number of steel tubes, 2 ¼ in. in diameter, through which the hot gases pass on their way to the smokebox. The tubes are expanded into the tube plates in order to make them steam-tight and, where there is a risk of corroding deposits accumulating on the projecting ends, are beaded over to reduce the possibility of subsequent leakage.

SMOKEBOX

The smokebox is riveted to the end of the barrel and, with the door, which is of sufficient size to allow the tubes to be withdrawn or cleaned, forms an air-tight compartment through which the products of combustion are drawn on their way to the chimney. After the steam has performed its useful work in the cylinders, it is exhausted through the blast pipe and chimney to the atmosphere. Some of the air contained in the smokebox is carried out with each jet of steam, and, to take its place, air flows in by way of the firebox and tubes. This produces the intense draught necessary for the combustion of the fuel. When starting or when working heavily on an ascending gradient, the volume of steam which is emitted from the blast pipe is so great that it would exert too fierce a pull on the fire, and so an automatic 'jumper' top is fitted to the blast pipe. This 'jumper' lifts when the exhaust exceeds a certain amount and provides an additional exit for the steam, thus softening the effect on the fire.

A spark arrester is fitted in the smokebox to induce an even draught through all the tubes, as due to the position of the blast pipe top, there is a tendency for an excessive draught to be created through the top tubes. This plate gives the gases a downward trend, with the result that any ash drawn through the tubes is deposited in the bottom of the smokebox, so preventing sparks being thrown from the chimney.

At the base of the chimney is a combined blower and ejector exhaust ring. The blower portion directs live steam from the boiler up the chimney, through a series of inclined holes drilled through the inner wall of the ring, thus assisting the action of the blast. The blower is, of course, only required under exceptional running conditions or when it is necessary to raise steam quickly in the shed.

The regulator box containing the main steam valve and its 'jockey' or pilot valve is fixed at the top of the tube plate and controls the amount of steam admitted to the cylinders. The pilot valve not only permits of a very gradual admission of steam, but also facilitates the opening of the regulator as, with the full steam acting on the valve, it is almost impossible to open the main valve directly.

The superheater is also located in the smokebox and consists of two chambers within one casting. Saturated steam – that is, steam in contact with the water from which it is produced – is picked up by the upturned mouths of the main steam pipe in the boiler and, passing through the regulator pipe, is then admitted to one chamber of the superheater header, from which it passes into the superheater tubes which are surrounded by hot gases. The steam is here superheated above the temperature of that in contact with the water and it returns to the other chamber of the header, from which it is distributed to the steam chest and cylinders.

CONSTRUCTION

Hydraulic flanging of both steel and copper plates has always been a strong feature of Swindon practice and one of the first steps in boiler construction is the preparation of the blocks and dies in which the various shapes are pressed. The blocks are of cast iron and are machined to the finished dimensions so that it is unnecessary to correct the shape of the plates after pressing. A particularly good example of hydraulic flanging is that of the front casing or throat plate. This is made from ¾ in. mild steel plate and is pressed out to the finished form in one heat. Reduction in the number of heats means not only economy in the cost of manufacture, but also a minimum of distortion in the material. Before being used the blocks are warmed up in order to avoid

any sudden chilling of the plate as the two come in contact.

Two presses are provided in the boiler shop; the larger of the two deals with the heaviest classes of flanged plate work, while the smaller is used principally for flanging smokebox tube plate and for levelling smokebox rings. Operating at a pressure of 1,500 lb. per square inch, the larger press exerts a total pressure of 650 tons, and the other a pressure of about 200 tons.

The heating of the plates preparatory to pressing is carried out in either of two furnaces, the larger of which is coal fired and the other gas fired. The plates are manipulated mechanically when charging and discharging the furnaces with considerable saving in labour and time, besides enabling the work to be carried out with a minimum of physical discomfort to the workmen.

After having been in the press, the rough-edged flanges of the steel plates are trimmed to the correct finished dimensions by an oxy-coal gas flame cutter. For this operation the plates are secured on a specially arranged table which can be adjusted to suit any of the standard plates. The copper plates are trimmed in horizontal band-sawing machines, the band-saw being supported in hardened steel guides carried on adjustable sliding brackets which permit of any sized plate being dealt with.

The barrel and wrapper plates are marked out to templates, the outline of the steel plates being cut by portable oxy-acetylene flame cutting machine. The stay holes in

Fitting the wheels of a King at Swindon. The partly completed chassis with boiler in place is lifted up by a powerful travelling crane and is lowered on to the wheels on the track beneath. The outer boiler covering of steel plate has in this instance been attached, but the insulation on the firebox has still to receive its protective coating of steel. Note method of lifting by two massive hooks under the buffer beam. Why two lifting holes were ever drilled is a mystery. Only Kings, Counties and Modified halls had them.

The engine lifted for wheeling – the coupled wheels are being run into position.

the crown plates are drilled, together with a few 'tacking' holes along the seams, enabling the plates to be bolted together temporarily in assembling. Where one edge of a plate has to butt against another edge, such edges have to be carefully machined, and you will appreciate that very accurate work is required when, for example, the barrel plates are to fit one inside the other. The copper and steel wrapper plates and the barrel plates are rolled to the correct shape in large bending rolls, three sets of which are used for rolling the plates and one for levelling them. Should the radius which it is desired to roll be smaller than that of the rolls themselves, use is then made of an auxiliary wooden roll placed between the main roll and the plate. The barrel plates are rolled conical throughout their length, but the ends require to be parallel as the rings fit one inside the other. The ends are therefore placed in a press consisting of a central block, the diameter of which is the exact internal diameter of the ring to be pressed, and a series of radial sectors which are pressed inwards with a force of 1,500 lb. per square inch.

The inner firebox and the outer casing are separately assembled on jigs, the plates being held together temporarily by means of the 'tacking bolts' previously mentioned and which can be seen in this picture. These jigs can be adjusted to suit the varying heights and lengths of different fireboxes and as the illustration shows, they incorporate an auxiliary feature in the shape of tubular legs which can be let down to support a platform upon which men may carry out work on the top of the box.

The rivet holes along the seams of the copper firebox are drilled while the box is assembled on its jig, but the outer casing is taken to a special drilling machine. The drilling head of this machine can be raised to any height which the table, to which the casing is secured, is capable of rotating through any angle and also of traversing in two directions at right angles to one another, with such a machine it is possible to drill, the necessary holes however awkward may be the position.

The various plates are next riveted together, the outer casing being riveted in a powerful hydraulic machine working in conjunction with a crane capable of dealing with loads up to a maximum of 30 tons. The throat plate has been removed. This is done in order that the copper firebox, to which the foundation ring has now been temporarily secured, may be placed inside the casing.

The foundation ring is of best Yorkshire iron, 4 in. by 3¾ in. in section, and has to be very accurately machined. The ring is set up on a large milling machine, to which it is secured by duplex jigs so that both the inside and outside surfaces can be milled with only one setting on the table.

When the copper box is placed inside the casing the two are correctly lined up in their relative positions and temporarily secured by means of a few crown stays and bolts.

A master template, with numerous indentations forming points of support for the pointed end of a pneumatic portable drilling machine, is fastened along the centre line of the inside box and from this are drilled the stay holes, the drill passing right through the copper and steel plates in order to ensure

perfect alignment. The holes are subsequently tapped ready to receive the large number of stays which are necessary to support the surfaces of the box.

The barrel is now carefully lined up with the firebox, special gauges being used to ensure correct alignment both laterally and vertically. The two parts are temporarily held in position with a few 'tacking' bolts before the throat plate connection is drilled ready for riveting in a powerful hydraulic machine having a gap 23 ft. in length, so that the whole boiler unit can be dealt with. An overhead crane, which lifts the boiler into position, is operated from the same platform as the riveting rams. Here are photographs of the boiler suspended from its crane over the jaws of the hydraulic riveter and lowered between the jaws to complete the riveting around the 'connection'. Note the size of the boiler compared with the man.

'Foot'-stays and 'palm'-stays, which are connected to the barrel of the boiler, are now put in and the smokebox tube plate is riveted in position, the tubes are inserted from the front end of the boiler and the front and back plates are secured by longitudinal steel stays before the boiler is handed over to the boiler mounters for the fitting of the regulator box, superheater, water gauges, safety valves, etc.

When completed, the boiler is tested under hydraulic pressure to 290 lb. per sq. in, - that is 40 lbs. per sq, in. above its working pressure. It is then further tested under steam to a pressure of 250 lb. per sq. in. The boiler now receives a coat of anti-corrosive paint before being handed over to the erecting shop ready for mounting on the engine frames. The smokebox is not **finally** secured to the barrel until the boiler has been tried in the frames, as the holes in the smokebox are marked off from those in the cylinder saddle casting.

BRICK ARCH

The brick arch extends in an upward direction from just below the bottom row of tubes in the firebox tube plate to about the middle of the firebox. It serves a twofold purpose as, by increasing the length of the passage of the gases, it enables complete combustion to take place before the gases leave the firebox and it also provides a reservoir of heat as the mass of firebrick becomes incandescent. To obtain complete combustion of the coal in the firebox some air must be allowed to enter over the top of the fire-bed and for this reason the Firehole doors are cast hollow so that, even when shut, a warm current of air may be admitted. A deflector plate, fitted inside the Firehole, prevents this additional air impinging directly on the tube plate and thus causing leaky tubes.

FIREGRATE

The firegrate is arranged in sections, each consisting of a number of cast-iron firebars carried on transverse supports. Each bar is cast with lugs at the centre and ends which, acting as spacers, ensure that sufficient air space is provided. The front sections slope downwards towards the front of the firebox and, with the vibration of the engine, assist in getting the coal well forward.

ASHPAN

The ashpan, built up from 3/16 in. steel plate, is secured to the bottom of the foundation ring and is made up in two portions so that, if necessary, it can be readily assembled over the trailing axle, which at this point is shielded from the heat of the fire by an asbestos lagging attached to the ashpan. The four doors provided can be opened or closed from the footplate, and their adjustment enables the amount of air admitted to the underside of the grate to be controlled.

ERECTING THE LOCOMOTIVES

The frames as received from the machine shop are placed on low trestles with their inner faces uppermost, and on these inside faces are marked the more important locating lines, such as those for the centres of the inside cylinders, the inside motion plate, and the saddle casting – also those for the valve gear casting, auxiliary shaft bearings, frame cross-stays and drag box casting. The frames are then turned over so that their outer surfaces are uppermost, and these are marked with the centre lines for the outside cylinders, motion plates, and the box angle irons which support the footplate.

This done, the frame plates are lifted into a vertical position and mounted in adjustable forked stands, six being used for each plate, as it is important that the plates shall not sag under the weight of the many parts which are attached to them. Cross-stays, temporarily bolted into position, ensure that the frames are the correct distance apart.

The next step is to ensure that the frames are dead level both lengthwise and crosswise.

And this is tested by means of a spirit level. Not only have the frames to be perfectly level, but also perfectly square, and, if necessary, one or other of the plates must be moved slightly until the diagonal distance between the centres of the leading horn on one side of the engine and the intermediate horn on the other side is the same, whichever pair of opposite horns is taken. 'Centre-pop' marks are made on the top edge of the frame immediately above the centres of the horns and the diagonal distances between them are tried with long trammels.

The frames are now tested for straightness by trying them over with long straight-edges, and any portions which may be even slightly bent are lightly tapped on the concave face with a 'knobbling' hammer while the opposite face is supported by holding a much heavier hammer against it. By this process the bent portions are drawn into line with the rest of the frame.

With the work so far properly squared and levelled it is possible to set up the trailing cheeks of the leading horns. These are the foundation from which other parts of the engine are set, so it is extremely important that these be correctly fitted. The greatest care is exercised in keeping the cheeks both square and plumb. The front cheeks are set to the trailing cheeks by means of a 'feeler' or gauge thus ensuring that each pair is perfectly parallel.

The inside cylinders and motion plate can now be bolted temporarily in the frames, the correct position being obtained from lines passing through the bore of the cylinders,

The engine lowered onto the coupled wheels.

Construction proceeds on that line of Kings.

through the motion plate, and over a straight-edge so placed across the frames that one edge (that over which the string line passes) coincides with an imaginary line between the exact centres of the leading horns. Before the holes for the bolts which carry the cylinders and motion casting can be broached out to their finished sizes, the cylinders and motion casting must be set so that they are absolutely central with the 'lines' which must themselves be parallel with the top of the frames. The lines must also be at the correct distance from the cheeks of the leading driving horns, and these must be the correct gauge distance from the face of the cylinders.

The valve gear and saddle castings can now be tried in the frames and their positions

determined from that of the inside cylinders. The holes for the carrying bolts are marked off, the castings are removed for drilling, again inserted in the frames (while the holes are broached out), and then temporarily bolted up in order to give the frames sufficient rigidity while the outside cylinders and motion plate are being fitted up. this latter process is very similar to that for the inside cylinders, lines being set through to a straight edge across the centres of the intermediate driving horns, and every care taken to ensure that they are square with the frames as well as central with the cylinders and motion plates. The cheeks of the intermediate driving horns are set from those of the leading driving horns, and here again the greatest care must be exercised in spacing the horns, for this determines the

distance between the wheel centres which, in turn, must be rigidly adhered to, for the adoption of coupling rods with solid bushed ends does not permit of any adjustment afterwards. For similar reasons it is also essential that the face of the outside cylinders shall be the correct gauge distance from the intermediate driving horns, in this case due to the solid bushed ends of the outside connecting rods.

It is owing to the limitations of space with which the locomotive designer is continually confronted, that at this stage a little difficulty is encountered, a portion of the outside cylinders and the valve gear casting are in the same relative position on opposite sides of the frame with the result that, while some bolt holes pass through both the frame and castings, others are 'blind'. The valve gear casting is taken down while the outside cylinder holes are broached from the inside of the frame (the holes in the frame having been previously broached with the valve gear casting in position), and, after taking the cylinders down, the valve gear casting is finally secured with countersunk bolts. In this way the difficulty is overcome. The whole of the castings and cylinders can then be bolted up ready to be passed by an examiner.

With the various angle irons and stays riveted up and the framing practically complete, as much as possible of the motion work is erected before the boiler is dropped on the frames, since there are several details which would be extremely awkward to place after the boiler was in position. The inside cylinder covers are now fitted, together with the motion bars, reversing shaft and brackets, quadrants and auxiliary levers, brake cylinders and reservoirs, brackets and shafts; in fact anything which would prove difficult to get in if left till later on, is fixed at this stage.

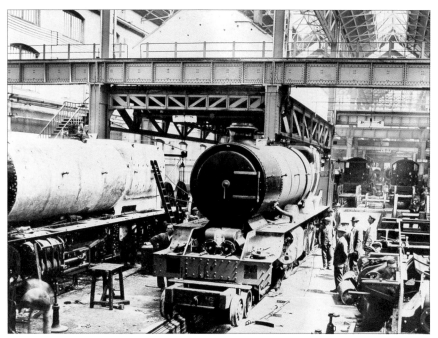

The engine on a temporary bogie ready for valve setting.

Now the boiler can be tried on the frames, the smokebox being held loosely in position ready for marking off from the cylinder and saddle castings. The carrying brackets, which are attached to the firebox casing side plates, are carefully marked off so that not only is the boiler central with the frames transversely, but the centre line of the boiler is also parallel with the top line of the frames. Before finally securing the boiler, it is tried on a second time to check the smokebox holes, and to mark off on the underside of the carrying bracket a groove to house the flat bearing springs which are interposed between the frame and bracket. Were it not for these springs (which are some 8 in. in length), it would be exceedingly difficult to ensure an even distribution of weight on the frames with a firebox as long as that of the 'King' engines.

Although the boiler is firmly secured to the cylinder and saddle castings at the front end, it is necessary to make some provision for its expansion under working temperatures and that consequently the back end must be free to slide. The boiler is prevented from lifting at the back end by the provision of a bracket attached to the frames, which fits over the carrying bracket. Nowadays the ashpan is fitted to the boiler before the latter is 'tried on', instead of assembling it separately over the trailing axle as was formerly the case.

Many parts are now added with a view to wheeling the engine. The axle boxes are fitted in the horns and bedded on the axles; eccentric sheaves and straps are secured in position, and pistons, valves, crossheads, and air pump assembled. Oiling gear and

all such fitments as the exhaust steam grease separator and injector pipe, which would be very difficult to fix after wheeling, are added, and the engine, ready for wheeling, is lifted off its supports by an electrically operated overhead crane capable of dealing with loads up to 100 tons.

The driving wheels are run underneath ready for the attached axle boxes to be guided into the horns as the engine is lowered on to them. The front end of the engine is carried on screw jacks. These are to support the weight of the overhanging until the bogie is placed in position.

Coupling and connecting rods are now erected, and valve gear and reversing gear coupled up ready for valve setting. This operation is of great importance, for the successful running of the engine in service is largely dependent on the correct distribution of the steam to the cylinders. The frames are set to their normal running position and, while valve setting is proceeding, the front end of the engine is carried on a 'dummy' bogie which enables the engine to be moved backwards and forwards as required.

The springs (if not already fitted), cylinder cock and brake gear, injector, cab, smokebox fittings, chimney, and the many other items which go to make the completed engine, may now be put in position. In the meantime, the boiler and cylinders have been coated with a non-conducting composition of magnesia and asbestos, and this, in turn, covered with thin sheet cleating plates. The ejector and hand rails are now fitted, and the painters get busy removing all dirt and grease and then applying a 'priming' coat

to all the surfaces which have to be painted. This is followed by a 'working down' of the surfaces with 'stopping', so obtaining an absolutely smooth surface with all hollows filled up. a coat of lead colour is next applied, followed by the finishing coats of green and 'lining out'. The painted surfaces are then given one or more coats of varnish.

During painting the engine has been lifted at the front end and the bogie run under and secured to its correct position so that the engine can now be weighed and levelled at the correct running height. This weighing is carried out on an ingenious machine which shows simultaneously the weight on each wheel of the engine, and, by suitable adjustment of the springs, the total weight is correctly distributed over the whole wheel base.

The new 'King' is now ready for a short trial run, during which it will be possible to see if the various parts are functioning properly, and to make any small adjustments that may be necessary. It will then be handed over to the Running Department at Swindon and employed for a short time on local trains so that any slight defect which may possibly develop can be corrected before being finally 'passed out' for express passenger train working.

Below. **Approaching completion with cab front and side plates now fitted. Front of engine lifted to allow bogie to be fixed.**

6005 KING GEORGE II reverses out of Paddington with the stock of an express from Plymouth in 1927. It appears to still be coupled to the leading coach and is working out to Old Oak with a station pilot at the front end. In the background is the original Paddington Goods Station which was rebuilt in the late 1920s with longer covered roads. The semaphore signals have not yet been replaced by the colour light signals which were introduced as part of a major modernisation of the station in the early 1930s. F.R. Hebron/Rail Archive Stephenson.

3. At Work

The initial distribution of the first six Kings, four to Old Oak and two to Laira, emphasised the intention to use the class on the high-profile Paddington-Plymouth route, a line which had, over the years, usually been worked by the newest and/or best engines, not least because of the difficult gradients west of Newton Abbot. The Plymouth expresses included the boat trains from Millbay Docks, but the Kings were officially prohibited from the quayside lines. That said, a King was used for a Coronation Day special from the quayside in 1953, albeit with a modest load of just five or six coaches. The Kings' prohibition from the quayside lines at Millbay Docks was just one of many restrictions imposed on the class. Due to their axle weights, for many years they were allowed on only four routes: Paddington-Westbury-Plymouth, Paddington-Bristol-Plymouth, Newton Abbot-Kingswear (which included six miles of single-track line), and Paddington-Wolverhampton.

The Kings' sphere of activity expanded slightly after nationalisation but, along with the big 47XX 2-8-0s, they were the most restricted of all Great Western engines. On official GWR maps, the routes on which the Kings could work were indicated by 'hatched red' lines over the existing 'red' routes. The restriction was shown on the engines by twin red discs, usually referred to as 'Double Red' - on the cab sides. On 6000

KING GEORGE V, the discs had to be painted below the number plate, the usual position above the number plate being occupied by the two medals brought back from America.

As more of the class entered service, they were divided among Old Oak Common, Plymouth Laira, Newton Abbot and Wolverhampton Stafford Road sheds. Intriguingly, the odd-numbered engines in the 6001-6019 series all went to Old Oak, except for 6019 which was at Stafford Road, and the even numbered engines to the south west sheds. Those at Newton Abbot were used principally on trains between Paddington and Kingswear. In later years, the only other sheds to have a permanent allocation of Kings were Exeter between 1939 and 1942, Bristol Bath Road and, finally in September 1960, Cardiff Canton.

Allocation at	1/8/28	1/8/32	1/8/38	1/8/47	1/8/53	1/8/59
Old Oak Common	10	14	14	8	12	13
Laira	8	8	8	13	12	8
Stafford Road	1	6	5	4	6	9
Newton Abbot	1	2	3	5	-	-
	20	30	30	30	30	30

Over There

Given the publicity surrounding the debut of 6000, it was somewhat inevitable that the locomotive would undertake a round of special appearances. It spent the first few days of July on show at Paddington as part of a fund-raising exercise for the Social

and Educational Union – the 'Helping Hands' fund. It then went 'on tour', exhibited to great acclaim, naturally, at Reading, Taunton, Exeter, Newton Abbot, Plymouth and Swindon stations.

As mentioned earlier, even before 6000 had been delivered it had been earmarked for a trip to the United States of America, where it was to participate in the Baltimore & Ohio Railroad's Centenary Exhibition and Pageant, which had the wonderful title of 'Fair of the Iron Horse'. The arrangement for a Great Western locomotive to attend the celebrations had been made as early as 1925; at the Stockton & Darlington centenary exhibition that year Sir Felix Pole had met a representative from the Baltimore & Ohio and, on learning about the American company's forthcoming centenary, Pole had offered to send a GWR engine as an exhibit. At the time, Pole had naturally assumed that the locomotive would be a Castle; little did he realise that the engine would be the first of a much-heralded new class. Prior to its American trip, which was funded by the Baltimore & Ohio, 6000 was fitted with Westinghouse brake apparatus so that it would be able to operate their air-braked stock – the pump was carried on the right-hand side of the smokebox. Its trans-Atlantic trip started at Roath

In 1930, a significant event in the railway calendar was the centenary of the Liverpool & Manchester Railway, and the Great Western was represented at the celebrations by new 6029 KING STEPHEN. www.rail-online.co.uk

KING GEORGE V, fitted with Westinghouse brake pump, on display at Paddington before its USA tour in 1927. The trip was funded by the Baltimore & Ohio Railroad and 6000 was fitted with Westinghouse brake apparatus so that it would be able to operate their air-braked stock. **Rail Archive Stephenson**

Dock in Cardiff on 3 August 1927, where 6000 had been separated into two sections – boiler and chassis – on the quayside prior to being loaded aboard the Bristol City Line's SS CHICAGO CITY. Separation into boiler and chassis was required firstly, because the biggest available crane – sent down from Swindon for the loading – had a capacity of only 70 tons and, secondly, for security of stowage during the voyage.

On arrival in America, 6000 was re-assembled at the Baltimore & Ohio's Mount Clare workshops. It was also necessary to make and fit new coil springs to its bogie, as had been done to the five other Kings following 6003's partial derailment at Midgham on 10 August (see later). Matters in America were supervised by William Stanier who, since 1922, had been principal assistant to Charles Collett. The 'Fair of the Iron Horse' lasted from 24 September to 15 October 1927. 6000 was not the only British representative, the GWR also having sent along a full-size 14-ton replica of Daniel Gooch's 2-2-2 NORTH STAR. To the American public, the two Great Western engines represented not only the company, but all of Britain's railways. It was another triumph for the GWR's well-oiled publicity machine.

6000 was the star of the show, its subtle lines, impressive finish and relative compactness providing a marked contrast to the modern American locomotives which, on the whole, adhered to the 'big is beautiful' school of thought. An American journalist wrote that '...the Great Western Railway of England had easily the most popular exhibit in that triumph of British locomotive design, the King George V...it took me a solid half-hour to get on to the footplate when the pageant was over'. Among the British reports, *The Locomotive* said that KING GEORGE V '....did more than any press or eloquent speakers could accomplish in assuring our cousins that we are far from being down and out. A nation in the doldrums could hardly build and send out such a machine as this'. This was a reference to the economic gloom of mid- and late-1920s Britain.

At the exhibition, all the locomotives paraded on a circular track at Halethorpe, Maryland, seven miles from Baltimore itself. It had been arranged for 6000 to be tested on the 'open road' after the exhibition was over, and on 17 October it made a 272-mile triangular trip from Baltimore to Washington, on to Philadelphia, and then back to Baltimore. The load was six coaches plus a dynamometer car but, due to the American penchant for substantial construction, that ensemble weighed 543 tons.

Despite the crew's unfamiliarity with the route and the poor-quality hard gas coal which produced large amounts of clinker, 6000 performed superbly. It achieved a maximum drawbar pull of 23,700lb and boiler pressure never fell below 200lb per sq in. American engineers who witnessed the trip were positively astounded by the engine's clear exhaust; to them, hard work was usually synonymous with a steady stream of dense black smoke.

6000's departure from America was slightly delayed. The problem, according to the Captain of the SS CHICAGO CITY, was that the only suitable crane at Baltimore was owned and operated by a family concern, a father and his four sons and all five were in jail at the time! For the sake of good PR, the local judiciary released the family temporarily so that the locomotive could be loaded on board the ship. The SS CHICAGO CITY arrived back at Cardiff on 24 November 1927 and KING GEORGE V was re-assembled on the quayside, and returned to Swindon.

6000 had created a lasting impression in America. That was evidenced shortly after its visit when a number of the Baltimore & Ohio's locomotives were treated to copper-capped chimneys! In order to commemorate the visit, 6000 retained the regulation bell which had been attached to its buffer-beam during its test run, although in GWR service the bell was mounted directly on to the front platform, instead of on a block, as had been the case in America.

It had been arranged for 6000 to be tested on the 'open road' after the exhibition was over, and it made a 272-mile triangular trip from Baltimore to Washington, on to Philadelphia, and then back to Baltimore. The bell which was fitted to its buffer-beam to conform with US regulations was, on return to the GWR, mounted directly on to the front platform, instead of on a block, as had been the case in America. It was inscribed:

PRESENTED TO LOCOMOTIVE KING
GEORGE V
BY THE BALTIMORE AND OHIO
RAILROAD
COMPANY
IN COMMEMORATION OF ITS
CENTENARY CELEBRATION
SEPT. 24th - OCT. 15th 1927

There has been much discussion in enthusiast circles about the fate of the original bell, whether it was modified, replaced or is still in existence. An article in the 'Great Western Echo' in 2002 stated that a replacement had been produced in July 1943. Certainly, some of the parts shown in this picture are not present on photographs of 6000 in service, in particular the operating lever on the left and the 'tubing' fastened to the ball on the right. Peter Kerslake recalls that in 1954 the bell was fixed in position without the clapper and had a dull, almost pewter like appearance. After preservation, there is no doubt that another bell was made and photographs of it alongside the 'original' have been published.

The engine also carried two medals fixed to its cab sides - another gift from the American hosts. That said, it appears that the medals were, in fact, replicas of those presented by the Baltimore & Ohio, the originals, which were affixed on the inside of the cab for special occasions, having been stolen in the early 1930s. The bell and the medals remained a distinctive feature of the locomotive, although the former didn't always find favour. It hindered maintenance work on the inside piston valves, and at Laira – where the shed fitters became acquainted (sometimes infuriatingly so) with the engine during the 1940s – the bell was sometimes removed and 'mislaid'. There were, of course, other occasions when it went missing, though these were usually pranks. On the subject of pranks, the bell served another purpose. 'Initiation

ceremonies' for new employees were as common on the railways as in any other industry, and a speciality at Old Oak Common shed was to tell a new fireman that, if he was strong enough to throw a shovelful of coal and hit the far end of the locomotive's lengthy firebox, the bell on the buffer-beam would ring automatically. But, of course, no matter how well the fireman did, the bell did not ring. A senior fireman would then step up to demonstrate what was expected of his colleagues, and each time he threw a shovelful of coal into the firebox, the bell would duly ring. The new fireman was given a second opportunity to prove that he was capable of doing the job for which he had been hired, but no matter how far he threw that coal the bell would not ring. How was it done? A long piece of string had been tied to the clapper of the bell and then run along the outside of the frames to the cab, where the other end was tied to the driver's leg. When a ring of the bell was required, the driver merely gave a little kick of the leg at the appropriate moment.

The American trip had, as already mentioned, been arranged by Sir Felix Pole. After his retirement in 1929 Sir Felix went to live at Calcot Grange, almost alongside the GWR main line just to the west of Reading, and until his sight failed completely he enjoyed watching the trains pass. As a sign of their respect for their former general manager, the crews in charge of the 'Riviera' or a directors' special (usually to Newbury races) would sound the engine whistle as they passed Sir Felix's home. If the

6028 KING GEORGE VI is slowed by the extensive PW work near Reading in the late 1930s. The advertisement on the bridge is for Newbery's Furniture Store which was situated in an imposing building at Friar Street in Reading.

Only four months after it entered traffic, 6003 KING GEORGE IV at Newton Abbot on 24 November 1927. It still has straight top feed pipes and there is no footstep on the smokebox door.

engine was KING GEORGE V, the bell would also be rung.

Although the American trip generated a large amount of positive publicity for the Great Western, it has been suggested that there was a cost. Despite its public status, in ordinary service 6000 was not the best of the Kings – far from it. Until refurbished in the 1950s, KING GEORGE V was considered by some railwaymen to be something of a dud – hot 'boxes were its speciality, and during the 1940s it seemed to spend a fair amount of its life under the hoist at Laira. There was a feeling that the engine's trans-Atlantic trip, which had necessitated a partial dismantling and re-assembly on two occasions and a less-than-smooth on-deck sea voyage, had had a long-term negative effect on the frames. It was

6010 KING CHARLES I waiting in the sunlight to leave Exeter St. David's with a Down express from Paddington, probably in mid-1928. Original features visible are the smooth casing over the inside cylinder block and the polished covers to the inside valve covers with the original spindle end covers. The upper lamp bracket is in its original position above the smokebox with the step providing access to that bracket on the smokebox door. www.rail-online.co.uk

Watched by another lineside lensman, 6004 KING GEORGE III approaches Dainton summit with an Up express in 1929. Note the bullion van at the front of the train. Robert Brookman/Rail Archive Stephenson

also considered that the speed with which the locomotive had been completed – due to its booking in America – hadn't helped.

Back Home
On the West of England main line, the best-known express was, of course, the 'Cornish Riviera' (also referred to as the '10.30 Limited' on account of its departure time from Paddington). This nominally ran non-stop between Paddington and Plymouth, a distance of 225½ miles via Westbury but, in normal service with a train over the prescribed weight, the usual practice was to stop at Newton Abbot to attach (or detach) a pilot engine. For several years a stop at Exeter St. David's was also scheduled, but from the early 1950s it was omitted all year round.

The first King-hauled 'Riviera' was on 20 July 1927, with 6000 in charge as far as Plymouth. The crew were Driver Young and Fireman Pearce of Old Oak – the same men who were to accompany 6000 to America. The train left Paddington loaded to around 425 tons – nine 70ft coaches, a set of articulated dining cars, and two coaches which were slipped at Westbury for Weymouth. *It was brought to a halt by signals four miles out of Paddington, and passed Southall over five minutes late, though KING GEORGE V had managed to accelerate to 60 mph over the five miles since the stop. The crew were also working with a partially failed injector from Acton but, with a very creditable performance, the schedule had been regained by Castle Cary.*

Slough to Exeter was covered at an average speed of 61.3mph, but the

biggest test was on the gradients west of Newton Abbot. After leaving the slip coaches at Westbury the train weight was 350 tons. 6000 nonetheless hauled it with relative ease and, significantly, without assistance, over the South Devon banks into Plymouth, where it arrived five minutes early, against its four hours seven minutes schedule.

At this date, Castles were allowed 288 tons unaided west of Newton Abbot. The loading for an unpiloted King on the South Devon banks was officially set at 360 tons (390 tons on the Kingswear line) but on 22 July, just two days after 6000's well-publicised trip with the 350-ton 'Riviera', 6001 KING EDWARD VII hauled a 400-ton train up Rattery, Hemerdon and Dainton unaided. This paved the way for the schedule of the 'Riviera' to be formally accelerated, as from 26 September, to four hours.

The partial derailment of 6003 KING GEORGE IV at Midgham on 10 August 1927, described later in this chapter, somehow stayed out of the limelight and so, for all the right reasons (for the GWR, at least) the Kings quickly became one of the best-known locomotive classes in Britain – helped enormously by the American trip. The Great Western wasn't exactly shy when it came to milking the publicity, and on 3 November 1927 the company arranged a special excursion from Paddington to Swindon, which included a conducted tour of the works where the already famous KING GEORGE V had been built. No less than 700 passengers bought tickets for the excursion, which was guaranteed to be hauled 'at high speed' in both directions

by one of the Kings. The fare was 5/- (25p), which included the tour of the works. The demand for tickets had, in fact, out-stripped supply, and so another excursion was arranged for the following Thursday, 10 November. This time, *two* trains, both King-hauled, were laid on.

British railway enthusiasts were eager to hear more about the Kings, and it was somewhat inevitable that they would be featured in that time-honoured tradition of railway journalism, *Locomotive Practice and Performance* (known to non-believers as the 'racing pages') in the *Railway Magazine*. The December 1927 issue described a trip with 6005 KING GEORGE II on the Down 'Riviera' in mid-October and compared the King's performance with those of a Star and a Castle in mid-October 1921 and 1924 respectively. The 'Riviera' was at its heaviest in mid-October, the Taunton and Exeter slip portions having been restored after the summer, and the trip with 6005 started with a load of fourteen coaches – 491 tons tare and some 525 tons gross.

It seems that there had been some unusual laxity in the preparation of 6005 at Old Oak, especially as the *Railway Magazine*'s correspondent, Cecil J. Allen, and Chief Locomotive Inspector Robinson were to be on the footplate. The tender contained a considerable quantity of slack ('little better than dust', according to Allen), and despite strenuous efforts by the fireman, by the time Taunton was reached the boiler pressure had dropped from 240lb to 220lb. From then on, the engine was driven with less cut-off than would normally have been applied; indeed, the cut-offs subsequently used were fairly similar to those noted during the trip with a Castle in 1924. Nevertheless, the South Devon banks were climbed with comparative ease (Allen likening the passing of Rattery signalbox to 'running over the gable end of a house') and the train was brought into North Road station at Plymouth nearly two minutes early. Allen remarked that, on inspection at Laira, the engine proved to be perfectly cool in every bearing and was apparently quite fit for an immediate return to London. However, he added that his clothing 'bore no uncertain evidences of the character of the coal which had been burned'.

Another report of a run on the 'Riviera' appeared in 'The Locomotive' magazine on 14 January 1928. This report was of a trip on 21 November 1927, with 6005 in charge once again. Poor quality coal was not a problem this time, and a pressure of 250lb was maintained all the way save for a short stretch near Starcross when it fell to 240lb. The load at the start of the trip was 489 tons tare but, after dropping off the slip coaches, a less daunting 256 tons remained for the Exeter-Plymouth leg. Plymouth was reached one minute inside the four-hour schedule: *...226 miles over a difficult road with a heavy train in under four hours; and this is to the Great Western Railway an ordinary everyday performance*, wrote Douglas Seaton. During the journey 8,300 gallons of water had been used, 6,500 gallons from the four troughs *en route*. Some four and a half tons of coal – a fairly acceptable 44lb per mile – had been consumed.

The latter report on the 'Riviera' trip was far more favourable than the one filed earlier by C.J. Allen. His account generated much debate in the letters pages of contemporary magazines, and there were several suggestions that the effects of inferior coal were worsened by the Kings' boiler design. There was a consensus of opinion that the wider fireboxes used on LNER designs were better suited to varying qualities of coal, but Swindon seems to have been unimpressed. However, as we shall see in chapter 4, this would come back to bite them in the early 1950s.

Pre-war to the West of England

The route to the West of England was, from the very earliest years of the Great Western's existence, the most important and prestigious, and therefore the latest form of motive power was put to work first on its services. When Dean's 4-4-0s began to be replaced by Churchward's new 4-6-0s in the early 1900s, the first batch of the Saint class went initially to the route and were followed a few years later by the four-cylinder Stars, the first ten of which were allocated to either Old Oak Common or Laira.

In July 1906 a new cut-off line to the west via Westbury was opened, which meant that trains to Devon and Cornwall no longer had to travel via Bristol. Limited-stop running between London and the West of England became commonplace, and engines now worked through between London and Exeter, Newton Abbot or Plymouth. When the Castles were introduced in 1923, they too were rostered predominantly on the West Country services during their first few years in traffic. Their reign was quite short-lived because the need for heavier trains on a more regular basis soon became apparent on the West Country route, especially in the summer months, and an assisting engine often had to be used to keep time when traffic was heavy. There was a need for a more powerful engine for the heaviest services which could work unaided over the South Devon banks without the expense of a second engine, and so it was inevitable that when the first Kings appeared in summer 1927, they were immediately put to work on the route.

The next three engines quickly followed 6000 from the Swindon Factory: 6001 appeared at Old Oak on 6 July, whilst on 22 July, 6002 went to Laira and 6003 to Old Oak. On 2 August, 6004 was allocated to Laira, and 6005 to Old Oak on the 6th, completing the initial

6005 KING GEORGE II at Norton Fitzwarren with the Up 'Cornish Riviera' in 1929. This location was near the scene of the worst accident involving a King when 6028 KING GEORGE VI overran two successive stop signals at danger in November 1940. The engine and the first six coaches were derailed, five of the coaches wrecked and 26 people were killed. F.R. Hebron/Rail Archive Stephenson.

From July 1929, the Kings were used on the newly inaugurated, but short-lived, 'Torquay Pullman'. 6010 KING CHARLES I at Torquay after arrival with the Down Pullman in 1929/30. Rail Archive Stephenson.

6000 KING GEORGE V is admired by the photographer's wife at Plymouth North Road after bringing in a half day excursion from London on 3 April 1931. Note the lever on the driver's side of the bell is still in place but has been removed on the fireman's side. H.C. Casserley.

6000 KING GEORGE V near Taunton in September 1931. ER Morten.

6021 KING RICHARD II arrives at what looks like Newton Abbot with a 'Holiday Haunts' express in around 1932. C.R. Gordon-Stuart/Rail Archive Stephenson.

6012 KING EDWARD VI climbs Dainton bank with a Down express in 1933. Originally allocated to Newton Abbot, it quickly moved on to Laira in July 1928 and remained there until 1954. Robert Brookman/Rail Archive Stephenson.

6025 KING HENRY III on a Down express at Newton Abbot, probably soon after a General repair completed in August 1933.

batch. However, on 3 August, 6000 departed to the United States, leaving the other five to handle the summer traffic.

For the winter 1927/8 timetable, Old Oak's engines had six West Country diagrams:

```
Old Oak
10.30am Paddington-Plymouth (to Penzance)
12.30pm Plymouth-Paddington (10.0am ex-Penzance)
Old Oak
11.15am Paddington-Bristol (to Weston-super-Mare)
1.45pm Bristol-Plymouth (10.40am Wolverhampton-Penzance)
6.20pm Plymouth-Paddington
Old Oak
12.0pm Paddington-Kingswear
11.25am Kingswear-Paddington
Old Oak
1.30pm Paddington-Plymouth (to Penzance)
2.5pm Plymouth-Paddington (11.0am ex-Penzance)
Old Oak
3.30pm Paddington-Plymouth (to Truro)
4.11pm Plymouth-Paddington (12.55pm ex-Penzance)
Old Oak
5.15pm Paddington-Plymouth
3.55pm Plymouth-Bristol (12.10pm Penzance-Crewe)
7.32pm Bristol-Paddington (12.55pm ex-Penzance)

All except the 11.15am Paddington were balanced with Laira or
Newton Abbot diagrams.
```

Building recommenced in late 1927, with 6006 entering traffic on 9th March 1928, and the last engine of the batch in August; two of these went to Stafford Road, for the Wolverhampton and Birkenhead expresses. By September 1928, when the first twenty engines were all in traffic, the allocation was:
Old Oak (9): 6000, 6001, 6003, 6005, 6007, 6009, 6011, 6013, 6015
Laira (8): 6002, 6004, 6006, 6008, 6010, 6012, 6016, 6018
Newton Abbot (1): 6014
Stafford Road (2): 6017, 6019

From July 1929, the Kings were also used on the newly inaugurated (though short-lived) 'Torquay Pullman', with 6018 of Newton Abbot noted as the regular engine early in August that year; however, patronage was poor and the Pullman cars were withdrawn the following year. The West of England route was indeed the 'glamour' one for the Kings, typified by a contemporary magazine report of arrivals at Paddington on 19 July 1930: 6007 with the Kingswear train at 3.50pm, 6010 with the second part of the Penzance train at 4.30pm, 6011 with the 'Riviera' at 4.45pm, 6003 with the Penzance train at 7.0pm, and 6013 with the Newquay train at 7.10pm. The correspondent enthused that all five arrivals were on or before time.

Although twenty engines were sufficient for the winter traffic, the Traffic Department decided that, during the busier summer periods, additional power was required for the increasingly heavily loaded services, especially on Saturdays and so ten more Kings were ordered. Building commenced at Swindon Factory in early 1930, and 6020 and 6021 appeared in traffic in early July for that summer's schedules, followed by 6022-6026 by the end of the month. The final engine, 6029, was delivered to Old Oak Common on 8 September 1930. The full allocation was then:

Old Oak (15): 6000, 6001, 6003, 6005, 6007, 6009, 6011, 6013, 6015, 6021, 6025-6029
Newton Abbot (2): 6018, 6023
Laira (8): 6002, 6004, 6010, 6012, 6016, 6020, 6022, 6024
Stafford Road (5): 6006, 6008, 6014, 6017, 6019

Half of them were based at Old Oak Common, which had one daily turn to Wolverhampton, with the remainder to the West Country. Laira's quota remained at eight, but Newton Abbot increased to two, with a Plymouth and London turn in addition to the 'Torbay'. For the winter of 1930, King West of England diagrams were as immediately below:

```
1 DOWN (Old Oak M,W,F; Laira Tu,Th,Sat)
10.30am Paddington-Plymouth
1 UP (Laira M,W,F; Old Oak Tu,Th,Sat)
8.35am Plymouth-Exeter and 11.0am Exeter-Paddington
2 DOWN (Old Oak M,W,F; Newton Abbot Tu,Th,Sat)
12.0pm Paddington-Kingswear
2 UP (Newton Abbot M,W,F; Old Oak Tu,Th,Sat)
11.25am Kingswear-Paddington
3 DOWN (Old Oak M,W,F; Laira Tu,Th,Sat)
1.30pm Paddington-Plymouth
3 UP (Laira M,W,F; Old Oak Tu,Th,Sat)
12.30pm Plymouth-Paddington
4 DOWN (Old Oak M,W,F; Laira Tu,Th,Sat)
3.30pm Paddington-Plymouth
4 UP (Laira M,W,F; Old Oak Tu,Th,Sat)
3.55pm Plymouth-Bristol and 7.32pm Bristol-Paddington
5A DOWN (Laira)
4.30pm Paddington-Plymouth
5A UP (Laira)
4.10pm Plymouth-Paddington
5B (second Laira)
same as 5A
6A DOWN (Old Oak)
6.30pm Paddington-Plymouth
6A UP (Old Oak)
2.0pm Plymouth-Paddington
6B (second Old Oak)
same as 6A
7 DOWN (Old Oak M,W,F; Newton Abbot Tu,Th,Sat)
11.15am Paddington-Bristol, 1.45pm Bristol-Kingswear, 5.40pm Kingswear-Newton Abbot
7 UP (Newton Abbot M,W,F; Old Oak Tu,Th,Sat)
6.20am Newton Abbot-Plymouth and then 8.10am Plymouth-Paddington
```

The Kings gained a new duty in March 1934 when they started working the newly introduced 12.50am Paddington-West of England newspapers, the first such train being hauled by 6027 KING

RICHARD I, which gained seven minutes on the schedule to Plymouth. In addition to the Paddington expresses, they also worked cross-country traffic daily between Bristol and Plymouth, usually in conjunction with a Paddington express to or from Temple Meads as shown below in the winter 1934/35 diagrams for West Country expresses: *(see bottom table)* In reality, these services were not always worked by the Kings because, during the months between autumn and early summer, the opportunity was taken to put many of the engines through Works, so that as many as possible were available for the summer traffic, when the loads were heavy and trains sometimes divided, especially on Saturdays.

In 1935, a King was officially rostered for the first time to one of the GWR's best-known trains, the 'Cheltenham Flyer'. It was customarily Castle-hauled – its loading was rarely enough to warrant the muscle power of a King

	Arrive/details
Old Oak	
1.30pm Paddington-Plymouth	6.35pm (for Penzance)
8.45am Plymouth-Bristol	12.11pm (for Crewe)
4.18pm Bristol-Paddington	5.35pm (1.30pm ex-Taunton)
Laira/Old Oak	
8.35am Plymouth-Paddington	1.5pm
1.40am Paddington-Plymouth	6.8am
Laira	
3.55pm Plymouth-Bristol	7.3pm (12.15pm Penzance-Manchester)
7.35pm Bristol-Paddington	10.25pm (6.50pm ex-Weston-s-Mare)
3.30pm Paddington-Plymouth	8.5pm
Old Oak/Laira	
6.30pm Paddington-Plymouth	12.25am
4.10pm Plymouth-Paddington	9.0pm (1.15pm ex-Penzance)
Old Oak/Laira	
10.30am Paddington-Plymouth	2.34pm (for Penzance)
12.30pm Plymouth-Paddington	4.45pm (10.0am ex-Penzance)
Old Oak/Laira	
4.30pm Paddington-Plymouth	10.13pm
2.0pm Plymouth-Paddington	6.50pm (11.10am ex-Penzance)
Old Oak/Laira	
5.30am Paddington-Plymouth	12.25pm
12.15pm Plymouth-Paddington	7.10am (9.0pm ex-Penzance)
Old Oak/Laira	
12.0pm Paddington-Kingswear	4.6pm
11.25am Kingswear-Paddington	3.45pm

and, besides, Kings were not permitted on the Swindon-Gloucester section. However, on 18 May 1935 the newly-streamlined 6014 KING HENRY VII broke with tradition and became the first

6003 KING GEORGE IV arrives at Kingswear with the 12.0pm from Paddington, the 'Torbay Express'. The Down train was worked by an Old Oak engine on Mondays, Wednesdays and Fridays; Newton Abbot provided the motive power on Tuesdays, Thursdays and Saturdays. Colour-rail

The original 6007 KING WILLIAM III blasts its way unassisted up Hemerdon with a nine coach load on an Up express. Ten coaches or 360 tons was the maximum load without a pilot between Plymouth and Newton Abbot over the South Devon banks. 6007 was theoretically written off and replaced by a new engine after the Shrivenham accident in January 1936, although this appears to have been an accountancy exercise rather than an actual replacement since the 'new' engine had the same frames and boiler as the original. transporttreasury.

6014 KING HENRY VII at Westbury on the 3.30pm Paddington-Penzance after the coverings over and around the cylinders were removed - along with the tender cowling - in August 1935. The 'bull nose' would remain until the end of 1942. Note the Reporting Number frame fixed to the special bracket welded to the front of the inside valve chest because it was impossible to attach the frame in the usual position over the smokebox door handles. This was fitted after 6014 went back into traffic and it was realised that it was impossible to attach a Reporting Number frame to the rounded nose.

In the classic seafront spot at Sprey Point, Teignmouth, 6015 KING RICHARD III with an Up express on 11 June 1936. Colour-rail

6015 KING RICHARD III runs through Dawlish Warren in the late 1930s on an express with three parcels vehicles at the front, two Siphon Gs and a Dean 40ft brake. Its upper lamp bracket has been moved down onto the smokebox front.

6022 KING EDWARD III on a Paddington – Penzance express on Dainton Bank, before entering Dainton Tunnel. www.rail-online.co.uk

The Kings were in the 'Special' power category and although that permitted them to take a load of 485 tons unassisted between Wellington and Whiteball, they were restricted to 360 tons from Newton Abbot to Rattery or Brent. 6027 KING RICHARD I is piloted by 3441 BLACKBIRD on a Down express climbing Dainton Bank, before entering Dainton Tunnel. The 4-4-0 was from the 'Bird' class, which was developed from the 'Bulldog' with deeper outside frames and a new type of bogie based on the French de Glehn design. www.rail-online.co.uk

of its class to be officially rostered to the 'Flyer', albeit only on the Swindon-Paddington leg. The train was driven by Jim 'Quality' Street, and took a mere 60 minutes – that was fast, but by no means a record.

The turn did not last long, because it was more by way of a 'filling-in' duty than one requiring such King power. The class did work a number of these shorter legs between their main duties to or from the West at various times, including the 2.30am Paddington-Bristol News, and the 3.15pm and 6.35pm Paddington to Cheltenham trains as far as Swindon, together with a number of balancing Up duties.

The Great Western's Centenary fell in 1935, and on 31 August a celebration was held in the Great Hall of Bristol University. There was the obligatory round of speeches, and the address given by the GWR's chairman, Sir Robert Horne, included an important announcement: *Up to now the best trains between Bristol and London have taken two hours. We propose – starting on September 9 – a new service in which a train from London to Bristol will take only one and three-quarter hours. The train will be called 'The Bristolian', and will be scheduled to do the 118¼ miles on the Down journey, via Bath, and the 117 and a half miles, on the Up journey via Badminton, in each direction, at an average speed of 67.6 miles per hour*

and 67.1 miles per hour respectively. The new train will leave Paddington at 10am and Bristol at 4.30pm on Mondays to Fridays inclusive, and will be the fastest in the country for a run of over 100 miles. The train will travel, for the greater part of its journey, at a speed of 80 miles per hour.

The party attending the centenary luncheon was taken home to London in a special train hauled by 6000, which was timed to run to the proposed 'Bristolian' schedule. The *GWR Magazine* subsequently reported that: *The run was so smooth that tea could be taken in comfort without being spilt.* A little over a week later, on Monday 9 September, the 'Bristolian' was formally inaugurated. The train comprised seven coaches – 230 tons gross – and was again hauled in both directions by 6000 with Driver Field at the helm. It left Paddington at 10.0am and returned from Temple Meads at 4.15pm. It was scheduled to cover the 118¼ miles on the Down journey (via Bath) and the 117½ miles on the Up (via Badminton) in 105 minutes, with average speeds of over 67 mph, requiring speeds in the mid- and upper-70s to maintain time.

Humphrey Baker, writing in the *GWR Magazine*, attributed the success of this fast service partly to 'the capacity of the 'King' class of locomotive for speed (and particularly for quick acceleration from rest or from a check)', but also to the

'keenness of the engine crews, who have seen to it that the fast schedule has been kept with time in hand'. He reported that, in the first month of operation, the 'Bristolian' had arrived at its destination either on or before time on every Up trip, and on all except two of the Down, neither of which were attributable to the locomotive. (one was caused by single-line working at Swindon following a derailment, and the other by a track circuit failure at Goring).

Although the 'Bristolian' was a prestige service, the Kings did not have a permanent role on the duty. As with the 'Cheltenham Flyer', the normal train loadings of the 'Bristolian' were comparatively light and, with speed more important than power, a Castle was perfectly adequate, and from 16 June 1936, the 'Bristolian' was diagrammed for an engine of that class.

There was little change in the distribution of the Kings during the 1930s, except that Newton Abbot gained one engine and Old Oak lost one. In March 1938, the allocation was:

Old Oak (14): 6000, 6001, 6003, 6007, 6009, 6011, 6013-15, 6021, 6025, 6027-6029

Newton Abbot (4): 6018, 6023, 6024 (Swindon Factory)

Laira (8): 6002 (on loan to NA), 6004, 6010, 6012, 6016, 6019, 6020, 6022

Stafford Road (4): 6005, 6006, 6008, 6026

Although the Kings were the primary GWR 'heavy express' class, they regularly filled in their time on lighter duties, including newspaper, milk and parcels, and at one time on a vacuum meat train from Exeter to Paddington.

Pre-war on the Northern Route
The demands of traffic and operation meant that the Northern line to the Midlands, Chester and Birkenhead was for many years the poor relation of the West of England route in terms of motive power. Until the opening of the cut-off route via Bicester in 1910, the shed at Wolverhampton did not have any 4-6-0s on its books while Old Oak had 35 Stars and Saints, Bristol 17, the West Country sheds 27, and Cardiff 10. Churchward's new engines were not entirely absent from the route; some of the Old Oak allocation could be seen on the heavier services, but the trains were mainly worked by 4-4-0s. The Great Western route to the Midlands via Reading and Oxford was about 16 miles longer than the competing LNWR, which effectively meant an extra 20 minutes journey time. The completion of the cut-off route via Bicester reduced the mileage by 19 miles, and Saints were introduced to a regular two-hour schedule; three were transferred to Stafford Road in June 1910, with another two by the end of that year. In winter 1912, they were joined by three Stars sent to Wolverhampton and by the end of the First World War, the 4-cylinder engines had taken over the majority of the heavily loaded services. The introduction of the Castles in 1924 had little effect on the Northern line, with the new class allocated to the West Country services and the Stars continued to handle the tasks allotted to them. In the spring of 1928, strengthening work on bridges in the Birmingham area was completed, which enabled the Kings with their 22½ ton axle loading to operate between Paddington and Wolverhampton, via Bicester.

On 16 July of that year, 6000 took over the working of the 6.50am Wolverhampton-Paddington, returning with the 11.10am from Paddington, and 6017 KING EDWARD IV took over the 11.37am Wolverhampton-Paddington, returning with the 6.10pm from Paddington. Despite starting and finishing its day at Wolverhampton, 6000 retained its status as an Old Oak engine, but 6017 was transferred to Stafford Road shed, where it was joined two weeks later by 6019 KING HENRY V. When the final batch of the class was built during 1930, they were joined by another four engines, 6005, 6006, 6008 and 6014, in August of that year.

The 'two-hour' Birmingham expresses were entertainingly described by W.A.

Tuplin as 'hell for leather, hammer and tongs' jobs. The heaviest trains usually departed from Paddington with loadings close to 500 tons, and although coaches were slipped at Banbury and Leamington, that still left 400-odd tons for the remainder of the journey. The schedule for the 110½ mile Paddington-Birmingham trip was actually a fraction under two hours which, after a period of familiarisation on the part of the crews, rarely presented the Kings with any real problems.

By 1931 the expresses were worked as follows:

Stafford Road
6.50am Wolverhampton-Paddington; 11.10am Paddington-Wolverhampton
8.35am Wolverhampton-Paddington; 2.10pm Paddington-Wolverhampton
9.33am Wolverhampton-Paddington; 4.10pm Paddington-Wolverhampton
11.37am Wolverhampton-Paddington; 6.10pm Paddington-Wolverhampton
3.14pm Wolverhampton-Paddington; 7.10pm Paddington-Wolverhampton
Old Oak
9.10am Paddington-Wolverhampton; 2.30pm Wolverhampton-Paddington

The allocation of six Kings to Stafford Road continued until May 1935, when 6019 was transferred away; a couple of months earlier, 6026 KING JOHN had arrived, replacing 6014. From May 1935, the daily pattern of King turns utilised one Old Oak and four Stafford Road engines, each working a double journey, and this arrangement lasted until the outbreak of war in September 1939.

After the introduction of the 1¾ hour non-stop 'Bristolian' in 1935, it was mooted that a similar schedule with a King and a 300 ton train would be possible to Birmingham, a distance eight miles shorter, but over a more difficult route with numerous permanent speed restrictions. In the event the idea was not pursued, and the 2-hour trains (with a 3 minute stop at Leamington) remained the fastest on the Northern line.

Off the Beaten Track
While the engines were settling down to the routine of everyday service, special occasions had not been overlooked. Going back to 1930, a significant event in the railway calendar was the centenary of the Liverpool & Manchester Railway, and the Great Western was represented at the celebrations by 6029 KING STEPHEN which was in the care of Agecroft shed in Manchester between 10 September and 7 October. Earlier that year, the GWR's metaphorical flagship, 6000, was used in January on three special workings for the Crusaders Union (from Paddington to Swindon and back), and an educational excursion from Paddington to Swindon on 24 April. In 1931 6000 undertook another round of Public Relations duties when it was used to promote the Empire Marketing Board's 'Buy British Week', the second week of the campaign being launched on 23 November at Paddington station with 6000 as the main attraction. The smokebox door was adorned with a circular 'EMB' headboard. Between 30 September and 17 December of the

same year, 6005 was exhibited at Swindon.

On 26 March 1934, alternative duties with a difference came the way of four Kings. Three Stafford Road engines, 6005, 6014 and 6017, and Old Oak's 6001 were used to test the new steel bridges on the recently quadrupled Olton-Lapworth section of the Birmingham line. The presence of 6001 was required as it was fitted with the latest type of speedometer, and some of the test runs had to be made at a fairly precise speed. During the tests, the engines worked in pairs (coupled together, one pair without a train, the other pair with two carriages), and they made several runs side by side on adjacent tracks, thereby subjecting the bridges to the maximum possible stress.

A King broke new ground on 9 June 1937, but in a fairly modest manner. With the turntable at Reading out of action, 6018 was turned on the Reading triangle – the first recorded occasion of a King on the West Loop. A somewhat more intriguing foray was made in 1938. Between the end of January and late February, 6004 of Laira and 6015 of Old Oak were temporarily attached to Bath Road shed in Bristol, and on Sundays during that period they undertook clearance tests through the Severn Tunnel and on to Newport. The tests involved one of the engines running chimney first and the other tender-first, with four vacuum-fitted wagons between them to help spread the weight, but despite the unorthodox formation, local speculation was that the tests were conducted with a view to Kings being used on South Wales expresses. Such speculation was, however, some twenty years premature.

It later became known that, during the tests, the two Kings had ventured beyond Newport. The principal purpose was, in fact, to see how large four-cylinder engines coped on the heavy ore trains to Ebbw Vale. One of the Kings was tried with a 950-ton train (32 loaded wagons) from Newport to Aberbeeg, stopping and starting on some of the steepest gradients. At Aberbeeg, twelve more wagons were added, bringing the load to some 1,350 tons, and the second King was attached to the rear of the train. The awesome pairing apparently coped well, despite gradients which peaked at 1 in 56.

No official account of the tests seems to have survived but whatever information the GWR gleaned from all this activity, previously-held ideas of a purpose-built locomotive (a 2-10-2T had been proposed) were discarded. Instead, the heavy ore trains from Newport to Ebbw Vale continued to be hauled by 2-8-0Ts, albeit with similar engines taking over from 0-6-0PTs as the usual bankers. That situation prevailed until February 1954 when, after satisfactory clearance

One of six Kings at Stafford Road in the early 1930s, 6005 KING GEORGE II at Swan Village, now part of West Bromwich, on 7 July 1934. It had just been transferred to Stafford Road from Old Oak for the second time, and remained at the Wolverhampton shed until September 1962. It has a Jaeger speedometer and the top lamp iron has been moved to the smokebox.

tests, Standard 9F 2-10-0s arrived at Ebbw Junction shed for use on the ore trains.

Apparently, Ebbw Vale wasn't the only place to get its first glimpse of a King in 1938. It is believed that, in the late spring or early summer of that same year, at least one underwent trials across the Royal Albert Bridge to Cornwall – territory which, according to the rule book, was out of bounds. The engine was 6028 KING GEORGE VI which, on a Sunday morning, was observed a little beyond Saltash station with a one-coach train, presumably for test purposes. It has been suggested that there were, in fact, two separate test runs, roughly in the period in question – one as far as St.Germans and the other just beyond Doublebois. Frustratingly, no official documentation relating to such trials seems to be available, and details of proceedings appear to have eluded the contemporary railway press. Considering that the Kings were among the highest-profile engines of the day it is somewhat remarkable that their trials in Cornwall were kept out of public view, throwing doubt on the authenticity of the report. On that score, the oft-repeated tale of 6000 working through to Penzance in 1934/35 with a special centenary train can surely be discounted – the GWR would surely have sought maximum publicity from such a trip, and said publicity is conspicuous by its absence. It would be another sixty years before there could be no doubt that a King crossed over

the Royal Albert Bridge, when the preserved 6024 KING EDWARD I worked into Cornwall in May 1998.

Kings in Trouble

When only a little over a month old, 6003 KING GEORGE IV was involved in a potentially disastrous incident at Midgham, near Newbury. On 10 August, it was hauling the Down 'Cornish Riviera' at 60mph when the bogie left the track; fortunately (miraculously perhaps, since it had just cleared some pointwork) the train remained on the track and there were no casualties. In later years, it was also suggested that, during its initial trials, 6000's bogie had left the track. Prior to the incident involving 6003, crews had filed reports that the Kings had been prone to 'rolling' at high speeds, something not hitherto associated with GWR four-cylinder 4-6-0s. Armed with this information, it seemed that the cause of 6003's partial derailment might have something to do with the bogie, and a prompt but thorough investigation revealed that the springing provided the axleboxes with only a limited margin for drop. If the axlebox dropped more than about three quarters of an inch (which, as had been seen, was far from impossible on anything other than perfectly-laid track) the wheel 'floated'.

The Midgham derailment could easily have been a major incident, but luck was on the side of the Great Western. The derailment, moreover, largely

stayed out of the public eye, and so the fast-growing reputation of the Kings was not impaired. The cause of the derailment having been identified, the problem was quickly solved by the addition of coil springs between the bogie frame and the hangers of the laminated springs, which softened the springing. Plates were also inserted in the trailing axleboxes to reduce the lateral clearance from one inch to a sixteenth of an inch. This was a relatively simple procedure in the case of five of the six Kings, and 6003 was back in traffic on 18 August, but 6000 was, at the time, halfway across the Atlantic. The only solution was to make and fit the new springs in America, and this was done under the supervision of William Stanier, as mentioned earlier. The later engines, 6006-6029, had the new style bogie coil springs from the outset.

On 15 January 1936 a King was again in the limelight but this time for the wrong reason. 6007 KING WILLIAM III had taken charge of the 9.0pm Penzance-Paddington express passenger train at Newton Abbot, the train, which included sleeping cars, being routed via Bristol. From Wootton Bassett, it was following in the wake of an Aberdare-Old Oak coal train, hauled by 28XX 2802 and comprising fifty-three loaded wagons plus a six-wheeled brake – a train weight of 1,108 tons. Unknown to all concerned the coal train had suffered a breakaway near Shrivenham, and the last five wagons and the brake van

46

(some 122 tons in all) were completely stationary on the line in the path of the express.

The express was travelling at between 50 and 60mph when, at 5.24am, it hit the wagons. Much of the force of the collision was taken by the frame of the goods brake van, but the engine of the express derailed and turned over on its right-hand side, its train inevitably coming to a violent standstill. The steel frame of the leading carriage, corridor third 4000 built in 1921, was thrown out sideways, clear of the train and across the Down line, but the body was projected beyond the frame and rolled down the bank, coming to rest almost upside down. Its five rear compartments were completely destroyed, as was the whole of the second coach (a twelve-wheeled newspaper and guard's van). The third and fourth carriages were modern steel-built sleepers, but although both were derailed, neither overturned.

The express was carrying about 100 passengers. Miraculously, there were just two fatalities, a lady who was believed to have been in the leading coach, and Driver Starr. Ten passengers, most of whom had been in the leading carriage, were seriously injured, while seventeen others and Fireman Cozens suffered minor injuries or shock.

The Ministry of Transport report into the accident revealed that, although the prime cause was the failure of a drawhook coupling on the coal train (which resulted in the breakaway) human failings contributed to the ensuing collision. The guard of the coal train was heavily criticised for not having reacted promptly to the obvious deceleration of the stray wagons, but the greatest proportion of the blame was apportioned to the signalman at Shrivenham for his failure to notice that the coal train had been incomplete when it had passed the signalbox. As for engine 6007, the official report listed the damage as:

Frames: R.H. mainframe, front end, bent (not cracked), standing off inside cylinders three eighths inch, wants rebolting. R.H. Footplate wants renewing, front and back. R.H. front corner brackets bent. R.H. hanging bar, bent front and back. R.H. motion plate bent. L.H. main frame, front end, bent and broken. L.H. corner bracket missing. L.H. hanging bar, front end, bent. L.H. motion plate, outside, bent. Buffer bar, box angle iron, angle irons and screw connection, broken.
Cylinders: All cylinders good. R.H. back cover broken.
Valve gear: R.H. valve spindle bent.
Reversing gear: Reversing screw and box bent; will not reverse.
Cab: Weather board, cab sides, leg plates, windows, cab handrails, pillars and T-irons, smashed. 4 cone, handrails, top feed pipes R.H. side, all smashed.
Boiler mountings: Good.
Sand gear: R. trailing sandbox, smashed.
Brake gear: Brake hangers, cross stays and rods, smashed.
Bogie: Both frames bent. Leading cross stay and life guard missing. R.H. bogie centre controlling spring and case smashed. L.H. inside T-springs and hangers all bent. Bogie centre pin casting broken in two webs only.
Springs: Engine springs good. Spring hanger brackets and spring hangers on L.M.D. bent.
Miscellaneous: Damper gear and cylinder cock gear on footplate damaged. Cylinder cock gear and cocks on R.H. outside cylinder broken off.
Tender 2572: All axleboxes broken. Brake rods, stays and hangers bent. Brake column broken and shaft bent. One brake hanger bracket missing. Draw gear side and centre links bent. Four handrails and two lamp irons back of tender bent. Tank water indicator gear column broken. Water pick-up scoop broken. Leading and trailing dragboxes damaged. Number plate broken. Intermediate buffers bent. Vacuum pipes damaged trailing end. Vacuum drip tap plate bent. Toolboxes badly damaged. Draghook bent. Middle wheels slightly out of gauge. Back and front footplates broken and buckled. Right hand side footplate broken and buckled, back end. Two toolbox angle irons broken, right side. Coal door broken, right side. Coal door wing broken, right side. Coal plate bent front end, right side. Shovel plate broken. Footboard supports broken. Tank, back end, badly bent and broken. Tank, back end, inside plates and top angle irons broken.

For accounting purposes, the badly damaged engine was condemned on 5 March 1936, and a replacement ordered under Lot 309 at a cost of £4,393. Despite the seemingly damning report on the state of the original locomotive, the replacement – also numbered 6007 – incorporated a not insignificant proportion of the old one; indeed, it was not even necessary to lift the boiler of

6026 KING JOHN, on a northbound express in 1938 at Warwick, had arrived at Stafford Road in March 1935, replacing 6014. From May 1935, the daily pattern of King turns on the Northern line utilised one Old Oak and four Stafford Road engines, each working a double journey, and this arrangement lasted until the outbreak of war in September 1939. Coltas Trust

the damaged engine from the frames. The 'new' 6007 entered traffic on 24 March 1936. It was paired with tender 2572; this too had its accident damage repaired, and, for book-keeping purposes, had also been written off and replaced by a 'new' tender, constructed under Lot A144.

A far less serious accident, little more than a minor bump in fact, occurred at Newton Abbot on 21 August 1936 when 6028 KING HENRY II was run into by Castle 5051, the driver of the latter having misread a signal. 6028's bogie was forced off the track at catch points, but there was no damage.

The next incidents occurred early in the Second World War. On 20 August 1940, 6010 was slightly damaged during an air raid at Newton Abbot, the cab roof and sides, the left-hand side of the tender and the water tank being holed. Just over two months later, on 4 November, 6028 KING GEORGE VI was involved in a far more serious accident, at Norton Fitzwarren near Taunton, resulting in a considerable loss of life. 6028 was in charge of the 9.50pm Paddington-Penzance passenger train, which comprised thirteen bogie coaches carrying some nine hundred passengers, many of them service personnel. The train was travelling at an estimated speed of 40-45mph on the Down relief line, and passed two successive stop signals at danger before becoming derailed, at 3.47am, at the catch points protecting the Down main line, where the two lines converge at the west end of Norton Fitzwarren station. The engine and the first six coaches were

derailed, five of the coaches being wrecked. Twenty-six people were killed, thirteen Naval personnel, twelve civilians and Fireman Seabridge. Fifty-six passengers sustained injuries serious enough to warrant hospitalisation, and eighteen complained of minor injuries or shock. Sixteen of the injured were members of the Services.

It could have been even worse. The 12.50am Paddington-Penzance newspaper train, also hauled by a King, was travelling on the Down main line at 55-60mph and overtook the passenger train as the derailment actually occurred. Somehow, the newspaper train got clear momentarily before 6028 derailed across its path. An inspection of the newspaper vans revealed just how close things had been – a rivet head from the bogie of the derailed engine had broken a window of the fourth van, and the panelling of the fifth van had been marked by flying ballast, caused by 6028 having derailed virtually alongside it.

Initially, there was speculation that the accident had been caused by enemy action or sabotage, but it quickly became clear that human error was to blame. The driver of the passenger train had assumed that he was on the main line (as was usually the case) and not the relief line, and he mistook the main line signals (which were set clear for the newspaper train) for his own. Lt-Col Mount, who chaired the Ministry of Transport enquiry, was sympathetic towards the driver: '...he frankly admitted his responsibility, but his account of what happened, given in good faith, appears to have been

affected by his experiences'. Lt-Col Mount declared that the driver's error '...must have been the outcome of failure to concentrate...', and that '...his breakdown may be partly attributed to operating conditions in the black-out, and to the general strain (for example, his house at Acton had been recently damaged) which Railway Servants, in common with other members of the community, are undergoing at the present time'. In the official report, it was emphasised that the driver was an experienced and capable man in the top link at Old Oak, who had forty years' service and an excellent record.

Many years later, the signalman on duty at the time of the accident privately admitted that, at the enquiry, he had been 'economical with the truth'. He had been less than diligent in his observance of the rule book, and his word had been taken in preference to that of the driver's. It did not, however, detract from the fact that the driver had made a simple but disastrous error in his reading of the signals. Following the accident, 6028 was taken to Taunton shed for inspection, and then spent the following ten weeks being repaired at Swindon. That was the second and last fatal accident involving a King, although some of them were not immune to the occasional minor scrape. For example, on 6 March 1941, 6012, running light near Ladbroke Grove, passed an automatic signal at danger and collided with the tail of a train 250 yards beyond. There were no casualties.

In August 1945, a work-stained 6006 KING GEORGE I at Bentley Heath near Solihull heads a 14-coach northbound express, typical of such workings at that date. 6006 was in the simplified wartime livery with the letters G and W with badge between on the tender. It was allocated to Stafford Road for virtually the whole of its working life and had the unhappy distinction of being the first King to be condemned, in February 1962. www.rail-online.co.uk

Old Oak's 6013 KING HENRY VIII at Leamington Spa on 9 February 1946. It appears to be in unlined green, some four years after its last General repair in late 1942.www.rail-online.co.uk

War and Post-War

When war broke out in September 1939, there was at first a significant reduction in regular services as troop and evacuation trains took priority, but after the initial 'emergency', a more sustainable timetable was introduced. There were fewer daytime services to and from the West, but they were heavier (generally loading to at least 12 coaches), and nearly all had Plymouth/Penzance and Paignton/Kingswear portions. The timings were naturally much slower, and more of them ran via Bristol.

During the war, train loads of fifteen bogies or more – sometimes much more – were far from uncommon, and the haulage capabilities of the Kings proved extremely useful. One particular occasion was on 25 October 1941, when an unidentified King brought the fifteen-coach Down 'Riviera' into Exeter fifteen minutes early, an average of 53.4mph despite the decelerations of the period! The availability of the Kings was, however, rather poor during the war years, and on more than one occasion at least eight of them were under the jurisdiction of Swindon Works simultaneously. Indeed, there were weeks when up to half of the Paddington-Plymouth expresses had to

be hauled by Castles, simply through a lack of serviceable Kings.

Within two months of the outbreak of the war, three engines were transferred in November 1939 from Old Oak to Bristol Bath Road, and two to Exeter from Wolverhampton Stafford Road. The revised position was:

Old Oak (11): 6001, 6003, 6007, 6009, 6013-6015, 6021, 6025, 6027, 6028
Bristol Bath Road (3): 6011, 6017, 6026
Exeter (2): 6000, 6002
Newton Abbot (3):6018, 6023, 6024
Laira (8): 6004, 6010, 6012, 6016, 6019, 6020, 6022, 6029
Stafford Road (3): 6005, 6006, 6008

These changes were probably made because of the increased weight of services in the West Country, with trains previously worked by Castles transferred to King diagrams. The Bath Road engines worked two turns to London:

	Arrive/details
Bath Road King	
7.40am Bristol-Paddington	10.30am (7.0am ex-Weston-s-Mare)
1.15pm Paddington-Bristol	3.58pm (to Penzance)
Bath Road King	
6.20pm Bristol-Paddington	9.35pm (4.0pm ex-Taunton)
12.0am Paddington-Bristol	3.25am (to Penzance)

The Exeter Kings regularly worked the 10.10 p.m. Paddington Postal, and

although 6004 went there in October 1941, all had left Exeter by February 1942. In summer 1943, the Bath Road ones were transferred away, leaving the engines at their four pre-war sheds:
Old Oak (12): 6001, 6003, 6007, 6009, 6011, 6013-6015, 6021, 6025, 6027, 6028
Newton Abbot (3): 6018, 6023, 6024
Laira (12): 6000, 6002, 6004, 6010, 6012, 6016, 6017, 6019, 6020, 6022, 6026, 6029
Stafford Road (3): 6005, 6006, 6008

The West Country diagrams for summer 1943 show the heavy utilisation of the Kings in this period. Excluding the weekend-only workings, Old Oak had seven engines diagrammed daily, Newton three and Laira ten, although with this level of planned usage, it was probably not unusual to see Castles or other classes substituting. The diagrams were now in 'blocks', with up to three engines from each shed carrying out a sequence of services over a number of days (see table page 53).

The wartime disruption to conventional working patterns threw up numerous unusual workings. For example, 6000, 6010 and 6019 of Laira and 6017 of Bath Road were all observed on Paddington-

Post-war drabness illustrated by 6015 KING RICHARD III at Warwick with a Down Birkenhead train on 10 August 1947. www.rail-online.co.uk

6013 KING HENRY VIII passes the distinctive Birmingham Snow Hill North box as it lifts its train out of Hockley tunnel into the station with a Shrewsbury to Paddington express on 5 August 1947. John P. Wilson/Rail Archive Stephenson.

6015 KING RICHARD III recovers from a signal check as it passes Princes Risborough with the 11.35am Birkenhead Woodside to Paddington express in June 1948. The tender has **BRITISH RAILWAYS** branding but the lined green 6015 does not yet have a BR smokebox plate. Hugh Harman/Rail Archive Stephenson.

6017 KING EDWARD IV at Leamington Spa in 1948 shows no evidence of lining or either GWR or BR branding. Its next visit to Swindon for a Heavy Repair was not until March 1949, although it did not appear in BR blue until 1950. www.rail-online.co.uk.

6018 King Henry VI leaves Exeter St.David's with an express for Plymouth on 6 June 1949. It is still in almost ex-works condition, having completed a three-month long Heavy General the previous month. John P. Wilson/Rail Archive Stephenson.

6019 KING HENRY V near Kintbury with the Down 'Cornish Riviera Express' in 1948. F.R. Hebron/Rail Archive Stephenson.

	Arrive/details
Three Laira Kings	
11.15pm Plymouth-Paddington	5.35am
4.15pm Paddington-Plymouth	11.40am
8.30am Plymouth-Paddington	2.0pm
11.30pm Paddington-Plymouth	7.32am (to Penzance SX)
11.45pm Paddington-Plymouth	5.45am (News, to Penzance SO)
Two Old Oak and One Laira Kings	
12.15am Paddington-Plymouth	5.50am (News, to Penzance)
2.2pm Plymouth-Paddington	7.25pm (11.0am ex-Penzance)
10.30 Paddington-Plymouth	3.24pm (to Penzance)
11.15 Plymouth-Paddington	4.50pm (8.0am ex-Penzance)
Three Old Oak Kings	
5.30am Paddington-Plymouth	12.45pm (to Penzance)
7.55pm Tavistock Jct-Paddington	2.5am (3.0pm ex-Penzance Perishables) (with 11.5am and 9.10am Paddington-Wolverhampton & Returns)
Two Old Oak Kings	
11.15am Paddington-Bristol	1.45pm (SX)
4.0pm Bristol-Paddington	6.40pm (SX)
9.5am Paddington-Bristol	11.50am (SO)
1.50pm Bristol-Paddington	4.35pm (SO)
10.40am Paddington-Kingswear	3.50pm
4.40pm Kingswear-Newton Abbot	5.28pm
12.36am Newton Abbot-Paddington	7.30am (7.20pm ex-Penzance)
Three Laira Kings	
12.30pm Plymouth-Paddington	5.30pm (9.30am ex-Penzance)
2.43pm Plymouth-Paddington	8.35pm (11.35am ex-Penzance-Suns)
2.15am Paddington-Bristol	5.5am
7.50am Bristol-Paddington	10.30am
6.30pm Plymouth-Paddington	1.40am
Three Newton Kings	
4.25am Newton Abbot-Plymouth	5.20am (9.50pm Paddington-Penzance)
10.40am Plymouth-Bristol	2.10pm (7.45am Penzance-Crewe)
3.55pm Bristol-Newton Abbot	6.35pm (9.15am Liverpool-Plymouth)
7.15am Newton Abbot-Paignton	7.48am (Parcels)
8.50am Paignton-Paddington	1.35pm
9.50pm Paddington-Newton Abbot	4.14am (SX, to Penzance)
10.40am Paddington-Kingswear	3.52pm (Suns)
5.10pm Kingswear-Newton Abbot	5.57pm (Suns)
Three Laira Kings	
8.22pm Plymouth-Bristol	12.7am
12.35am Bristol-Paddington	4.5am (Sun/MO, 4.45pm Penzance-Crewe & Paddington)
3.50pm Plymouth-Bristol	7.9pm
7.35pm Bristol-Paddington	11.10pm (3.55pm ex-Exeter)
1.30pm Paddington-Plymouth	7.5pm (to Penzance)
9.50pm Paddington-Plymouth	5.20 (Sun, 2nd part, to Penzance)
Old Oak King	
9.50pm Paddington-Newton Abbot	4.14am (SO)
1.0pm Newton Abbot-Paignton	1.26pm (Sun)
2.40pm Paignton-Paddington	7.55pm (Sun)
Newton King	
4.20am Newton Abbot-Plymouth	5.20am (Sun) (9.50pm (Sat) Paddington-Penzance)
7.5am Plymouth-Paddington	3.50pm (Sun)
9.50pm Paddington-Newton Abbot	4.14am (Sun)
Old Oak King	
4.35pm Paddington-Plymouth	11.50pm (Sun)
12.20pm Plymouth-Paddington	5.20pm (MO) (Relief to 9.30am Penzance)

Wolverhampton expresses during February 1943, while in July and August of that same year 6006 and 6005 had visited Plymouth for the first time since the 1930s. During 1944, all thirty Kings were seen in Plymouth at one time or another.

In early summer 1944, Newton Abbot's allocation increased to five, with Old Oak transferring 6027 and 6028. By 1946, a fourth, 6011 KING JAMES I, was allocated to Stafford Road, and that shed's turns increased to three, with Old Oak's turns to the Midlands reduced to one daily, as in pre-war days.

The 1948 Exchanges

Although enthusiasts viewed the 1948 Locomotive Exchanges organised by the newly nationalised British Railways otherwise, the official line was that: *They were not intended to be a contest between locomotives of similar types which .... had been designed to fulfil the requirements of their particular Region.* The tests began on 20 April 1948 and engines were to be worked in normal service on existing timings over selected routes, with dynamometer cars attached to the trains to record speeds and other essential data. The locomotives to be tested were divided into three groups: express passenger, freight and mixed traffic, and in the former category the King was paired with the LMS Coronation 4-6-2 and rebuilt Royal Scot 4-6-0, LNER A4 4-6-2, and Southern Railway Merchant Navy 4-6-2. Unfortunately, the King's participation was limited because it could not work on the London Midland and

The Western Region was represented by 6018 KING HENRY VI in the express passenger category in the 1948 Locomotive Exchanges organised by the newly nationalised British Railways. The engines were to be worked in normal service on existing timings over selected routes, with dynamometer cars attached to the trains to record speeds and other essential data. Unfortunately, the King's participation was limited to the Western and Eastern Regions because it could not work on the London Midland and Southern Regions, its width over cylinders being too great for their platform clearances. The engines running on 'foreign' lines firstly worked pre-test familiarisation runs and then the following week, the actual test runs with dynamometer cars attached. 6018 KING HENRY VI departs from Kings Cross with its first test run with the 1.10pm to Leeds 18 May 1948. John P. Wilson/Rail Archive Stephenson.

Southern Regions since its width over cylinders was too great for their platform clearances. The trials were spread over a period of about four months, the express passenger tests taking place in the first ten weeks, and the routes used for these were: Euston-Carlisle, King's Cross-Leeds Central, Paddington-Plymouth and Waterloo-Exeter Central.

The engines were to have run between 15,000 and 20,000 miles since the last general repair and each was to be specially examined before leaving the parent Region to minimise repairs during the trials. It was intended that the same engine of each class should work throughout the tests and the Kings were represented by 6018 KING HENRY VI from Newton Abbot. The coal normally used on each Region was to be provided, apart from on the Western Region where hard coal was to be supplied instead of the soft Welsh coal normally used. The principal dimensions of each class are listed top right.

The engines were to have crews who normally worked them in their home Regions, and all were returned to their home sheds at week-ends. The trains chosen were to be made up to agreed weights to facilitate comparison. The engines running on 'foreign' lines worked pre-test familiarisation runs on Mondays and Wednesdays with the Down trains, and on Tuesdays and Thursdays with the Up trains. The following week, the actual test runs with dynamometer cars attached to the trains were on Tuesdays and Thursdays with the Down trains, and Wednesdays and Fridays with the Up trains. Summaries of all the runs on the two Regions where 6018 took part are provided at right.

Paddington-Plymouth
KING HENRY VI began

	King	A4	Coronation	Merchant Navy	Royal Scot
Year introduced	1927	1935	1937	1941	1943
Cylinders – diameter	(4) 16¼ in.	(3) 18½ in.	(4) 16½ in.	(3) 18 in.	(3) 18 in.
Cylinders – stroke	28 in.	26 in.	28 in.	24 in.	26 in.
Driving wheel diameter	6 ft. 6 in.	6 ft. 8 in.	6 ft. 9 in.	6 ft. 2 in.	6 ft. 9 in.
Heating surface total sq.ft.	2,201	2,576	2,807	2,451	1,850
Superheating surface sq.ft.	289	749	830	822	420
Firegrate area sq ft.	34.3	41.3	50.0	48.5	31.3
Working pressure (lbs/sq.in.)	250	250	250	280	250
Adhesion weight (tons)	67.5	66.0	67.0	63.0	61.0
Tractive effort (85% w.p.)	40,300lb	35,455lb	40,000lb	37,500lb	33,150lb

PADDINGTON-PLYMOUTH

Pre-test runs	6018		46236		60033		35019		46162	
	Down	Up	Down	Up	Down	Up	Down	Up	Down	Up
Date	20/04	21/04	18/05	19/05	4/05	5/05	27/04	28/04	25/05	26/05
Load (tons) between										
Paddington-Newton Abbot	482	491.8	486.2	493.1	482	491.8	471.8	491.8	436	456.1
Newton Abbot-Plymouth	324.5	330.2	328.7	330.2	324.5	330.2	317.9	330.2	281.5	293.1
Running time (minutes)	282.4	287.8	297.8	297.5	296.3	287.3	295.1	284.7	302.6	296.5
Average speed (mph)	47.8	47.1	45.4	45.5	45.6	47.2	45.8	47.6	44.6	45.7
Average DBHP	2,820	2,897	2,804	2,998	3,000	2,919	3,164	2,915	2,355	2,979
Coal										
Pounds	10,730	10,602	9,024	9,898	8,950	9,710	11,708	10,804	8,482	11,308
lbs/mile	47.66	46.96	40.09	43.84	39.76	43.00	52.01	47.83	37.68	50.08
lbs/DBHP.hour	3.81	3.66	3.22	3.30	2.98	3.33	3.70	3.71	3.60	3.80
Water										
Gallons	8,145	7,910	8,426	8,975	7,409	7,145	9,786	9,590	6,594	8,094
Gallons/mile	36.2	35.0	37.4	39.8	32.9	31.6	43.5	42.5	29.3	35.8
lbs/DBHP.hour	28.87	27.30	30.04	29.93	24.70	24.47	30.92	32.91	28.00	27.17

PADDINGTON-PLYMOUTH

Test runs	6018		46236		60033		35019		46162	
	Down	Up	Down	Up	Down	Up	Down	Up	Down	Up
Date	22/04	23/04	20/05	21/05	6/05	07/05	29/04	30/04	27/05	28/05
Load (tons) between										
Paddington-Newton Abbot	482	491.8	486.2	491.2	482	491.8	472	490	436	456.1
Newton Abbot-Plymouth	324.5	330.2	328.7	326.3	324.5	330.2	318.2	328.3	281.5	293.1
Running time (minutes)	288.9	282.6	290.4	287.2	295.5	288.1	293.7	294.2	293.8	290.2
Average speed (mph)	46.8	48.0	46.5	47.2	45.7	47.0	46.0	46.1	46.0	46.7
Average DBHP	3,220	2,841	2,693	3,087	2,930	3,174	2,974	2,933	2,437	2,800
Coal										
Pounds	11,730	10,966	8,632	10,022	9,494	10,132	10,352	10,452	8,118	10,662
lbs/mile	52.11	48.56	38.34	44.39	42.18	44.87	45.98	46.27	36.06	47.22
lbs/ton mile (exc engine)	0.113	0.105	0.083	0.096	0.092	0.097	0.102	0.100	0.087	0.109
lbs/ton mile (inc engine)	0.088	0.081	0.061	0.071	0.067	0.071	0.077	0.076	0.065	0.083
lbs/DBHP.hour	3.64	3.86	3.21	3.24	3.24	3.19	3.48	3.56	3.33	3.81
lbs/sq.ft.grate/hr	71.0	67.9	35.7	41.9	46.8	51.2	43.6	44.0	53.0	70.5
Water										
Gallons	8,510	8,029	7,848	8,638	7,406	7,562	9,033	8,930	6,777	7,596
Gallons/mile	37.8	35.6	34.9	38.3	32.9	33.5	40.1	39.5	30.1	33.6
lbs/ton mile	0.635	0.594	0.557	0.614	0.524	0.531	0.670	0.649	0.546	0.59
lbs/DBHP.hour	26.42	28.26	29.14	27.98	25.27	23.82	30.38	30.45	27.82	27.12
lbs water/lbs coal	7.25	7.32	9.09	8.62	7.80	7.46	8.87	8.55	8.35	7.12

KINGS CROSS-LEEDS

Pre-test runs	6018		46236		60034		35017		46162	
	Down	Up	Down	Up	Down	Up	Down	Up	Down	Up
Date	18/05	19/05	4/05	5/05	20/04	21/04	25/05	26/05	27/04	28/04
Load (tons) between										
King's Cross-Wakefield	494.5	423.3	501.5	428.8	500.5	425.3	508.5	427	503.3	422.3
Wakefield-Leeds	366.8	299.8	373.8	298.5	372.8	298.5	381.5	299.8	378.5	295.5
Running time (minutes)	238.6	235.6	233.1	238.5	239.5	241	236.4	236.7	243.3	251.6
Average speed (mph)	46.7	47.3	47.7	46.7	46.5	46.7	47.1	47.1	45.8	44.3
Average DBHP	2,773	231	2,823	2,701	2,513	2,557	2,689	2,248	2,801	2,684
Coal										
Pounds	9,630	7,451	8,382	8,210	7,453	7,500	10,755	8,250	9,207	8,690
lbs/mile	51.85	40.12	45.16	44.18	40.12	40.35	57.92	44.40	49.60	46.80
lbs/DBHP.hour	3.48	3.21	2.97	3.04	2.97	2.93	4.00	3.67	3.29	3.24
Water										
Gallons	7,985	6,989	7,129	6,880dy	5,217	6,150	8,086	6,865	6,667	6,691
Gallons/mile	43.0	37.6	38.4	37.0	28.1	33.1	43.5	37.0	35.9	36.0
lbs/DBHP.hour	28.82	30.12	25.25	25.48	20.82	24.10	30.07	30.55	23.80	24.94

KINGS CROSS-LEEDS

Test runs	6018		46236		60034		35017		46162	
	Down	Up	Down	Up	Down	Up	Down	Up	Down	Up
Date	20/05	21/05	6/05	7/05	22/04	23/04	27/05	28/05	29/04	30/04
Load (tons) between										
King's Cross-Wakefield	495	427.3	502.8	425.3	499.3	428.8	510.8	429.3	501.8	430.0
Wakefield-Leeds	367.8	299.8	372.8	298.5	371.5	298.5	383.8	300.5	377.0	298.5
Running time (minutes)	238.5	232.5	238.1	233.5	236.0	241.0	242.5	232.6	257.1	236.1
Average speed (mph)	46.7	47.9	46.7	47.7	47.2	45.8	46.0	47.9	43.3	47.7
Average DBHP	2,921	2,338	2,838	2,393	2,469	2,420	2,645	2,255	2,644	2,498
Coal										
Pounds	10,023	7,996	8,573	7,557	7,023	7,060	9,505	8,200	8,819	7,950
lbs/mile	53.93	43.01	46.18	40.74	37.80	38.00	51.20	44.14	47.40	42.80
lbs/ton mile (exc engine)	0.110	0.092	0.093	0.086	0.077	0.081	0.101	0.094	0.096	0.091
lbs/ton mile (inc engine)	0.086	0.072	0.070	0.064	0.057	0.060	0.078	0.071	0.075	0.070
lbs/DBHP.hour	3.43	3.42	3.02	3.15	2.84	2.92	3.59	3.42	3.33	3.18
lbs/sq.ft.grate/hr	73.40	60.20	43.18	38.84	43.30	42.20	48.50	43.60	65.90	64.60
Water										
Gallons	8,285	7,389	7,190	6,446	5,139	6,031	7,562	6,822	6,655	6,148
Gallons/mile	44.6	39.8	38.7	34.7	27.6	32.5	40.7	36.7	35.8	33.1
lbs/ton mile	0.715	0.662	0.589	0.545	0.419	0.509	0.624	0.593	0.566	0.545
lbs/DBHP.hour	28.35	31.61	25.32	26.93	20.8	24.92	28.58	30.25	25.15	24.61
lbs water/lbs coal	8.27	9.24	8.38	8.53	7.32	8.56	7.96	8.32	7.54	7.73

54

6018 KING HENRY VI arrives at Kings Cross on the return test run with the 12.15pm from Leeds on 19 May 1948. The engines were manned by enginemen who normally worked them in their home Regions, and all were returned to their home sheds at week-ends. The trains chosen were to be made up to agreed weights to facilitate comparison. AG Forsyth/Initial Photographics

the trials on familiar territory, working the 1.30 pm Paddington-Plymouth and the 8.30 am Plymouth-Paddington, which slipped a coach at Reading, reducing the load by 37 tons. The distance between Paddington and Plymouth was 225 miles with a schedule of 287 minutes in each direction and there was a reduced load west of Newton Abbot. The King was worked with 'Maximum cut-off 50% with full regulator on Hemerdon Bank. Usual cut-off 19% on easy stretches. Several rough starts and rough brake applications occurred during the runs'. 6018 beat the scheduled running time on the Down pre-test and the Up test runs, but dropped around a minute on the Up pre-test and Down test runs. However, even though it was on home ground, its coal consumption on the two test runs was significantly higher than all the other participants.

King's Cross-Leeds
A month later 6018 became the second GWR 4-6-0 to work on the East Coast main line almost 25 years after 4074 CALDICOT CASTLE had shown the LNER the advantages of long travel valve gear married to high superheat, resulting in the development of the A3

Pacifics. The 185.7 miles journey had booked times of 236 minutes for the 1.10 pm King's Cross-Leeds Central and 241 minutes for the 7.50 am Leeds Central-King's Cross. The load was around 130 tons lower between Wakefield and Leeds in both directions as the Bradford portion ran separately to and from Wakefield. On the Up journey, one coach from York was added at Doncaster and another at Grantham, from Lincoln. 6018 was reported to have 'steamed freely with boiler pressures varying between 225 and 240 lbs/sq.in. For normal running steam chest pressures were generally 195 to 200lb/sq.in rising to 210lb on gradients'. Once again, KING HENRY VI had a much higher coal consumption than the A4 and Coronation on the test runs.

Summary
Major interest in the Official Report centred on the coal and water

Average fuel consumption related to power output			
	lb.coal per dbhp/hr	lb.water per dbhp/hr	lb of water per lb of coal
King	3.57	28.58	8.07
Coronation	3.12	27.08	8.67
A4	3.06	24.32	7.92
Merchant Navy	3.60	30.43	8.45
Royal Scot	3.38	25.81	7.70

Avg. coal consumption	Eastern Region		Western Region	
	lb. per mile	lb per dbhp/hr	lb. per mile	lb per dbhp/hr
King	47.25	3.39	48.82	3.74
Coronation	44.05	3.04	41.67	3.24
A4	39.08	2.92	42.45	3.19
Merchant Navy	49.41	3.73	48.02	3.61
Royal Scot	46.66	3.26	42.76	3.64

Avg. water consumption	Eastern Region		Western Region	
	lb. per mile	lb per dbhp/hr	lb. per mile	lb per dbhp/hr
King	41.2	29.60	36.2	27.71
Coronation	37.2	25.71	37.6	29.27
A4	30.3	22.63	32.7	24.57
Merchant Navy	39.5	29.82	41.4	31.17
Royal Scot	35.2	24.62	32.2	27.53

6018 KING HENRY VI leaves Wood Green tunnel with the 1.10pm Kings Cross to Leeds express, its second test run, on 20 May 1948. It reached Leeds in 238.5 minutes against a scheduled 236 minutes. 6018 was reported to have 'steamed freely with boiler pressures varying between 225 and 240 lbs/sq.in. For normal running steam chest pressures were generally 195 to 200 lbs/sq.in rising to 210lbs on gradients'. However, KING HENRY VI had a much higher coal consumption than the A4 and Coronation Pacifics on the test runs. In its defence, 6018 had to burn hard coal instead of the soft Welsh coal which it was designed for. F.R. Hebron/Rail Archive Stephenson.

consumption during the tests; this occupied the first three pages of results. The three tables on page 55 are the only ones which gave a direct comparison between the participants; the detailed information on the running of the test trains was presented using separate tables for each class showing the results for each run made. There was no attempt to directly compare the performance on each route between the engines.

The Merchant Navy and King had by far the worst fuel consumption figures, although the latter had the excuse of having to burn hard coal instead of the soft Welsh coal which it was designed for. The summary in the official report of the exchanges acknowledged this, saying: *The Western Region locomotives had grate and smokebox arrangements specifically designed to suit Welsh coal and these, together with the firing technique to which the Western Region enginemen had been trained, differed from what is customary with the types of coal used on the trials. In view of these conditions it was arranged that, on completion of the trials, additional tests should be carried out on the Western Region using Welsh coal.*

These duly took place in November and December 1948 between Paddington and Plymouth. The opportunity was taken to compare two engines, 6001 KING EDWARD VII with the standard 2-row superheater and 6022 KING EDWARD III, which in February of that year had been fitted with a modified boiler having a four-row high-degree superheater (see chapter 4). The results for 6001 showed a significant improvement in coal consumption over the hard coal used in the original tests (42.28lb/train mile compared with 48.82lb) and the higher superheat reduced consumption on 6022 by a further 10% to 41.23lb per mile; water consumption decreased similarly.

Naturally, much was written about the trials in the contemporary railway press, in most cases singling out individual performances which beat the scheduled times or clawed back operating delays, but some of these were on the pre-test runs where the crew were familiarising themselves with

the routes and their characteristics. Whether the interchange trials had any material effect on the new British Railways standard designs is questionable.

British Railways
As already discussed, the Kings' heavy axle weights meant that they were effectively restricted to a handful of main lines, and although their sphere of activity expanded slightly during the BR era, changes were gradual. Kings returned to Bristol Bath Road at the end of 1948, when 6000 and 6019 were transferred from Laira, and 6018 from Newton Abbot. This was part of a major reorganisation of rosters in which Stafford Road's allocation increased to seven, with changes elsewhere:
January 1949
Old Oak (10): 6001, 6003, 6007, 6009, 6013-6015, 6017, 6021, 6028
Bath Road (3): 6000, 6018, 6019
Laira (10): 6010, 6012, 6016, 6022-6027, 6029
Stafford Road (7): 6002, 6004, 6005, 6006, 6008, 6011, 6020

There were now ten each at Old Oak and Laira, but Newton Abbot lost its Kings entirely, although it did acquire one for a few weeks in the summer. After the last King had left Bath Road, the allocation was:

October 1952
Old Oak (12): 6000-6003, 6007, 6009, 6013, 6015, 6018, 6019, 6021, 6028
Laira (12): 6008, 6010, 6012, 6014, 6017, 6022-6027, 6029
Stafford Road (6): 6004-6006, 6011, 6016, 6020

Apart from the six engines at Stafford Road, the rest were thus shared equally between Old Oak and Laira.

By July 1958, five of Laira's engines had moved to Old Oak:

Old Oak (15): 6000, 6002, 6003, 6007, 6009, 6012, 6013, 6015, 6016, 6018, 6019, 6022-6024, 6028
Laira (9): 6004, 6008, 6010, 6017, 6021, 6025-6027, 6029
Stafford Road (6): 6001, 6005, 6006, 6011, 6014, 6020

The new Warship diesel-hydraulics were delivered in the winter of 1958/59, marking the beginning of the end for Laira's Kings; they were reduced to eight by January 1959, but only six remained in July for the summer service. The winter timetable saw a further decline, and only three Kings were left at Laira by December, while Old Oak now had 17. Stafford Road had increased to ten in preparation for electrification work on the former LMS line, when the main Birmingham expresses were transferred to Paddington from the Euston line.

Old Oak (17): 6000, 6003, 6004, 6009, 6010, 6012, 6015, 6018, 6019, 6021, 6023-6029
Laira (3): 6002, 6013, 6016
Stafford Road (10): 6001, 6005-6008, 6011, 6014, 6017, 6020, 6022

6013 left Laira in March 1960, followed in September by the final two, 6002 and 6016, which by that time were little more than spares kept to cover against diesel failures.

West of England
At the start of the British Railways era, the 'Cornish Riviera', a long-standing regular duty on the West of England route, was scheduled at 4hr 30min for the Down run to Plymouth and 4hr 40min Up. That timing was retained until the summer of 1952, when a 4hr 15min timing was re-introduced. A good start was made to the summer schedules when, on 30 June, 6008 KING JAMES II brought the Down 'Riviera' into Plymouth four minutes early, having made up almost ten minutes of lost time since Westbury.

All of the winter 1952 diagrams for Old Oak Kings, and part of those for Laira, have survived, providing details of most of the workings to and from the West of England: *(above)*

For the summer of 1955, the 'Riviera' had, at long last, its four-hour timing

Days	Train	Arrive/detail
Old Oak - 3A		
MWF	2.25am Paddington-Bristol (News)	4.55am
MWF	7.45am Bristol-Paddington	10.10am (7.0am ex-Weston-s-Mare)
MWF	6.30pm Paddington-Bristol	8.59pm (to Weston-s-Mare)
MWF	9.10pm Bristol-Plymouth	12.45am (4.9pm ex-Crewe)
TThS	11.12am Plymouth-Paddington	4.17pm (8.0am ex-Penzance)
Old Oak - 3B		
Sun	3.30pm Paddington-Plymouth	9.10pm
MWF	11.12am Plymouth-Paddington	4.17pm (8.0am ex-Penzance)
TThS	2.25am Paddington-Bristol (News)	4.55am
TThS	7.45am Bristol-Paddington	10.10am (7.0am ex-Weston-s-Mare)
TThS	6.30pm Paddington-Bristol	8.59pm (to Weston-s-Mare)
TThS	9.10pm Bristol-Plymouth	12.45am (4.9pm ex-Crewe)
Sun	10.10am Plymouth-Paddington	3.30pm
Old Oak - 6A		
Sun	10.30am Paddington-Plymouth	3.24pm (to Penzance)
MWF	12.15pm Plymouth-Paddington	4.30pm (9.45am ex-Penzance)
TThS	10.30am Paddington-Plymouth	2.45pm (to Penzance)
Sun	12.20pm Plymouth-Paddington	5.20pm (9.45am ex-Penzance)
Old Oak - 6B		
MWF	10.30am Paddington-Plymouth	2.45pm (to Penzance)
TThS	12.15pm Plymouth-Paddington	4.30pm (9.45am ex-Penzance)
Old Oak - 7 (with OOC 8, Laira 2A & 2B)		
MF	3.30pm Paddington-Plymouth	8.0pm (to Penzance)
TS	8.30am Plymouth-Paddington	1.30pm
TS	9.50pm Paddington-Plymouth	4.39am (to Penzance)
W	7.50pm Plymouth-Paddington	2.0am (3.45pm ex-Penzance Perishable)
Th	11.0am Paddington-Plymouth	4.35pm
F	12.0am Plymouth-Paddington	7.25am (8.45pm ex-Penzance)
Sun	11.45pm Plymouth-Paddington	5.0am (9.30pm ex-Truro)
Old Oak - 8 (with Old Oak 7, Laira 2A & 2B)		
MF	11.0am Paddington-Plymouth	4.35pm
MF	12.0am Plymouth-Paddington	7.25 (8/45 Penzance)
TS	3.30pm Paddington-Plymouth	8/0 (to Penzance)
W	8.30am Plymouth-Paddington	1.30pm
W	9.50pm Paddington-Plymouth	4.39 (to Penzance)
Th	7.50pm Plymouth-Paddington	2.0am (3.45pm ex-Penzance Perishable)
Sun	7.5am Plymouth-Paddington	3.45pm
Old Oak - 9		
Sun	9.15am Paddington-Bristol	12.20pm (to Weston-s-Mare)
Sun	5.30pm Bristol-Paddington	8.40pm (1.20pm ex-Plymouth)
Laira - 2A (with Laira 2B, Old Oak 7 & 8)		
MF	7.50pm Plymouth-Paddington	2.0am (3.45pm ex-Penzance Perishable)
TS	11.0am Paddington-Plymouth	4.35pm
T	12.0am Plymouth-Paddington	7.25am (8.45pm ex-Penzance)
W	3.30pm Paddington-Plymouth	8.0pm (to Penzance)
Th	8.30am Plymouth-Paddington	1.30pm
Th	9.50pm Paddington-Plymouth	4.39am (to Penzance)
Laira - 2B (with Laira 2A, Old Oak 7 & 8)		
MF	8.30am Plymouth-Paddington	1.30pm
MF	9.50pm Paddington-Plymouth	4.39am (to Penzance)
T	7.50pm Plymouth-Paddington	2.0am (3.45pm ex-Penzance Perishable)
W	11.0am Paddington-Plymouth	4.35pm
W	12.0am Plymouth-Paddington	7.25am (8.45pm ex-Penzance)
Th	3.30pm Paddington-Plymouth	8.0pm (to Penzance)

restored. Prior to the official reintroduction of the faster schedule, 6013 KING HENRY VIII was tested on a four-hour timing on 8-11 March, working Down and Up trains on alternate days. Apart from a few relatively minor gremlins on the first Down run, 6013 met all targets concerning the margins of reserve. More spectacularly, on 9 September of that same year 6019 KING HENRY V gained no less than nineteen minutes with the Down 'Riviera'. It should be noted that, at the time, both 6013 and 6019 were still single-chimney engines.

Commencing on 28 January 1956, two other established West of England

services – the 1.30pm Paddington-Penzance and the 11.0am Penzance-Paddington – were jointly christened the 'Royal Duchy' and equipped with 'chocolate and cream' liveried stock. The inaugural Down train was hauled as far as Plymouth by 6000.

In the summer of 1956, Old Oak had four King diagrams (involving one, two, three and four engines respectively), including the Down 'Riviera' and both Up and Down 'Torbay' expresses, with the usual filling-in milk and parcels duties. Laira Kings worked four diagrams daily:

Laira - 1			
Passenger	MF	12.30pm Plymouth-Paddington	4.40pm (10.0am ex-Penzance)
News & parcels	TF	12.30am Paddington-Plymouth	5.0am
Sleeper	SO	12.35am Paddington-Plymouth	5.33am
Passenger	SO	12.30pm Plymouth-Paddington	5.20pm (10.0am ex-Penzance)
News & parcels	MO	12.30am Paddington-Plymouth	5.2am
Laira - 2A			
Passenger	SunF	4.10pm Plymouth-Paddington	9.0pm (1.20pm ex-Penzance)
Passenger	SO	12.14pm Laira Jct-Paddington	4.55pm (10.0am ex-Newquay)
Passenger	D	1.30pm Paddington-Plymouth	6.25pm (to Penzance)
Passenger	Sun	3.30pm Paddington-Plymouth	9.10pm
Laira - 2B			
Passenger	SO	12.0am Plymouth-Paddington	7.25am (8.45pm ex-Penzance)
Passenger	Sun	9.50pm Plymouth-Paddington	4.50am (to Penzance)
Passenger	MS	8.30am Plymouth-Paddington	1.25pm
Passenger	MS	9.50pm Paddington-Plymouth	5.50am (to Penzance)
Laira - 2C			
Milk	SX	10.5pm Plymouth-Wood Lane	4.50am (6.20pm ex-Penzance)
Passenger	Sun	12.0am Plymouth-Paddington	7.25am (8.45pm ex-Penzance)
Passenger	D	4.15pm Paddington-Plymouth	10.55pm
Laira - 7			
Passenger	MO	12.0am Plymouth-Bristol	3.35am (8.45pm ex-Penzance-Sun)
Passenger	MO	6.45am Bristol-Plymouth	10.42am (12.35am Manchester-Penzance)

6012 KING EDWARD VI working wrong line at Southcote Junction, south of Reading West where the Basingstoke and Newbury lines diverge, on the Down 'Cornish Riviera' in 1951. It had been repainted in standard blue livery in May 1950 during a Heavy General overhaul.

Waiting to depart from Paddington with 'The Bristolian' on 10 June 1952, 6021 KING RICHARD II. The name had been re-introduced in June 1951 for the 8.45am departure from Paddington but the light weight high speed service was more suited to the Castles and Kings were not used regularly at this date. Note the GWR 70ft Concertina coach in the background.
www.rail-online.co.uk

6028 KING GEORGE VI threads its way over Paddington's approach pointwork as it arrives with an express from Plymouth. It is in the British Railways standard light blue express passenger livery which it had from November 1950 until September 1953. 6028 had been transferred from Newton Abbot to Old Oak at the end of 1948. www.rail-online.co.uk

6012 KING EDWARD VI ready for the 'off' on Platform 2 at Paddington with the 'Cornish Riviera Limited' in 1956. The 10.30am departure had become the 'Limited' from June 1956 when 'chocolate and cream' liveried coaching stock was introduced together with a GWR-style train headboard; it reverted to 'Express' in 1957. The picture is uncannily similar to the one on page 168. www.rail-online.co.uk

6018 KING HENRY VI waits at Bristol Temple Meads on 30 May 1950. It is in lined green with BRITISH RAILWAYS on the tender. It was one of three Kings transferred to Bath Road in 1948. They regularly worked the 8.20am from Weston-Super-Mare, returning with the 1.15pm from Paddington, and the 12.0 noon from Bristol and the 4.15pm from Paddington back. The allocation was reduced in June 1950, when two of the engines were transferred to Old Oak, leaving just 6000, which stayed until in October 1952. John P. Wilson/Rail Archive Stephenson.

Blue liveried 6017 KING EDWARD IV waits at Newton Abbot with the 5.8pm to Paddington on 2 June 1952. It would revert to green a few weeks later, after a Heavy General completed on 7 August. P.W. Gray.

There was one King which needed no further identification because of the bell on the front platform presented following its visit to the United States in 1927. 6000 KING GEORGE V is on the 8.50am Saturdays Only Paddington to Paignton train in 1956. The sea wall path is unusually quiet, but it is apparently a warm day as there aren't many coats or jackets to be seen, although there is a strong sea running and it is also high tide with the sea wall taking a bit of a pounding. 6000 has an impressive load of fourteen coaches and it may be that there is a Plymouth portion which would be detached at Newton Abbot, the next stop. www.rail-online.co.uk

The hand-written Reporting Number shows this to be the 7.15am (SX or the 7.0am SO) from Plymouth to Paddington with Old Oak's 6007 KING WILLIAM III in charge at Westbury in 1955. 6007 was officially withdrawn following its accident at Shrivenham in 1936, but was in fact repaired and put back into service although masquerading as a new engine. This must have been an accounting 'fudge' to gain a tax advantage. www.rail-online.co.uk

The easy drop down from Plymouth North Road to the River Plym at Marsh Mills has allowed Laira's 6023 KING EDWARD II to build up a good head of steam and it is blowing off from the safety valves before the climb to Hemerdon summit on 11 March 1956. 6023 has charge of a relatively lightly loaded Sunday 'Cornish Riviera' and therefore does not need a pilot engine over the banks to Newton Abbot. The Gas Company storage area in the centre background is now a Sainsbury's supermarket. P. Kerslake/www.rail-online.co.uk

In the mid-1950s, the weekday 'Riviera' consisted of a nine-coach formation for Penzance, with a single slip coach for Weymouth at the rear. On Saturdays, most of the train was destined for St. Ives. This fifteen-coach service was taken as far as Newton Abbot by the King, from where it was usually replaced by a pair of lesser 4-6-0s for the slog over the South Devon banks.

On summer Saturdays during much of the 1950s, two Kings could often be observed working double-headed between Newton Abbot and Plymouth. This was the only section of the Western Region where such a practice was officially permitted, authorisation having been given in January 1949. The regal double-heading resulted from the Down 'Riviera's' routine engine change at Newton Abbot, where the King on the Saturday train came off. It then continued to Plymouth by piloting the next Down train, the 10.35am ex-Paddington which, itself, was often King-hauled. That practice, which continued (nominally at least) until the start of the summer 1960 timetable, could cause much confusion to onlookers, because the King which had been taken off the 'Riviera' sometimes retained the train headboard while piloting the 10.35am.

In the Up direction, the use of double-headed Kings had been routine during part of 1949. On Sunday nights, the 8.40pm Penzance-Paddington sleeper (which ran via Bristol) was sometimes hauled from Plymouth (dep. 11.55pm) by two Kings, although one was acting as pilot only as far as Newton Abbot. The sleeper was, in effect, the return working for the two Kings - one had worked into Plymouth with the 4.15pm local from Bristol, the other with the 5.45pm from Bristol (10.40am ex-Liverpool/10.45am ex-Manchester).

For the winter of 1956, three new 'out and back' West of England diagrams were established for Old Oak's newly double-chimneyed Kings:

7.15am Plymouth-Paddington
6.30pm Paddington-Plymouth
12.30pm Plymouth-Paddington
9.50pm Paddington-Plymouth
2.0pm Plymouth-Paddington
12.30am Paddington-Plymouth newspapers

Matters are a little uncertain, but it seems that the above diagrams might have been changed before too long. The uncertainty stems from a contemporary report which refers to an Old Oak engine working the 12.30am newspaper train to Plymouth and returning with the perishables ex-Penzance. In January 1958 the Western Region's first Warship diesel-hydraulics (the heavy-weight North British built D600 A1A-A1A series) went into service. As described at length in The Book of the Warships (Irwell Press, 2009) they proved very unsatisfactory, but the light-weight D800 series (the ones the Western Region really wanted) which made their debut in August 1958, were altogether better machines. They were drafted first to the West of England route to work the principal trains and, as their numbers increased, the scope for steam locomotives diminished. Nevertheless, the Kings would have one final fling, on the 1958 summer services,

as shown by the diagrams on page 63 which used seven Old Oak engines daily, with a couple more over the weekend period, with five from Laira.

By March 1959 there were nine Warships at Laira and they now regularly worked the 'Riviera'. As more Warships arrived, the Kings gradually reduced, from eight in January 1959, down to just six in July for the summer service. Surprisingly, the Saturday Down 'Riviera' was still worked by the Kings, although the following 10.35am from Paddington was a diesel turn, giving the sight of the old and new together on the banks between Newton and Plymouth. However, by the end of the year, there were only three Kings left at Laira. The last to leave were 6002 and 6016, in September 1960. Perhaps ironically, they had been at Laira for just fifteen and eighteen months respectively, the shed's longer-term residents having already departed.

As for the diesel take-over, further emphasis (as if it were required) was supplied by local observers; during the summer of 1960 there were days when not one single King was spotted at work in Devon. Considering that 6002 and 6016 were still based at Laira at the time in question, that shows just how complete a take-over it was. Yet all was not lost for the West Country steam enthusiast – at least, not quite yet. During the Easter period of 1961, 6000 was noted at the head of the 10.10am Plymouth-Paddington (Easter Sunday), 6010 was observed with the Kingswear portion of the Up 'Royal Duchy' on the Tuesday, and on 17 April 6026 worked

Days	Train	To
Old Oak - 4 One King		
SO	10.35am Paddington-Plymouth	3.10pm (to Penzance)
SO	11.45pm Plymouth-Paddington	4.55pm (8.15pm ex-Penzance)
Old Oak - 6 Three Kings		
Sun	4.15pm Paddington-Plymouth	11.15pm
SX	10.30am Paddington-Plymouth	2.30pm (to Penzance)
SO	10.30am Paddington-Newton Abbot	2.0pm (to Penzance)
SO	2.7pm Newton Abbot-Plymouth	3.5pm (Assist 10.35am Paddington-Penzance)
MX	10.0pm Plymouth-Southall	4.22am (6.20pm Penzance-Kensington Milk)
MX	4.27am Southall-Old Oak LE	5.0am
MO	10.0pm Plymouth-Southall	4.12am (6.20pm Penzance-Kensington Milk)
MO	4.25am Southall-Old Oak LE	4.55am
D	5.30pm Paddington-Plymouth	10.0pm
SX	12.5pm Plymouth-Paddington	4.20pm (9.30am ex-Falmouth)
SO	11.5am Laira Jct-Paddington	4.3pm (8.35am ex-Falmouth)
Sun	2.0pm Plymouth-Paddington	7.20pm (11.0am ex-Penzance)
Old Oak - 7 Two Kings		
SX	3.30pm Paddington- Plymouth	8.0pm (to Penzance)
SO	11.0am Paddington- Plymouth	3.40pm (to Penzance)
Sun	3.30pm Paddington- Plymouth	9.10pm
SX	4.10pm Plymouth- Paddington	9.0pm (1.20pm ex-Penzance)
SO	11.15am Plymouth- Paddington	4.18pm
Sun	12.0am Plymouth- Paddington	7.25am (8.45pm ex-Penzance)
Old Oak - 8 Two Kings		
Sun	5.0pm Paddington- Plymouth	10.10pm
D	4.15pm Paddington- Plymouth	10.55pm
SX	7.15am Plymouth- Paddington	12.15pm
SO	7.0am Plymouth- Paddington	12.15pm
D	6.35pm Paddington- Swindon	8.10pm (to Cheltenham)
D	9.45pm Swindon-Wood Lane	11.55pm (3.50pm Whitland-Kensington Milk)
D	12.0am Wood Lane-Old Oak LE	12.30am
Sun	12.20pm Plymouth-Paddington	5.30pm (9.45am ex-Penzance)
Old Oak - 9A One King		
FO	10.35pm Paddington-Plymouth	3.32am (to Penzance)
SO	10.52am Laira Jct-Paddington	3.55pm (8.15am ex-Perranporth)
SO	9.50pm Paddington-Plymouth	4.29am (to Penzance)
Sun	9.45pm Paddington-Southall	3.46am (5.40pm Penzance-Kensington Milk)
Old Oak - 9B One King		
Sun	10.40am Paddington-Plymouth	3.44pm (to Falmouth)
Sun	11.45pm Plymouth-Paddington	5.0am (8.25pm ex-Penzance)
Old Oak - 247 One King		
Sun	9.5am Paddington-Bristol	12.15pm (to Weston-s-Mare)
Sun	6.55pm Bristol-Paddington	9.45pm
Laira - 1 - One King		
SX	8.30am Plymouth-Paddington	1.25pm
SX	6.30pm Paddington-Bristol	8.50pm (to Weston-s-Mare)
SX	9.5pm Bristol-Plymouth	12.43am (4.11pm ex-Crewe)
SO	8.30am Plymouth-Paddington	1.35pm
SO	6.30pm Paddington-Bristol	8.50pm (to Weston-s-Mare)
SO	9.5pm Bristol-Plymouth	12.43am (3.10pm ex-Manchester)
Laira - 2 - One King		
SX	12.30pm Plymouth-Paddington	4.40pm (10.0am ex-Penzance)
SX	9.50pm Paddington-Plymouth	4.29am (to Penzance)
SO	12.30pm Plymouth-Paddington	5.20pm (10.0am ex-Penzance)
Sun	10.30am Paddington-Plymouth	3.23pm (to Penzance)
Laira - 3 - One King		
SX	2.0pm Plymouth- Paddington	7.15pm (11.0am ex-Penzance)
SO	12.14pm Laira Jct- Paddington	4.55pm (10.0am ex-Newquay)
D	12.15am Paddington-Plymouth	4.45am (News to Penzance)
Laira - 4 - One King		
MX	12.0am Plymouth-Paddington	7.25am (8.45pm ex-Penzance)
SX	1.30pm Paddington-Plymouth	6.25pm (to Penzance)
SO	2.30pm Paddington- Plymouth	8.0pm (to Penzance)
Laira - 5A - One King		
D	7.50pm Plymouth-Paddington	2.0am (3.40pm ex-Penzance Perishable)
SX	9.30am Paddington-Plymouth	2.0pm (to Falmouth)
SO	9.30am Paddington-Plymouth	2.17pm (to Newquay)
Laira - 5B - One King		
Sun	7.15am Plymouth-Paddington	3.55pm
Sun	9.50pm Paddington- Plymouth	4.29am (to Penzance)
Laira - 26 - One King		
Sun	12.0am Plymouth-Bristol	3.37am (8.45pm (Sat) Penzance—Paddington)
MO	10.21am Bristol-Newton Abbot	12.53pm (7.30am Plymouth-Paignton)
MO	3.11pm Newton Abbot-Plymouth	4.20pm (Assist 11.30am Paddington-Penzance)

the 4.10pm Plymouth-Paddington. To the pleasant surprise of many, the start of the 1961 summer timetable saw the restoration of a fairly regular King working to Plymouth. It was on the 11.30am Paddington-Plymouth, the engine returning on the following day's 12.5pm from Plymouth. That, however, was short lived and, by July, sightings of Kings in Devon were once again few and far between. Among the infrequent appearances were those of 6018 with a fourteen-coach Colchester-Plymouth troop train on 13 July, and 6016 on the 12 noon Penzance-Crewe on 22 July.

For the winter 1961 timetable, so far as express operations were concerned, steam traction was effectively eliminated west of Taunton. Nevertheless, 6000 was noted at the head of the 'Riviera' on 22 December while, on 27 January 1962, 6009, 6015 and 6027 worked football specials to Plymouth, where the Argyle were playing Tottenham Hotspur in the F.A. Cup. Other sightings of the period included those of 6025, in charge of the 3.25pm Bristol-West of England parcels on 16 February, and 6016 (at least as far as Exeter) on the second part of the 10.30am Paddington-Penzance on 26 May 1962.

During the summer of 1962 King-hauled relief workings on the West of England route included three on 2 June: 6018 on the 9am Paddington-Plymouth, 6015 on the 10.10am, and 6019 on the 10.35am. On 9 June, 6025 worked the 12.15pm Plymouth-Paddington. A regular relief working during that summer - the 10.40am Paddington-Penzance - was rostered for an Old Oak King and was said at the time to be probably the last working to take a King to South Devon with any consistency. One-off workings included those of 6029 on the northbound 'Devonian' on 19 June, 6009 on a Paddington-Minehead train (but, of course, only as far as Taunton) and 6018 on a Paddington-Penzance train on 30 June, 6019 on the Down Torbay Express' on 26 July, and 6026 on the first part of the Down 'Riviera' on 4 August. However, following the use of 6000 on the 2.45pm Plymouth-Old Oak parcels on 10 August, no more Kings were observed in the West Country for the rest of the summer.

The class had a final, if sporadic, flourish in Devon towards the end of 1962. On 4 October 6000 worked the 5.30pm Paddington-Plymouth (at least as far as Exeter) while on 14 December 6011 worked the 10.40pm Paddington-Plymouth parcels, and on 17 December 6025 was seen on the Up 'Royal Duchy'. What is believed to be the last King

6017 KING EDWARD IV at Taunton with the 8.30am Plymouth-Paddington in the early 1950s, after it was returned to green livery in August 1952 and before it was fitted with a double chimney and new front frames and inside cylinders at the end of 1955. transporttreasury

The cameraman has found a high vantage point here for an overhead view of Laira's 6017 KING EDWARD IV making an unassisted assault of Dainton bank on 17 February 1957 with the Down 'Cornish Riviera' heading to Plymouth on the Newton Abbot side of the bank. There's not much coal visible in the tender and the load is within the ten coach maximum for an unassisted King over the South Devon banks between Newton Abbot and Plymouth. www.rail-online.co.uk.

6023 KING EDWARD II sets off from Plymouth North Road in the early 'fifties at 12.30pm with the Up 'Cornish Riviera'. The prevailing south west wind has provided a great smoke effect, taking the exhaust up over the signals and Modified Hall 7905. P. Kerslake/www.rail-online.co.uk.

An unidentified King passes through Plympton on 17 March 1956 with the 9.30 am from Paddington. P Kerslake/www.rail-online.co.uk

The driver watches the fireman move coal forward as Old Oak's 6028 KING GEORGE VI waits at Exeter St. David's with the 12.5pm Saturdays Only Paddington-Plymouth in the mid-1950s. transporttreasury

Two of Laira's Kings, 6010 KING CHARLES I and 6023 KING EDWARD II head past Aller Junction, west of Newton Abbot on Saturday 13 August 1955 with the relief 'Cornish Riviera', the 10.35am from Paddington. 6010, working the main train, would have come off on a through road at Newton Abbot because the 'Riviera' did not stop at Plymouth on Summer Saturdays, and it would continue to Plymouth on the front of the following relief portion. If the latter was also King-hauled, as it usually was, there was the spectacle of double-headed Kings through to Plymouth. P. Kerslake/www.rail-online.co.uk

working in Devon was that of 6018 which, on 21 December 1962 worked the 12.5pm Paddington-Penzance.

Paddington-Wolverhampton and Shrewsbury

After nationalisation, two more Kings, 6002 KING WILLIAM IV and 6004 KING GEORGE III, joined the four at Wolverhampton in December 1948, and were followed by a seventh, 6020 KING HENRY IV, during the following month. The number of turns operated by Stafford Road Kings increased to five for a short time, before dropping down to four when 6002 was transferred to Old Oak in July 1950.

The post-war services to the Midlands did not return to the pre-war two-hour schedules, with trains taking at least an extra 15 minutes, even with just one stop. Most through trains now stopped at Banbury, whilst calls were often made variously at High Wycombe, Princes Risborough and Bicester too. However, in the early fifties, one train in each direction between London and Birmingham was re-scheduled for a two-hour run; these were the Down 'Inter-City' and the Up 'Cambrian Coast Express'.

Kings had been employed on the Wolverhampton expresses since 1928, and from 1951 had started to appear in Shrewsbury regularly on the West to North line, but although

Wolverhampton and Shrewsbury were less than twenty rail miles apart, the Kings were prohibited from working between those two points. The major stumbling block had been Shifnal Viaduct, but in 1953 it was reconstructed, the work requiring the complete closure of the Wolverhampton-Shrewsbury line on two Sundays, 18 October and 29 November.

The reconstruction of the viaduct enabled Kings to work northwards from Wolverhampton, although such instances remained sporadic for some time. Prior to the upgrading of the viaduct, as a form of preliminary foray, a King had – in the autumn of 1952 – tentatively undertaken clearance tests between Wolverhampton and Shrewsbury. At Codsall, the cylinders had been found to be uncomfortably close to the platform edge and the tests had been halted. One must assume that action was later taken to improve the clearances, although the Kings were not used regularly north of Wolverhampton until 1959.

In 1952, the general condition of Stafford Road Kings (and, for that matter, many other locomotives at the shed) drew adverse comments from many quarters. The situation was partly excused by spare link men; that is, the less experienced drivers, working the Kings. One irate passenger commented on the occasion when a spare link crew

took over a Down express at Leamington: '...twelve bogies on a falling gradient and straight road, and the driver slipped the King so violently that the vibration could be felt in the second coach. This also occurred at the Knowle and Birmingham restarts'. Leaving driving techniques to one side, the best Paddington-Wolverhampton expresses were invariably hauled by Stafford Road or Old Oak Kings. One service on which they retained a monopoly until 1955 was the 6.10pm from Paddington but, subsequently, the 5.10pm took priority if there was a shortage of Kings. During the early 1950s, at least, a popular running-in turn for Stafford Road's Kings was the 8.28am Leamington-Wolverhampton semi-fast.

On 25 February 1958, 6005 KING GEORGE II was observed running light through Oakengates in the direction of Wellington, although the reason is unknown. Later that year, on November 6, 6000 worked the 'Cambrian Coast Express' through from Paddington to Shrewsbury - only the second King, it seems, to penetrate beyond Wolverhampton in everyday service. The Up working that day was given to 6028 KING GEORGE VI. At the time, those sightings of a King north of Wolverhampton were certainly considered newsworthy, as was the sight of 6022 KING EDWARD III heading the 'Cambrian Coast' through to

Shrewsbury and returning with the balancing working on 1 January 1959. Before very long, however, Kings ceased to have a rarity value on the Wolverhampton-Shrewsbury line, after the class was given the official all-clear following satisfactory clearance trials with 6011 on 13 April. As from 20 April, Kings formally took over the Paddington-Shrewsbury 'Cambrian Coast' diagram formerly worked by Castles. For the first week 6024 KING EDWARD I was in charge, giving way to 6000 on 25 April. This came to an end in late August when Castles returned, albeit interspersed with sporadic appearances by 6010 and 6019.

For most of the 1950s, Stafford Road retained an allocation of six Kings, and of those, 6005, 6006, 6011 and 6020 would stay until the final days of the class in 1962, being joined in 1954 by 6001 KING EDWARD VII and 6014 KING HENRY VII. The allocation increased to ten Kings by the start of 1960, the stud having been boosted - directly and indirectly - by engines displaced from the West of England route by diesels. This coincided with an increase in services between Paddington and Wolverhampton, with sixteen through

6017 KING EDWARD IV and 6026 KING JOHN make light work of the Saturdays Only 10.35am Paddington-Penzance at Dainton on 30 June 1956. On summer Saturdays during the 1950s, two Kings could often be observed working double-headed between Newton Abbot and Plymouth – the only section of the Western Region where such a practice was officially permitted. This arose because the Down 'Cornish Riviera' routinely changed engines on Saturdays at Newton Abbot, where the King came off. The engine then continued to Plymouth by piloting the next Down train, the 10.35am ex-Paddington which, itself, was often King-hauled. The practice continued (nominally at least) until the start of the summer 1960 timetable. P.W. Gray.

trains running daily, each shed having eight turns.

The Monday-Friday diagrams for the winter of 1959/60 employed seven of Stafford Road's ten Kings each day, and eight on Fridays. The Old Oak engines engaged on the Wolverhampton route at that time had six diagrams on Monday-Thursday, and an additional one on Fridays. The diagrams and the usual loading were:

Departure	Train No.	Shed /Type	Balancing working	Load
DOWN				
8.30am	807	OOC King	1.34pm Wolverhampton	9
9.0am SX	808	OOC King	4.35pm Wolverhampton SX	11
9.10am	908	OOC King	2.35pm Wolverhampton	11
10.10am	911	OOC King SX	3.33pm Wolverhampton	9
	911	WSR King SO	ex 2.20pm Wolverhampton FO	9
11.10am	912	WSR King SX	ex 6.45am Wolverhampton	9
		OOC King SO	4.35pm Wolverhampton	9
12.10pm	826	Castle	ex 8.30am Banbury via Oxford	6
1.10pm	915	OOC King	5.33pm Wolverhampton	12
2.10pm	916	WSR King	ex 9.35am Wolverhampton	12
3.10pm	844	OOC King	7.29pm Wolverhampton	9
4.10pm	918	WSR King	ex 10.30am Wolverhampton	12
5.10pm SX	855	WSR King	ex 11.36am Wolverhampton	13
6.8pm FO	862	OOC King	7.25am Wolverhampton SO	10
6.10pm	919	WSR King	ex 7.25am Wolverhampton SX	11
	919	WSR King	ex 11.36am Wolverhampton SO	11
6.23pm	863	WSR King	ex 8.33am Wolverhampton	11
7.10pm SX	864	Castle	*12.10am Wolverhampton*	9
8.10pm	920	WSR King SX	ex 4.20pm Wolverhampton	11
	920	OOC King SO	*12.15am Birmingham MO*	11
UP				
6.45am SX	008	WSR King	11.10am Paddington	11
7.25am	009	WSR King SX	6.10pm Paddington	12 SX
	009	OOC King SO	ex 6.8pm Paddington FO	11 SO
8.33am	018	WSR King	6.23pm Paddington	12
9.35am	025	WSR King	2.10pm Paddington	11
10.30am	034	WSR King	4.10pm Paddington	12
11.36am	039	WSR King	5.10pm Paddington SX	11
	039	WSR King	6.10pm Paddington SO	11
12.20pm		Castle		
1.34pm	049	OOC King	ex 8.30am Paddington	9
2.20pm FO	069	WSR King	*10.10am Paddington SO*	10
2.35pm	065	OOC King	ex 9.10am Paddington	11
3.33pm SX	072	OOC King	ex 10.10am Paddington	9
4.20pm SX	077	WSR King	8.10pm Paddington	9
4.35pm	082	OOC King	ex 9.0am Paddington	11
5.20pm FO	091	Castle	*4.10pm Paddington (Sun.)*	8
5.33pm	094	OOC King	ex 1.10pm Paddington	11
7.29pm	103	OOC King	ex 3.10pm Paddington	12
Where a balancing working is shown in italics, this indicates it occurs on a subsequent day unless otherwise stated.				

Where a balancing working is shown in italics, this indicates it occurs on a subsequent day unless otherwise stated.

Services expanded further over the next two years as the route absorbed Euston's traffic to Birmingham and Wolverhampton in addition to its own, due to electrification work on the old

LNWR line. In order to give the engineers the longest possible occupation, this required some retrenchment of passenger train services, primarily affecting the expresses between Euston, Birmingham and Wolverhampton, which were replaced by an increased service on the Western Region line. Five weekday trains in each direction were suspended and of the four remaining trains each way, seven were diverted to the Northampton route. The Kings at Stafford Road consequently increased during 1961/62, with up to 14 of the class allocated there in the final months. Due to a diagram revision, as from 16 May 1960 the Down 'Cambrian Coast' became an almost everyday duty for the Kings,

the engine returning home with the 2.35pm ex-Birkenhead. There was an interruption to that pattern between January and June 1961, but the Kings resumed the duty for the summer 1961 timetable.

On 22 April 1961, 6002 KING WILLIAM IV reached Ruabon with the 'Ffestiniog Railway Special' from Paddington. Special permission was apparently required for 6002 to work to Ruabon, similar permission presumably being required for 6000 which, on 29 September 1962, arrived there with the 'Talyllyn Railway Special Train'.

Early in 1962 the Kings took over the 8.25pm Shrewsbury (Abbey Foregate)-Wood Lane milk train, the working having recently been diverted at its southern end from Marylebone. In June of that same year, several of the new 'Western' diesel-hydraulics took up residency at Oxley for use on the principal Paddington expresses, and this was at last the beginning of the end for the Stafford Road Kings. Nevertheless, the requirements of the summer timetable meant that the Kings remained surprisingly active on the Paddington-Birmingham-Wolverhampton route for a little while longer, albeit in what was described as a 'rapidly deteriorating mechanical condition'.

In the northbound direction, during the summer of 1962 Old Oak Kings retained a dominance of the Down 'Cambrian Coast' through to Shrewsbury while, due to a motive power shortage on 6 August, Stafford Road's 6016 was given the Up 'Cambrian Coast'. That was stated to be the first occasion since September 1959 that the train had been King-hauled between Shrewsbury and Wolverhampton.

The rostering of Kings to Birmingham expresses came to an end with the introduction of the winter 1962 timetable but, inevitably, that didn't bring about an immediate cessation of such outings. One revival was undoubtedly rather pleasurable to steam enthusiasts. It concerned 6002 KING WILLIAM IV which, in early September 1962, was exhibited at Snow Hill station (to mark the end of Kings on the Birmingham expresses). When, on 4 September, the diesel on a Wolverhampton express failed, 6002 stepped into the breach at a moment's notice. 6000 also came to the rescue of a failed diesel that same month, taking over the 6.40pm Shrewsbury-Paddington from D1005 on 29 September; the King had worked north that day with the Talyllyn Special, and its return trip to London with the 6.40pm was officially booked as a light engine working!

There were several other King workings on the Birmingham line during and after September 1962. For example, on 18 October, 6005 KING GEORGE II hauled the 8.20am Paddington-Shrewsbury (the 'Inter City') and returned with the 12.58pm Up 'Cambrian Coast Express' from Shrewsbury, relieved at Birmingham by 6011 KING JAMES I. On 30 October 6011 worked the two-hour (10am) Birmingham-Paddington, and on 3 November 6000 worked the Up 'Inter City'; on 17 November 6018 worked a special excursion to Wolverhampton while, on 21 December, the 10.50am Paddington-Shrewsbury relief to the 'Cambrian Coast Express' and its return was worked by 6011.

By now, the Kings were close to extinction. The first to have been withdrawn was 6006 KING GEORGE I, a Stafford Road engine since 1930, which had been taken out of service on 15 February 1962. Just seven months later, on 20 September, it was reported that 6012, 6014, 6015, 6017 and 6022 were stored in the open at Stafford Road (of those, 6012 and 6017 had been withdrawn). Stafford Road shed itself did not long survive the passing of the Kings and was closed in September 1963.

Paddington-Bristol
The three Kings transferred to Bath Road in 1948; 6000, 6018 and 6019, were seen frequently at Paddington, working the 8.20am from Weston-Super-Mare and returning with the 1.15pm from

A summer Saturday working, probably in 1956, and Laira's 6008 KING JAMES II is piloting a Britannia through Mutley Cutting into Plymouth North Road with the 10.35am relief 'Cornish Riviera' from Paddington. 6008's fireman has correctly removed the 130 Reporting Number from its frame, together with the headboard, something which was not always done and often led to confusion amongst observers. This viewpoint is now ruined by the presence of a carpark which has been built from the tunnel mouth and which extends down way to the extreme right of the photograph. P. Kerslake/www.rail-online.co.uk

In these two photographs taken on 5 August 1956, Laira's 6025 KING HENRY III pilots Old Oak Common's 6019 KING HENRY V through Mutley Cutting into Plymouth with the 10.35am second portion of the 'Cornish Riviera' from Paddington. The first part of this train, departing from Paddington just five minutes earlier, did not stop at Plymouth on Summer Saturdays in those years and 6025, which had been running ahead of 6019 on the first part, would have come off at Newton Abbot, to be coupled as pilot to the second part over the banks to Plymouth. The Royal Eye Infirmary is in the background and no wonder with all those engines in the siding that a notice on those railings asked enginemen to keep smoke and noise to a minimum for the benefit of patients! More than one footplateman ended up in there with smuts in his eye. Both: P. Kerslake/ www.rail-online.co.uk

Paddington, and the 12.0 noon from Bristol in and the 4.15pm from Paddington back. The allocation was reduced in June 1950, when two of the engines were transferred to Old Oak, leaving just 6000, which stayed until October 1952.

As already related, the fastest trains on the Paddington-Bristol route were not usually heavily loaded and, with speed more important than sheer power, Castles were normally considered more than adequate. However, Kings regained a brief monopoly of the prestige 'Bristolian' service in 1954. For that year's summer timetable, the train was accelerated to a time of just 105 minutes. A preliminary trial was undertaken on 30 April 1954 by 6003 KING GEORGE IV which, with an eight-coach loading (254 tons tare), easily kept ahead of the schedule. On the outward trip, 6003 was unofficially timed at 98mph on the descent of Dauntsey Bank while, on the return trip, Swindon to Paddington was covered in 60 minutes exactly. The first public working of the 'Bristolian' to the new schedule was on 14 June, and the seven-coach train arrived at Temple Meads three and a half minutes early. The return journey was via the Badminton line, 6000 bringing its six-coach train into Paddington four minutes early. Between Badminton and Old Oak the train had averaged 80mph. The usual 'Bristolian' loading was relatively light, and the

Kings had no trouble with the new schedule; indeed, on 17 June 6015 brought the Up train into Paddington no less than ten minutes early. It was, however, inevitable that the Kings would not be allotted indefinitely to such a lightly-loaded duty, and Castles gradually took over from early September.

During the first week of October 1954, Kings were given the 7.30am and 9.5am Paddington-Bristol trains, which had usually been Castle-hauled; as if to redress the balance, during much of that month several Paddington-Plymouth trains were worked by Counties instead of the customary Kings. Earlier in 1954 - on Sundays 9th and 16th May – an unusual sighting in Bristol had been that of the King-hauled 'Riviera', the train having been diverted from its normal route due to bridge renewal work at Newbury.

By 1956 the usual 'Bristolian' engines were still Castles, but later that year Kings reappeared on Mondays following an increase in the loading of that day's trains to eight coaches. Normally, anything over seven coaches on the 'Bristolian' resulted in an extra time allowance, but on 8 August 1957, 6019 KING HENRY V illustrated the inappropriateness of that practice by hauling a ten-coach special (some 350 tons) from Paddington to Bristol for a ship launching ceremony, in just 99 minutes, an average of 72.7mph.

Nevertheless, the practice of relaxing the schedule for a heavier than normal 'Bristolian' continued.

During 1956 and 1957, regular King duties on the Bristol line included the 2.25am Paddington-Bristol newspaper train, returning with the 7.45am Bristol-Paddington, and occasionally the TPO via Bristol. Another regular duty was the 6.35pm Paddington-Cheltenham as far as Swindon (due at Swindon at 8.10pm - not exactly 'Cheltenham Flyer' scheduling!), returning with the milk train (3.50pm ex-Whitland) for Wood Lane.

In 1958 the WR conducted trials with a view to introducing a 100-minute schedule for the 'Bristolian'. One of the test runs was undertaken by 6018 KING HENRY VI which, on 22 May, failed to achieve the target with a 247-ton train. The late arrivals (nearly four minutes with the Down train and more than six minutes with the up) were, however, not the engine's fault as crippling permanent way checks were in force in both directions. Despite top speeds of 91mph on the Down run and 86mph on the Up, the lost time couldn't be regained. The 100-minute timing was introduced in 1959, but with Warship diesels in charge. The last scheduled steam-hauled weekday 'Bristolian' ran on 12 June 1959, with Castles in both directions. (Continues Page 78).

A Sunday 'Cornish Riviera' in 1956 has no less than 6000 KING GEORGE V at its head as it drops down over Trefusis Bridge at Lipson Vale shortly after having left Plymouth North Road on its run to Paddington. The driver and fireman are taking in the view and will shortly see Laira shed on this side before they run along the River Plym and then tackle the 1 in 42 of Hemerdon Bank. 6000 has no pilot engine so its load must be within the 360 tons, ten coach maximum, which was not unusual for a Sunday working. P Kerslake/www.rail-online.co.uk

6029 KING EDWARD VIII at Reading with 'The Royal Duchy' in May 1957. The 1.30pm train to Penzance had only been given the title on 28 January. 6029 still has its original single chimney and was not fitted with a double chimney until the end of the year.

Driver Griffiths and Fireman Forester get ready to reverse 6008 KING JAMES II back to Paddington to work the 2.10pm to Wolverhampton on 17 July 1959. Normally the engine would be provided with sufficient coal at Stafford Road to cover the out and home workings, but there were occasions when the engine would arrive back at Stafford Road with the fireman sweeping up the remnants at the back of the tender coal space. To make the return trip easier for the fireman, a team of shedmen were employed at Ranelagh Bridge to shovel the remaining coal in the tender forward to be within the fireman's reach. Brian Penney.

Shortly before 4pm, two Kings wait for departure time at Paddington, probably during 1961. On the left, 6017 KING EDWARD IV is on the 4.10pm to Birkenhead, and on the right, the now preserved 6023 KING EDWARD II will take out the 3.55pm 'Capitals United Express' to South Wales. 6017 had been at Stafford Road since February 1959, while 6023 had been transferred to Cardiff Canton from Old Oak in September 1960 along with five others as diesel traction took over their former duties. This was a short-lived exercise which ended in March 1962 with the introduction of the Beyer-Peacock 'Hymeks' on the South Wales trains. www.rail-online.co.uk

On 4 September 1962, just a few days before its withdrawal, 6026 KING JOHN is being watered at Ranelagh Bridge after working the 8.55am Birkenhead-Paddington and is being prepared for its return to Wolverhampton. The facilities at Ranelagh were used regularly by engines arriving at Paddington on the shorter runs from Bristol, Cardiff and Wolverhampton, enabling them to be turned, watered and prepared for their return run without having to run down to Old Oak Common. Turn-round times were impressive, and often engines would be off back to Paddington within the hour. The yard was also used by diesels as shown by Warship D835 PEGASUS. www.rail-online.co.uk

6000 KING GEORGE V and North British Warship D601 ARK ROYAL provide super power for the relief Down 'Cornish Riviera Express' at Aller Junction on Saturday 23 August 1958, the first year of service for the diesel. In 1958 the '133' Reporting Number was used on the main 'CRE' train instead of the '130' used in previous years. The King will have brought this to Newton Abbot, where it came off because the train ran non-stop to Truro on summer Saturdays. KING GEORGE V has been attached in front of D601 which is on the 10.35am relief train, and is working down to Plymouth. www.rail-online.co.uk

6003 KING GEORGE IV in this 1958 view taken on the approach to Teignmouth station from the west was working the 8.30am Truro-Paddington. The picture was taken under the Sea Lawn footbridge which was demolished by the early 1960s. 6003 was fitted with its double chimney in April 1957, although it has not had new front frames and a new inside cylinder block. www.rail-online.co.uk

6009 KING CHARLES II coming up through Reading in 1958 on the Paddington-bound 'Mayflower' which it has worked from Plymouth, departing there at 8.30am. The sun is in the right direction for the cameraman, the engine has been turned out well by the cleaners at Laira and 6009 has steam to spare which adds to the scene. www.rail-online.co.uk

Old Oak's 6019 KING HENRY V at Taunton after arrival with the Sundays Only 11.15am from Paddington via Bristol. Colour-rail

6012 KING EDWARD VI emerges from the eastern portal of Dainton tunnel at the head of a Paddington-bound express in 1959. The coaches show the change in gradient, with the summit itself being within the tunnel. There is no pilot engine to spoil the view, so the load will be within the ten coach limit for a King over the South Devon banks from Plymouth. 6012 was one of fourteen of the class to have new front ends fitted whilst undergoing a Heavy Overhaul at Swindon a few years earlier. The work amounted to a new frame section and inside cylinders. An assembly was set up in Swindon Works in advance of the next King arriving for major attention. www.rail-online.co.uk

Laira's 6017 KING EDWARD IV nears the top of Dainton bank, with a London express in 1958 or early 1959. Both Up and Down sidings are visible, and it is worth remembering that those sidings are on the level, indicating the steepness of the 1 in 36 gradient here. One of Newton Abbot's large prairie tanks is just visible on the left, probably after having banked a freight up from Aller Junction and it is now waiting to cross over to run bunker first back down to Aller, or home to Newton Abbot once the line is clear. The large mirror mounted on a post, visible above the leading coach, was for the signalman to check that a tail lamp was present on workings coming up the bank and heading into the tunnel when his view may have been obscured by a train on the Down main line passing in front of his box. www.rail-online.co.uk

At Leamington Spa on 29 December 1957, only the wedge-shaped cab front panels and the bracket for the Reporting Number frame remain on 6014 KING HENRY VII from its 'streamlined' past. It had been fitted with a double chimney at the end of 1955. www.rail-online.co.uk

6005 KING GEORGE II descending west from the tunnel under Wooburn Moor and White House Farm above Loudwater between High Wycombe and Beaconsfield with the 4.10pm Paddington-Birkenhead in 1962. Apart from its first three years from 1927 to 1930, 6005 was a Stafford Road engine for its whole life. www.rail-online.co.uk

Stafford Road's 6011 KING JAMES I waits to depart from Paddington with the 1.10pm Wolverhampton on 30 May 1960. It was one of fourteen engines which received new front frames and inside cylinder block, and it has had replacement parallel shank buffers. B.W.L. Brooksbank/Initial Photographics.

6012 KING EDWARD VI emerges from Snow Hill tunnel and passes Birmingham Moor Street station with the Up 'Inter-City' in 1961. M. Mensing.

Two spotters chat with the crew as they admire 6018 KING HENRY VI in August 1962 waiting to depart from Wolverhampton Low Level with the original 'Inter-City' which had been introduced in September 1950. It is interesting that the name went on to be used by British Rail to describe all of its principal express services and was even adopted by German Railways (who still use the title). 6018 was returned to service in 1963, after the class had all been withdrawn at the end of 1962, to work the Stephenson Locomotive Society's 'Farewell to the Kings Tour' on 28 April 1963 from Birmingham to Swindon and back. www.rail-online.co.uk.

Despite the gradual diesel take-over, the Kings maintained a presence on the Bristol line until 1962, the last year of the class. During the summer of 1962 they were often used on the Down 'Bristolian' on Saturdays, which was usually loaded to 14 bogies. The return working was the 2.35pm from Weston-super-Mare. Among those noted were 6000 on 28 July and 4 August and 6026 on 11 August. In August 6018 worked an excursion train through to Weston-super-Mare (Locking Road).

West to North
Apart from the brief trials of Kings in South Wales and west of Plymouth, and the various 'guest appearances' and exchange workings, the class was restricted to familiar territory until 1948. Late that year, following track improvements, permission was given for them to be used between Bristol and Shrewsbury – this was the first time that route availability had been officially extended.

Bath Road's 6000 inaugurated the workings on the Shrewsbury route on 1 February 1951 – the first official revenue-earning King workings through the Severn Tunnel. The diagram took in the 4.30pm Bristol to Liverpool (9.55am ex-Penzance) as far as

Shrewsbury, returning with the 8.20pm ex-Crewe which was scheduled to arrive at Bristol at 12.46am. The diagram was changed as from 20 October 1952, and 6000 was transferred away from Bath Road, the last of its class to be allocated there.

Castles subsequently regained a domination of the 'west to north' trains, but on 20 May 1954, 6009 KING CHARLES II of Old Oak worked the Bristol-Shrewsbury leg of the 10.5am ex-Penzance. This unusual course for an Old Oak engine was due to the failure of the designated Castle, 5037 of Bath Road. The Kings had a reprise in the autumn of 1959, when one was rostered for the Shrewsbury-Newton Abbot leg of the 9.5am Liverpool-Plymouth on Mondays, Wednesdays and Fridays, returning on the remaining weekdays with the 5am Plymouth-Liverpool and Glasgow. During October, Stafford Road's 6011 was such a regular performer on that diagram that a *Railway Magazine* correspondent excitedly, if mistakenly, reported that it had actually been transferred to Shrewsbury.

As evidenced by 6009 in 1954, it was not unknown for 'foreign' Kings to appear on the 'west and north' route. Another instance occurred on 22

October 1960 when, as an indirect result of a roster change, 6021 KING RICHARD II of Old Oak had been noted working to Shrewsbury and back, on a Bristol diagram covering the 1.15pm Plymouth-Liverpool and the 7.0pm Liverpool-Bristol.

On 11 October 1961, after a DMU caught fire in the Severn Tunnel, 'west and north' trains were among those re-routed via Gloucester. One of the diverted trains was the 12 noon Penzance-Crewe, which was hauled by an unidentified King, and this brought about what is believed to be the first instance of a King in Gloucester. The engine was apparently taken off there and returned light to Bristol. Around that time, a regular King duty involved taking the 12.35am ex-Manchester-Penzance on from Shrewsbury, the engines usually being from Old Oak, taken off at Bristol. As late as 1962, Kings were still occasionally seen on 'north to west' duties and 6014 KING HENRY VII, for example, was noted hauling the 10.45pm ex-Manchester-West of England on from Shrewsbury in June. (Continues page 86).

Exactly four weeks before its official withdrawal date of 7 September 1962, 6015 KING RICHARD III has a 'clear road ahead' signalled out of Banbury. www.rail-online.co.uk.

In its final week in traffic, 6019 KING HENRY V slogs up Hatton Bank with the 2.10pm to Birkenhead on 1 September 1962. It had been transferred back to Old Oak from Canton in March. B.W.L. Brooksbank/Initial Photographics.

It was not until 1959 that Kings regularly worked through to Shrewsbury and beyond their former boundary at Wolverhampton. On 20 April they formally took over from the Castles the Paddington-Shrewsbury 'Cambrian Coast' diagram. Old Oak Common's 6021 KING RICHARD II waits for the train to depart westwards before backing out to Shrewsbury shed. Note Shrewsbury station's distinctive water bag extending over the platform track in order to allow locomotives on the through road to take water. www.rail-online.co.uk

6018 KING HENRY VI passes the industrial waste tips at Wednesbury, between Wolverhampton and Birmingham, with a southbound express in 1961. 6018 remained at Swindon following its official withdrawal in December 1962 and was re-instated to work the last King hauled SLS Special on 28 April 1963 before being cut up at Swindon in October of that year. www.rail-online.co.uk

6026 KING JOHN at Banbury with an express to London on 26 April 1962. www.rail-online.co.uk

On 29 September 1962 6000 KING GEORGE V worked the 'Talyllyn Railway Special Train' from Paddington through to Ruabon from Paddington. Special permission was required for the King to work beyond Shrewsbury. The return from Ruabon was scheduled to be Light Engine to Shrewsbury and then a local passenger from Shrewsbury to Wolverhampton from where it was to run light engine back to Old Oak Common. Events took a different turn, however, for when 6000 arrived that evening at Wolverhampton with its passenger working, a Western diesel had failed there on the 6.40pm from Shrewsbury to Paddington. 6000 was coupled inside the diesel, assisting it and its train to Paddington. www.rail-online.co.uk

The fireman climbs aboard as Canton's 6003 KING GEORGE IV waits to add an LMS BG van to a west-bound express at Bristol Temple Meads. 6003 was allocated to the Cardiff shed between September 1960 and February 1962. It was one of the class which did not receive new front frames and inside cylinder block in the late 1950s. It retains the original style of inside valve spindle covers and has no strengthening pieces welded to the lifting holes in the front frames. The mechanical lubricator is mounted ahead of the outside steam pipe to permit easier access to the lubricating points on the inside valve gear. www.rail-online.co.uk

Those houses up on the skyline at Totterdown are still there today, as is the Bath Road bridge under which 6008 KING JAMES II runs as it arrives at Bristol Temple Meads around 1958. It had been fitted with a double chimney in mid-1957 and was transferred from Laira to Stafford Road in February 1959. 6008 received new front frames and inside cylinder block in the late 1950s, has the later pattern of inside valve spindle covers, and strengthening pieces welded to the lifting holes in the front frames. www.rail-online.co.uk

6015 KING RICHARD III in the unmistakeable surroundings of Sydney Gardens at Bath with the Down 'Merchant Venturer' on 9 April 1956. During a lengthy works visit in 1955, it had been experimentally fitted with a double chimney fabricated from sheet steel. It returned to traffic on 8 September, and its performances were closely monitored. On its first official test run with the 'Cornish Riviera' on 26 September, it reached 103mph on a section where 85mph had been the norm for single chimney Kings. Three days later, during another trip on the 'Riviera', 6015 was timed at over 107mph, the highest authenticated speed achieved by any Great Western locomotive. H. Ballantyne.

There are three odd maroon coaches at the front of the 'Bristolian' 'chocolate and cream' set and 6021 KING RICHARD II is displaying the named train's B04 reporting number as it passes Oldfield Park, Bath on 7 July 1962. The probable explanation is that the weekday set had been strengthened for the Saturdays Only Paddington to Weston-super-Mare train. www.rail-online.co.uk

As suitable express passenger work for the Kings at Old Oak Common diminished in late 1960 the decision was taken to transfer Kings 6003, 6004, 6018, 6019, 6023 and 6028 to Cardiff Canton. Their duties were mainly Paddington expresses through the Severn Tunnel to and from Cardiff and also on the north and west line to Shrewsbury, but their use on the London jobs ended in early 1962 when the new 'Hymeks' took over. 6019 KING HENRY V was working the 'Capitals United Express' from Paddington on 11 May 1961. www.rail-online.co.uk

When diesels began to displace the Kings at Old Oak Common on the West Country workings, six were transferred to Cardiff Canton. One of them, 6028 KING GEORGE VI, was at Newport with the 10.30am Swansea-Paddington on 10 February 1961. Colour-rail

Canton's 6028 KING GEORGE VI, formerly an Old Oak engine, heads 'The Red Dragon' at Stoke Gifford on 23 May 1962. This working would have taken the loop at Patchway following its three mile climb up from the Severn Tunnel, leaving the direct line into Bristol at that location, and now heads eastwards on to the main line through Badminton and onwards to Swindon and Paddington. 6028 returned to Old Oak in June 1962 but went into store on 3 August and never returned to service. The work of the Kings on South Wales trains was generally regarded as unremarkable. www.rail-online.co.uk

6029 KING EDWARD VIII waits to leave Cardiff General with the 8.15am to Paddington on 6 May 1960. This was an Old Oak engine but was not one of the Kings transferred to Canton in September of that year. Kings began working to Cardiff on a regular basis in late 1959, the diagram involving the 12.45am Paddington-Cardiff newspapers and returning with the 8.0am from Cardiff, the 'Capitals United Express'. Time-keeping on the new diagram was poor and the Western Region reverted to Castles on the 'Capitals'. An Old Oak King continued to be rostered to the Down newspaper train, but the diagrams were revised so that it returned with the 8.15am from Cardiff. R.O. Tuck/Rail Archive Stephenson.

6003 KING GEORGE IV at Rumney Bridge soon after leaving Cardiff with the Up 'Red Dragon on 24 September 1960. It had been transferred to Canton from Old Oak on 13 September. R.O. Tuck/Rail Archive Stephenson.

South Wales

Although 6014 KING HENRY VII had reached Cardiff on a Paddington-West Wales special in 1935, it was not until April 1952 that a King, 6009 KING CHARLES II, undertook clearance tests at Newport and Cardiff, despite the fact that Kings had previously ventured through to Cardiff (albeit not on regular workings) seemingly without any mishaps. In April 1943 a King had made a tentative and low profile test run to South Wales. 6007 KING WILLIAM III of Old Oak was trialled on all the lines at Cardiff Canton shed, particular attention being paid to clearances at the coal stage and on the turntable.

It is believed that, during the 1952 tests, particular attention was paid to the Rumney River bridge, just to the east of Cardiff, which had recently been strengthened. At Newport, Kings had, of course, been seen regularly on Bristol-Shrewsbury workings since early 1951, but those trains had turned off at Maindee East Curve and had not penetrated the centre of Newport itself. It was suggested that the testing of Kings at Newport and Cardiff in 1952 was with a view to their use on the 'Red Dragon', but that didn't happen until 1959.

The Kings finally made it beyond Newport in a revenue-earning capacity in 1955. On 19 February, 6015 KING RICHARD III worked the 12.45am

Paddington-Carmarthen newspaper train as far as Cardiff, returning with the Up Irish boat train at 8.15am. This was the first appearance of a King, it is believed, on a regular working in the Welsh capital. Kings were subsequently used on a similar out-and-back working, but for only a short period before Castles regained their domination. Another South Wales incursion was observed on the morning of 24 August that same year, when 6022 KING EDWARD III of Old Oak was noted at Newport, heading in the direction of Cardiff with an unidentified fourteen-coach train.

A King made another rare appearance in South Wales on 30 September 1957 when 6000 headed the Down 'Capitals United Express' into Cardiff. An even more unusual South Wales working involved 6008 KING JAMES II of Laira which, on 10 May 1958, was turned out for the 9.5am Bristol-Cardiff. It returned from Cardiff with the 11.10am ex-Swansea, which it worked right through to Plymouth.

It was late in 1959 before Cardiff started to see Kings on a regular basis. As from 23 November of that year, the diagram involving the 12.45am Paddington-Cardiff newspapers was revised so that the return trip was with the 8.0am from Cardiff, the 'Capitals United Express', and the round trip was worked by an Old Oak King. Things

got off to an uninspiring start, the engine on the first day being 6024 KING EDWARD I which, at the time, was due for a works visit. It lost 25 minutes with the newspaper working and steamed so badly on the return trip that the 'Capitals' reached Paddington 43 minutes late.

Time-keeping on the new diagram continued to be poor. During the first fortnight, the only day the Up 'Capitals' arrived at Paddington on time was 30 November and that was when Castle 7029 had been turned out for the duty. It was not exactly the Kings' finest hour - on 5 December 6015 failed, on 7 December 6024 brought the 'Capitals' into Paddington 60 minutes late, and on 8 December 6015 had to stop for a 'blow up' and arrived at Paddington 65 minutes late. The Western Region quickly abandoned the experiment. An Old Oak King continued to be rostered to the Down newspaper train, but the diagrams were revised so that it returned with the 8.15am from Cardiff instead of the 'Capitals'. An unusual participant in that diagram on 14 December was 6020 KING HENRY IV of Stafford Road. The Kings were, however, not unknown on another Cardiff named train, the 'Red Dragon'. On 16 February 1960, for example, 6028 KING GEORGE VI of Old Oak took the Down 'Dragon' from Paddington, having worked Up from Cardiff with

6000 KING GEORGE V brings the 4.10pm Whitland to Kensington milk train past Rhymney River bridge on the outskirts of Cardiff on 15 May 1960. Kings had been regularly diagrammed on the heavy milk trains to London from the south west since GWR days and they worked the Whitland train in the mid-1950s and early 1960s, initially only from Swindon but later from Cardiff. R.O. Tuck/Rail Archive Stephenson.

A lone spotter carrying the inevitable duffel bag watches 6018 KING HENRY VI as it waits to leave Cardiff General with the 7.20pm Crewe mail on 6 May 1961 which it will take as far as Shrewsbury. R.O. Tuck/Rail Archive Stephenson.

6023 KING EDWARD II, checked by a PW slack, cautiously climbs Nantyderry bank, near Abergavenny, with the 12.15pm Manchester to Plymouth express, which it will work from Shrewsbury to Bristol, on 19 May 1962. Although Castles were the mainstay of the West to North services, after route restrictions on them were lifted in early BR days, Kings did work as occasional substitutes and for a short time in 1951/52 and again in 1959/60 had a regular diagram over the line. R.O. Tuck/ Rail Archive Stephenson.

6004 KING GEORGE III crosses Rhymney River bridge on the northern edge of Cardiff with the 7.20pm Cardiff to Crewe mail on 17 May 1962. By the summer of 1961, the Canton diagrams were revised and took a King only as far as Pontypool Road with the 7.20pm, then from Pontypool Road to Shrewsbury with the 12 noon ex-Penzance, and back with the following day's 2.25pm Shrewsbury-Cardiff. R.O. Tuck/Rail Archive Stephenson.

Stripped of its number plates and nameplates, 6017 **KING EDWARD IV** at Stafford Road, its final depot, where it had been condemned in July 1962 following a month stored out of use from mid-June. There's another King behind, 6012 **KING EDWARD VI**, which had also been transferred to Stafford Road in 1959. www.rail-online.co.uk

the 5am ex-Neyland. Despite the Kings' often unhappy experiences with South Wales workings, 6003, 6004, 6018, 6019, 6023 and 6028 were transferred from Old Oak to Cardiff Canton in September 1960. The influx was simply a reflection of the spread of diesel traction elsewhere; options were severely limited because of the weight of the Kings, and Canton offered what were the only real opportunities for alternative work. They were joined a year later by 6010 and 6024 when Canton transferred its Britannia Pacifics to the London Midland.

The Canton engines were used principally on the regular Paddington turns, the 8.0am Up and 1.55pm back, the 10am Up and 3.55pm back and the 12 noon Up and 5.55pm back. The Kings were allowed 500 tons on the Severn Tunnel line, compared to the 455 tons allowed for Castles, Counties and Britannias. Other duties in which the Canton Kings regularly participated were the Fridays Only 7.5am to Paddington and 5.35pm return (an Old Oak job for the rest of the week) the Sundays Only 7.10pm to Paddington and 1.20am (Monday) return, and two former Britannia workings as far as Shrewsbury and back - the 8.55am Cardiff-Manchester returning with the 12.15pm ex-Manchester-Plymouth, and the 11.50am ex-Swansea-Manchester, returning with the 3.5pm ex-Manchester-

Cardiff. The Kings were barred west of Cardiff.

By the summer of 1961 a variation had crept into the Canton diagram involving the 8.55am Cardiff-Manchester. The new pattern was for the engine to leave from Shrewsbury with the 2.25pm to Bristol, work the 7.15pm Bristol-Pontypool Road, and return home with the Cardiff portion of the 8.30pm ex-Crewe. Another diagram revision took a King from Cardiff to Pontypool Road with the 7.20pm, from Pontypool Road to Shrewsbury with the 12 noon ex-Penzance, and back with the following day's 2.25pm Shrewsbury-Cardiff.

The last outings of Kings on the Cardiff routes seem to have attracted little attention, but in March 1962 Beyer-Peacock Hymek Type 3 diesels took over much of the main line work to and from South Wales. Indeed, the following month it was reported that two Canton Kings were unserviceable and in store 'unlikely to work again'. The last two Kings left Canton in July 1962, when 6004 and 6024 (already withdrawn) were dispatched to Swindon.

Withdrawals

There were mutterings in the enthusiast press as early in 1952, casting doubts about the longevity of the Kings. It was noted that they required reboilering,

and that heavy repairs to the frames were frequently necessary. A visitor to Swindon on 10 February 1952 reported that no less than eight Kings were 'in or about' the works: 6003 (Light Casual), 6004 (Heavy Intermediate), 6009 (Light Casual), 6019 (Light Casual), 6023 (Heavy General), 6024 (Light Casual), 6025 (awaiting Heavy General), and 6028 (Heavy General).

Later that year, another report added fuel to the fire by noting that, in the last week of September, four of the class were in the works, nine were at sheds under or awaiting repair, one was stopped pending the delivery of material for repair, and another was fresh from the shops. In other words, half of the class was out of action at that particular time. There is no doubt that by the mid-1950s the Kings were showing increasing signs of the hard work which they had undertaken, almost incessantly, for the previous twenty-five years or so. However, in this respect they were no different than their contemporaries on the other Regions such as the LNER A3s and the LMS Princess Royals, both of which classes needed frequent frame repairs.

As chapter 4 describes in detail, the fitting in the 1950s of double chimneys, new boilers and front-end refurbishments revitalised the engines. To offset this, the declining standards

A forlorn 6022 KING EDWARD III on 7 April 1963 outside Stafford Road shed. Although withdrawn in the previous September and shorn of its plates, it is otherwise intact. It was one of the class given new front frames and inside cylinder block during an earlier overhaul at Swindon. 6022 had been allocated to Stafford Road since June 1959. www.rail-online.co.uk

Although officially withdrawn on 31 December 1962, 6018 KING HENRY VI was steamed again. It was sent to Tyseley and employed between 22 and 25 April 1963 on local passenger duties, as a prelude to its run on 28 April, when it hauled an SLS special on a circular Birmingham-Southall (where it is pictured)-Swindon-Birmingham trip. After that, 6018 came very close to being preserved when the Butlin's Holiday Camp company was purchasing steam locomotives for display but the sale fell through; Butlins bought a Stanier Pacific in its place and 6018 was duly cut up at Swindon in October 1963. P. Groom.

of maintenance in the early 1960s brought a resurgence of failures, the Birmingham line, in particular, being badly affected. When a King failed on a passenger working, the first suitable engine – often from a freight – was commandeered as a replacement, and such was the frequency of King failures on the Birmingham line that the freight services became notoriously unreliable. In the eyes of officialdom, the Kings had actually become a liability. However, their abrupt withdrawal – all thirty were retired by BR in 1962 – was effectively due to their size. They had been displaced from their traditional duties by diesels but, unlike most other displaced engines, with the exception of the LMS Coronations, the Kings couldn't be found suitable alternative work. They were simply too big or too heavy to be used on all but a handful of routes.

Throughout 1962 withdrawals made steady inroads into the class, but the remaining engines were not denied the occasional late flourish. For the opening of the Richard Thomas & Baldwins Ltd. steelworks at Llanwern near Newport on 26 October 1962, 6000 and 6018 hauled special VIP trains from Paddington. The two Kings were serviced at Newport Ebbw Junction shed in readiness for the return trip - the first time two of the class had been at Ebbw Junction simultaneously since the Ebbw Vale trials of 1938.

On 27 October, the day after the Llanwern trip, 6000, 6005 and 6011 all worked Paddington-Newbury race specials, the last steam-hauled trains to arrive at the racecourse station. 6005 and

6011, displaced from Stafford Road, had been transferred to Old Oak in September and from the 10th of that month were used on a diagram which involved the 6.35pm Paddington-Didcot, returning the following morning with the 7.10am from Didcot. The engine working the Down train on Fridays and spent the weekend at Didcot.

Rather late in the day, in November 1962, 6011 and 6018 broke new ground when they spent several days at Chepstow acting as test loads for the rebuilding work in progress on the Wye Bridge. By the beginning of December, only four Kings remained active. They were 6000 (withdrawn on 4th), 6011 and 6025 (both quoted as being withdrawn on either 18 or 21 December) and 6018 (which survived until the end of the month). Despite the official demise of all four during December, in the following spring it was rumoured that 6000, 6011, 6025 and 6026, which were all in store at Old Oak, might be held in reserve in case they were needed to help out on the forthcoming summer schedules. That, however, didn't come to pass.

Preservation

Three Kings have been preserved, one by design and two through good fortune, and each of them has worked on the main line at various times. An incorrect rumour of the period was that, due to a cracked frame, 6000 was to be broken up and 6018 KING HENRY VI would be preserved instead, the name and number plates and the bell being transferred accordingly and, as if to

emphasise 6018's reasonable health, it was steamed again. It was sent to Tyseley and employed between 22 and 25 April 1963 on local passenger duties, working the 6.5pm Birmingham-Leamington local and return. Those workings were a prelude to its run on 28 April, when it hauled a Stephenson Locomotive Society special on a circular Birmingham-Southall-Swindon-Birmingham trip (fare 30s 6d!) notching up a speed of 90mph *en route*. After that, 6018 came very close to being preserved when the Butlin's Holiday Camp company was purchasing steam locomotives for display. 6018 had been sent to Swindon for 'repairs' in preparation for a move to the Minehead camp but the sale fell through, apparently because the WR scrap value was £800 more for the King than the LMR wanted for one of its Coronations and so Butlins bought one of the Stanier Pacifics in its place, and 6018 was cut up at Swindon in October.

6023 KING EDWARD II and 6024 KING EDWARD I were more fortunate; after withdrawal on 19 June 1962 both engines were sold on 10 October to the scrap merchants T.W Ward Ltd at Briton Ferry near Swansea but, because the Kings were banned from the main lines west of Cardiff, they were re-sold to Woodham Brothers at Barry Docks on 26 November 1962. They both languished in the South Wales sea air for many years before they each began the long journey to restoration and main line working.

6000 KING GEORGE V
Despite the early doubts the first to be

With a headboard commemorating its fifty years in service, 6000 **KING GEORGE V** was in Bulmer's Railway Centre at Hereford on 7 June 1977. The authorities had given clearance for 6000 to work a one-off Enthusiasts' Special between Hereford and Newport using stock from the Severn Valley Railway and so shortly after the date of this view the engine headed the 'Great Western Venturer' between Newport and Shrewsbury on 3 July. 6000 languished at Swindon for nearly six years after withdrawal before eventually being removed from the Stock Shed in August 1968, and taken to Newport for restoration to working order by A.R. Adams and Son before it was officially handed over to Bulmer's on 13 November. www.rail-online.co.uk

KING GEORGE V, working a special at Chester in around 1980, was the trail blazer for the return of main line steam on the national network when it was allowed to work Bulmer's exhibition train from Hereford to Tyseley, and then on to Kensington Olympia in 1971. It subsequently operated regularly on the main line for almost two decades, but has since been a static exhibit at York and Swindon Museums. www.rail-online.co.uk

6023 KING EDWARD II and 6024 KING EDWARD I were both sold in October 1962 to the scrap merchants T.W Ward Ltd at Briton Ferry near Swansea but, because the Kings were banned from the main lines west of Cardiff, they were re-sold the following month to Woodham Brothers at Barry Docks. They both languished for many years in the South Wales sea air as shown by 6023 around 1966, before its rear driving wheels were cut through, making its subsequent restoration a long and costly process which saw it finally return to the main line for the first time in late 2017. www.rail-online.co.uk

Running through Saltash with the 'The Par King Pioneer' on 9 May 1998, 6024 KING EDWARD I had been fortunate to leave Barry scrapyard nearly ten years before 6023 and was restored to main line condition by 1990. It has since been used on many enthusiasts' specials, but one of the most notable was when it worked into Cornwall hauling 'The Par King Pioneer', the first authenticated working of a King into the county. P. Kerslake/www.rail-online.co.uk

Crowds gather to see 6000 KING GEORGE V near Box on the Bulmer's exhibition train working from Swindon to Hereford on 9 October 1971. This was the final journey in a week long tour which began at Hereford and went to both Tyseley and Kensington Olympia for display before returning to the Bulmer's rail centre. www.rail-online.co.uk

saved was, appropriately enough, 6000 KING GEORGE V, which had been earmarked for preservation as part of the National Collection. After it had been rejected by the GWR Museum at Swindon because of lack of space, KING GEORGE V languished at Swindon for over five years after withdrawal. Eventually, on 9 August 1968, it was ceremonially rope-hauled out of the Stock Shed and handed over, on loan for a period of two years, to Mr. Bertram Bulmer, chairman of the Hereford cider making firm who had undertaken to restore the locomotive for public exhibition. It was transported to Messrs. A. R. Adams and Son Ltd., at Newport for restoration to main line condition. The work was very swiftly carried out and KING GEORGE V arrived at Hereford on 30 October 1968 and was steamed again on 13 November at the opening of Bulmer's new Steam Centre at its Hereford factory.

After much behind-the-scenes negotiation, BR finally agreed in late 1971 to, temporarily at least, lift its ban on steam working on the main line. In October of that year 6000 was allowed to take five Bulmer's owned Pullmans from Hereford to Tyseley and after display there at an open day, on to Kensington Olympia where it was on show for a few days before returning to Hereford. There was no further

relaxation of the ban but, after evaluating the results of the exercise, BR concluded that it had been a success and, in June 1972, 7029 CLUN CASTLE became the first of many to follow in 6000's footsteps; KING GEORGE V itself worked regularly on the network for almost two decades.

In 1988 when its boiler certificate expired, its lease from the National Railway Museum was transferred from Bulmer's to the 6000 Locomotive Association, who had been stewarding the engine since 1971; their intention was to raise funds for an overhaul to restore the engine for main line running. It went on display at Swindon as part of the 'NRM On Tour' exhibition in 1990. There was then a difference of opinion with the NRM who did not allow the overhaul to take place and in 1992 it was placed in Swindon Museum in exchange for 4003 LODE STAR which was transferred to York.

In June 2000 KING GEORGE V was one of the principal exhibits at the new Swindon Heritage Museum, 'STEAM – Museum of the Great Western Railway', before returning to the NRM in 2008. It went back to Swindon again in 2015 as part of the GWR 175 celebrations and is expected to remain there until 2020.

6024 KING EDWARD I
6024 KING EDWARD I was bought from

Woodhams by the 6024 Preservation Society for £4,000 and taken by road from Barry to their base at Quainton Road in March 1973 to begin a planned restoration to main line condition. The work, carried out in the open air for the first twelve years, took sixteen years but on 2 February 1989, 6024 finally moved again under its own power. In October it went by low-loader from Quainton Road to the Birmingham Railway Museum, Tyseley from where it completed its main line test runs, and on 15 April 1990, it hauled its first revenue-earning train.

After running almost 10,000 main line miles, 6024 was withdrawn from traffic in March 1995 for a Heavy overhaul at the end of its boiler certificate and was moved to a secure MoD site at BAD Kineton in Warwickshire for the Society to carry out the work. In September 1996 it re-entered service after a number of small but significant modifications. These included the fitting of dual-braking equipment (air and vacuum) to increase flexibility in the use of passenger stock, and the reduction of its chimney, safety valves and cab-roof heights to permit it to fit within the standard 13ft 1in loading gauge. In 1998, KING EDWARD I was allowed to work over the Royal Albert Bridge into Cornwall – on 9 May it hauled 'The Par King Pioneer' railtour from Bristol to Par, before working for two weeks on the Bodmin & Wenford Railway. It returned to its base at Didcot on 30 May with 'The Clotted Cream' railtour and visited Cornwall on several more occasions over the following years.

After clocking up a further 15,000 main line miles, 6024 was withdrawn in October 2002 for its second major overhaul during preservation, which was carried out by the Society within the Tyseley Locomotive Works. 6024 returned to action in October 2004, now fitted with Train Protection Warning System (TPWS), to begin its third 7-year main line boiler certificate, and for three years it continued to work all over the country on steam charters.

Following the publication of the autumn 2007 issue of *King's Messenger*, the 6024 Society's journal, there began a dispute between the society and its former chairman. This ended up in the High Court, resulting in costs awarded against the society. It had no option other than to put KING EDWARD I up for sale. Following discussions with various interested parties, the Society agreed in December 2010 to sell 6024 to the Royal Scot Locomotive and General Trust. It was purchased by the Trust in 2011 and is currently being overhauled to main line condition by the 6024 Preservation Society who remain responsible for its care. During the overhaul, the opportunity is being taken to reduce the profile of the locomotive's cylinders. This will make KING EDWARD I slightly narrower and enable the engine to travel to more places on the national rail network when it returns to service in 2019.

6023 KING EDWARD II

The restoration of 6023 KING EDWARD II was finally completed in 2011, almost half a century after its withdrawal and nearly thirty years after it left Woodham Brothers scrapyard. 6023 suffered a shunting accident whilst awaiting scrapping at Barry, and this led to the rear driving wheel set being sliced through with a cutter's torch. This resulted in 6023 remaining in the open, exposed to salty sea air for nearly 20 years, eating through the boiler cladding and much of the steel plating, and it was also raided for parts for other preservation projects.

The hulk was eventually purchased by the Barry Steam Locomotive Action Group for £15,000 in 1982, but was quickly sold on to Harvey's of Bristol, the well-known purveyors of sherry, for £21,000. It was moved to a bay platform at Temple Meads station for restoration by the Brunel Engineering Centre Trust under the Manpower Services Scheme, a government initiative to reduce unemployment. KING EDWARD II was dismantled, much preservation work was done, and components were sent away for contract work or as patterns for new parts.

Restoration work continued until the autumn of 1988, but then ceased when the Manpower Services Scheme funding was withdrawn, leaving 6023 as a kit of parts ready for restoration. Some parts that were away for contract work were scrapped when funding dried up, notably the cab sides and tender tank. In 1989 the Great Western Society purchased what was left for around £16,000, including movement costs, and 6023, stripped down to boiler, frames, wheels and tender, was moved from Bristol to Didcot Railway Centre in March 1990. New rear driving wheels had to be cast at a cost of around £11,000, and almost the entire motion had to be replaced. One of the aims of the project was to restore 6023 to its original single chimney condition, while at the same time the overall height was reduced by 4 inches to fit within Network Rail's 13ft 1in loading gauge to allow operation on the present-day main line. In addition to these major tasks, the most time-consuming part of the restoration was the manufacture or refurbishment of hundreds of small components. Livery was now the 1949 blue. In early 2011, 6023 was steamed for the first time and operated on the demonstration line and finally, in September 2017, it ran along the GWR main line from Didcot to Paddington, albeit with assistance from 70013 OLIVER CROMWELL and a Class 47 diesel as back-up.

After crossing into Cornwall on 9 May 1998, 6024 worked for two weeks on the Bodmin & Wenford Railway (!) before returning to its base at Didcot on 30 May with 'The Clotted Cream' railtour, and is pictured crossing into Devon over the Royal Albert Bridge at Saltash. KING EDWARD I visited Cornwall on several more occasions over the following years. It is currently undergoing a major overhaul to allow it to return to the main line in 2019. P. Kerslake/www.rail-online.co.uk

The front end of 6001 KING EDWARD VII in original condition, with the upper lamp iron on top of the smokebox and a smokebox door footstep (added to each engine soon after building principally to improve access to the upper iron). The inside valve casing (in front of the smokebox saddle) has a curved top with no tread plate. Starting in 1932, the engines had their upper lamp irons removed from the top of the smokeboxes and re-sited on the smokebox doors. The reasons for this were twofold: firstly, in the new positions they were far easier to reach and, secondly, the currents of air around the smokebox door were far less than those above the smokebox and, consequently, the flame in the lamp would be less likely to be blown out. A side-effect of the re-siting of the irons was that the footsteps were rendered largely superfluous, and were eventually removed.

4. The Devil in the Detail

The Kings at a casual glance may appear to have had no significant differences, at least until they were fitted with double chimneys in the 1950s. However, on closer study, the dedicated engine picker can identify a number of variants, a few as built but most as a result of later modifications; livery variations naturally followed the prevailing fashion.

Bogies and Frames
The initial problems with the bogie springing which resulted in the derailment of 6003 at Midgham shortly after it entered traffic in 1927 have been discussed in chapter 3. One possible, but relatively minor, consequence was that one King bogie had a slotted front cross-stay. It could hardly have been intended as a weight saving measure for it would have had a negligible effect, and it is unlikely that it was done to aid the flow of air around the inside cylinders as cooling would not have been desirable but may have been intended to direct cool air to the inside bearings of the trailing wheelset. The bogie was fitted

to 6004, the first new King to be completed after the Midgham incident. The other engines known to have had the slotted bogie are:

6000 in July 1931
6023 in 1935 and maybe through to 1938 or later
6018 either to or from September 1948
6028 (unconfirmed) possibly circa 1950
6014 in 1954/55
6024 in 1957, possibly also 6000 in 1957
6005 seemingly from 1958 to 1961
6021 in 1962

The subject of bogies came to the fore again in the mid-1950s, at the same time as problems with the mainframes were discovered. In November 1954, a worried magazine correspondent reported: 'At Swindon, three Kings, 6013, 6016 and 6022, have recently undergone drastic repairs. The entire front halves of their frames have been cut away and replaced by new or spare parts'. Things weren't quite as drastic as they sounded and frame troubles were more general than might be

supposed at that time. On the London Midland Region, replacement work had been done on the Princess Royal Pacifics from early 1952 to address frame fractures, though of course the bogies were quite different from those on the Kings. Over at Doncaster, the LNER had, almost unnoticed, been replacing the front sections of the frames on its A1s and A3s since the 1930s, with many of them not much more than a decade in service.

The Kings' improved draughting and their new boilers with larger superheaters resulted in increased power but their frames were more than 25 years old, so it is not surprising that they were becoming in need of attention. From 1954 when the first twenty engines, 6000-6019, were undergoing a Heavy repair, twelve were fitted with new front half-frames, cylinders, valve gear and motion castings. These were 6000, 6002, 6004, 6005, 6007, 6008, 6009, 6012, 6013, 6015, 6016 and 6017. This work was carried out on fourteen engines between September 1954 and June 1958, with 6027

The driver is oiling the motion of 6028 on 13 January 1937, the day after it was renamed from KING HENRY II to KING GEORGE VI. Prominent is the long drive from the cab to the crank on the Jaeger type speedometer. These were also fitted to 6006, 6007, 6010, 6017, 6023 and 6025. It is believed that the whole class had been fitted with standard speedometers by the end of 1937.

6024 KING EDWARD I with its bogie removed at Stafford Road on 19 March 1961 shows the later pattern of inside valve covers which the final ten engines were built; twelve of the earlier engines were modified to this pattern. The footstep on the smokebox door has gone and the curved top inside valve cover has been replaced by one with a square top and tread plate. When the exhaust passages were later altered, the centre portion of the tread plate (above the valve covers) was raised to provide the necessary clearance. 6024 also has parallel shank buffers instead of the original tapered pattern. www.rail-online.co.uk

The Kings were given self-cleaning smokeboxes in the early 1950s and the mesh used to break up the char shows up well in this photograph. www.rail-online.co.uk

the last one. As always, there were exceptions and eight of the first twenty continued with their original frames until withdrawal, while two of the 1930 batch (6022 and 6027) were modified. At least one other, 6021 in early 1956, was planned to be treated.

In addition to the replacement front frames, the engines also had strengthening plates welded to their bogie frames and reinforced lifting holes in the front frames. These, curiously, were never used in works overhauls, during which massive hooks were employed instead. They seemed to have only been of use during shed repairs, when a loco could be lifted under a hoist to run out the bogie. Although the repairs were considered worthwhile at the time, a little over a year later serious flaws were revealed. In January 1956, there were two failures of King bogies in quick succession. The Western Region was extremely concerned, and on 23 January the 27 Kings which had had bogie frames welded during repairs were promptly taken out of service. Only 6000, 6006 and 6022 were considered immune. To help offset the WR's sudden and severe loss of motive power, two Stanier Coronation Pacifics, 46254 and 46257, were imported from the London Midland Region. The two Pacifics took up residency at Old Oak and were used on Paddington-Wolverhampton and Paddington-Bristol runs. Elsewhere, Castles deputised for Kings.

The King bogies were repaired by welding additional strengthening strips to the frames; in the case of at least eleven engines the bogies were removed at running sheds and sent to Swindon for the necessary work to be done. Contemporary reports noted that, on 27 January, 6007 and 6029 were at Bath Road minus bogies, on 28 January, 6003, 6013, 6019, 6024, 6025 and 6028 were all bogie-less at Old Oak, while on 12 February 6014, 6015 and 6016 were in a similar state at Stafford Road; in addition, 6017 was photographed at Laira in February awaiting its bogie.

January 1956 was not a good month for the Kings, but things were about to get worse. On the last day of the month, just when it seemed that the bogie problem had been rectified, a new cause for alarm was discovered. This concerned the mainframes, which appeared to be feeling the strain of the recent front-end modifications. That shouldn't have caused as much surprise as it actually did, since for the best part of twenty-five years the Kings had been used almost day-in and day-out on long-distance runs with the heaviest expresses. To emphasise the point, a couple of years earlier it had been revealed that the Kings were notching up an average of 259 miles every day - the highest figure of any ex-GWR locomotive. It had been a hard life.

The entire class was taken out of service and, as substitutes, Princess Royal Pacifics 46207 and 46210 arrived

from the London Midland Region to help out the two Coronations, and in addition eight Standard 5MT 4-6-0s, three from the LMR and five from the Southern Region, were loaned. On Wolverhampton duties, the Pacifics were turned on the Oxley triangle. The 5MTs released a number of Castles, which were more suitable substitutes for the Kings, albeit with a frequent need for double-heading. Four of Neasden's V2s had originally been offered, but the Western Region's Civil Engineer had prohibited them from working from Stafford Road shed. Fortunately, the 'King Crisis' as it was dubbed in the contemporary railway press was soon resolved, and six of the class were back in action by 18 February. By the end of the month, enough were returned to service to permit the Pacifics to be sent home.

In 1956, it was proposed to fit the King axles with roller bearings. Their plain Swindon bearings were perfectly sound in design, but almost thirty years of handling the heaviest expresses had, inevitably, increased the instances of overheating. An order for eight complete sets of roller bearings was subsequently placed with Messrs Timken, and the materials delivered to Swindon in 1957/58. It was, however, a case of bad timing. Further modifications to the Kings were suspended when construction of diesel-hydraulic locomotives commenced, and the bearings were never fitted. It is

The so-called 'rabbit-ears' outside slidebars and motion brackets were to appear on the first two of Stanier's LMS Princess Royals. There were many other similarities with the Kings including the 6ft 6in diameter driving wheels. However, the LMS engines had four independent sets of valve gear rather than the Kings' two sets with rocker arms to drive the other two valves. The external axlebox and springs on the front bogie wheel are also visible in this picture of 6001 KING EDWARD VII at Stafford Road on 19 March 1961. www.rail-online.co.uk

From late 1949, the class was fitted with mechanical lubricators for cylinders, valves and regulator. Initially, 23 had lubricators placed on the running plate immediately to the rear of the right-hand outside steam pipe, but this hindered access to the inside cylinder motion and so the lubricators were re-sited ahead of the right-hand outside steam pipe. The original fitting of the lubricators was usually undertaken during reboilering; the subsequent repositioning was, in some cases, not carried out until the engines were fitted with double chimneys. Following experiments with 6016 KING EDWARD V in 1953, the entire class was fitted with new outside steam pipes which had a larger radius at the cylinder end, thereby increasing their flexibility and reducing the tendency to fracture at that point.

The King tenders were the standard Collett 4,000-gallon type as shown by 6011 KING JAMES I at Newport Ebbw Junction in the 1960s. www.rail-online.co.uk

interesting to speculate how the Kings would have fared with roller bearings; in the late 1950s the fitting of roller bearings to ER/NER A1 Pacifics increased the average mileages between shoppings from 80,000 to no less than 120,000.

Steaming and Boilers
In May 1939, the Swindon Drawing Office issued a report comparing the steaming of its Kings and French compound locomotives. The report opened by explaining that, in the previous twenty years, the horse power per ton weight of French compound locomotives had increased from 23 to 37, whereas the best figure ever recorded by a King was a relatively modest 20.4. It was explained that the huge improvement with the French locomotives had been achieved by three relatively slight modifications: (1) fitting Kylchap double blastpipes, (2) increasing the degree of superheat, and (3) increasing the size of all steam passages.

The report – let it not be forgotten that it was prepared at Swindon – admitted that the Kylchap blastpipes were far superior to the GWR pattern blastpipes. The former enabled an equilibrium to be maintained between the supply and the demand of the steam whereas, during controlled tests in 1931, 6005 KING GEORGE II had shown that an equilibrium could be maintained only by the use of a blower. As for the superheat temperature, the Houlet superheater produced a temperature of around 350 degrees (Fahrenheit), while

100 was the norm for Swindon superheaters. Various figures were quoted for the steam passages on both types of locomotives, but it was emphasised that direct comparisons were unfair due to the different nature of the two types.

It was stated that, in the case of a King, at 60mph its tractive effort fell to 28% of the theoretical maximum, whereas the corresponding figure for the French compound was a remarkable 70%. This manifested itself in the French engine having greatly superior acceleration and hill climbing - it could maintain 60mph on a 1 in 120 gradient with a 500-ton load, while a King could manage only 200 tons under the same conditions. The report suggested that, if a King were able to maintain its tractive effort at speed to the same degree as that of the French engine, it '...would revolutionise train working over the undulating routes from Paddington to Plymouth and Birmingham... the existing maximum loads on main lines could be drawn at a practically constant speed (of the order of 75mph) regardless of gradient - a far more effective method of cutting down point-to-point times than by raising downhill speeds to the 100mph mark'.

The report concluded by recommending that extensive experiments with blastpipes be instigated, and that attention should be paid to increasing the superheater units by at least 50%. The potential problem of increased wear and tear – as had been

encountered in France, where steel fireboxes had been found essential – was considered unlikely as the train loads in England were lighter. With the benefit of hindsight, it can be appreciated that, although Churchward had learned much from the French in the early 1900s, by the late 1930s there was more to be learned.

The report was far-reaching in its content, but it appeared at a bad time. With the outbreak of war later in 1939, experimentation had to be shelved – energies had to be devoted to keeping the existing locomotives working, and unnecessary expenditure was out of the question. If it hadn't been for the war, then the modification of the Kings in the 1950s with high-degree superheat or double-blastpipes would almost certainly have occurred much earlier.

The first move towards higher superheating came in March 1948 when 6022 KING EDWARD III was fitted with a rebuilt boiler (4670, subsequently designated WB) which had a four-row high-degree superheater. This had a heating surface of 489sq ft (later reduced to 473.2sq ft) instead of the 313sq ft of the original. Conspicuously, the increase in the superheating surface was 56%, the 1939 report having asked for 'at least 50%'. A total of thirty-four new WB boilers (4695-4699, 8600-8628) were built between 1951 and 1955, and the reboiling programme was completed in October 1956 when 6014 and 6026 received their WB boilers. While the reboiling of the class was in progress, the remaining WA boilers had the superheater heating surfaces reduced to 289sq ft. As will be seen from the registers, six Kings; 6007, 6008, 6012, 6014, 6019 and 6021, never actually had brand-new WB boilers, only 'second-hand' ones, while some received brand-new WB boilers on more than one occasion.

Draughting experiments were carried out with 6017 KING EDWARD IV in the autumn of 1952 and with 6001 KING EDWARD VII early in 1953. These were conducted to see how revised draughting could improve steaming capacity, albeit with the retention of the self-cleaning plates in the smokebox. This was achieved by the fitting of a longer, but narrower, chimney liner and a smaller diameter blastpipe.

6001 was subsequently put through extensive tests on the road and at the test plant, the latter taking place in April and July. It was revealed that the locomotive's steaming ability had been increased by some 30 per cent and that, in many aspects, the performances were comparable with more recent designs such as LNER V2s, LMSR Coronations and even the new BR Britannias. With a test load of twenty-five bogies (almost 800 tons) from Reading to Stoke Gifford and back (on 23 July), 6001 covered the return leg at an average of 60mph. It was found that even with more conventional loads, the engine nevertheless had a rather hearty appetite for coal; while BR Standard designs in particular could cope well with most varieties, the King worked best on South Wales coal. The draughting experiments with 6001 being deemed satisfactory, most of the class were similarly modified. A slight variation was applied to 6000, 6003 and 6020, which were fitted with longer chimney casings and had their capuchons removed.

Despite the initial satisfaction with the modified draughting, it was soon decided that, to maximise the benefits, a reduction in exhaust pressure was required. The obvious way of achieving this was to use a double blastpipe and chimney; this was not uncharted waters for the technical staff at Swindon as they had been involved in the design of the front end for the three-cylinder Standard

Pacific 71000 DUKE OF GLOUCESTER, in which the twin blastpipes were based on those of a 2301 'Dean Goods' 0-6-0! The layout worked out by Sam Ell successfully took away the limitations on evaporation of the single chimney arrangement, with the engine's maximum capacity limited only by the ability of the grate to burn coal. Another advantage was the reduction in back pressure on the pistons as a result of a one third reduction in the blastpipe orifice discharge pressure, which produced a much freer running locomotive.

During a lengthy works visit in 1955, 6015 KING RICHARD III was experimentally fitted with a double chimney which had been fabricated from sheet steel. It returned to traffic on 8 September, and its performances were closely monitored. On its first official test run with the 'Cornish Riviera' on 26 September, it comfortably achieved a speed of 103mph on a section where 85mph had been the norm for single chimney Kings. Three days later, during another trip on the 'Riviera' with an inspector on the footplate, 6015 was timed at over 107mph. Those speeds became the subject of considerable debate and GWR partisans weren't

averse to 'inflating' the figure each time the tale was repeated. It is now generally accepted that 107mph was indeed exceeded - the highest authenticated speed achieved by any Great Western locomotive.

Returning to the subject in hand, it was, perhaps, a little ironic that on 8-11 March 1955, a few months before 6015 had been fitted with its highly effective double chimney, 6013 KING HENRY VIII had, with its single chimney, been tested on the 'Riviera' prior to the re-introduction of the four-hour schedule. 6013 had met all targets concerning the margins of reserve, and the runs included the hardest sustained efforts which had ever been made by a King. To further the case for the single chimney engines, on 9 September 6019 KING HENRY V gained no less than nineteen minutes on the four-hour schedule with the Down 'Riviera'. But, when it came to high speeds, it was conceded that a single chimney King would have to be steamed very hard indeed to reach 100mph.

Although the single chimney Kings were clearly no slouches, the double chimney adaptation of 6015 was such a success that, by March 1958, the entire class had been similarly treated. Initially, there were two types of double chimney. Twelve of the class originally received narrow fabricated chimneys similar to that of 6015, but from November 1956 a more pleasing cast iron chimney of elliptical cross-section was used, those engines with fabricated chimneys being later refitted with cast iron chimneys. The class was transformed, not only in terms of performance, but also reliability.

Steam Pipes
Following experiments with 6016 in 1953, the entire class was fitted with new outside steam pipes. These had a larger radius at the cylinder end, thereby increasing their flexibility and reducing the tendency to fracture at that point. It was later realised that the most common cause of fractures had been movement of the cylinders due to the flexing of the frames.

Feed Pipes
6000-6019 were built with straight boiler feed pipes, but 6020-6029 had feed pipes which curved back behind the nameplates. The feed pipes of the earlier engines were subsequently altered, the programme being virtually complete by the end of 1934.

Blow-down Apparatus
Between January 1935 and May 1936, 6021 KING RICHARD II was fitted with

6024 KING EDWARD I uncoupled from its tender at Wolverhampton Stafford Road on 19 March 1961 shows the fallplate between engine and tender, and the steam heat and vacuum pipe connections. Note the ATC shoe which on a King was at the rear. www.rail-online.co.uk

The unique design of plate-frame bogie caused problems in 1927 and again in 1956. The advanced positioning of the inside cylinders left insufficient room for overhung springs between the leading bogie wheels, and so it was necessary to use outside springs, axleboxes and frame-plates for the leading axle. The rear axle had conventional inside springs and bearings, features dictated by the position of the outside cylinders. The restricted clearances meant that the bogies had to be fitted with 3ft diameter wheels, the standard Swindon bogie wheel having previously been 3ft 2in. This close-up shows the additional strengthening pieces welded to the top sideframes of the bogies following the discovery of cracks which resulted in two bogie failures in January 1956. The leading additional section is just above the top three large bolts behind the second coil spring hanger, with the second piece above the similar three bolts just ahead of the trailing wheel. This picture also shows the rocker arms from the inside motion driving the valves of the outside cylinders. www.rail-online.co.uk

6017 KING EDWARD IV, minus its bogie, in Laira's Long Shed in February 1956 alongside the on loan Princess Royal 46210 LADY PATRICIA. When all the Kings were taken out of service after cracks were discovered in some of the bogie frames, four Pacifics were hastily sent to Old Oak Common from the London Midland Region to assist on the Paddington to Plymouth and Wolverhampton services; elsewhere, Castles deputised for Kings. 46210 worked the 'Cornish Riviera' to Plymouth on 10 February 1956, but suffered a collapsed firebox brick arch on the way down and is pictured here awaiting replacement bricks. Laira's fitters have taken the opportunity to replace 6017's piston valve rings whilst waiting the return of its bogie from Swindon Works where strengthening work on it would be carried out. P. Kerslake/www.rail-online.co.uk

non-automatic continuous blow-down apparatus. Externally, this was identifiable by a pipe leading from the nearside of the cab, along the side of the firebox, to the top side of the boiler. Blow-down was a method of discharging a quantity of water steadily *en route* and was used to help prevent a build-up of soluble salts in the boiler water. It was not, however, ideal; if the discharged water included water-softening chemicals, the permanent way could be adversely affected. Indeed, an accident on the LMS at Watford in the 1930s was blamed largely on a rail breakage, ascribed to blow-down of 'treated' water. Blow-down was, therefore, subsequently regarded with some caution.

Water Testing and Treatment
During its Heavy General in January/February 1954, 6014 KING HENRY VII was fitted with a new type of blow-down apparatus. It was also fitted with a device in the cab which enabled samples of boiler water to be taken, to check the formation of deposits in the boiler. The equipment was developed in conjunction with ICI, and after re-entering traffic 6014 was transferred to Stafford Road (being replaced at Laira by 6004) so that it could be nearer to the ICI technicians. They travelled with the engine in the course of their observations and for their comfort a temporary seat was provided, on the fireman's side of the cab.

In an attempt to find a long-term solution to the hardness of the water supply at Stafford Road, from 1954 its Kings and Castles were fitted with 'Alfloc' water treatment equipment which enabled them to run for thirty days between boiler washouts. Eventually, 'Alfloc' equipment was fitted to seventeen Kings: 6000-6002, 6005-6009, 6011-6017, 6020 and 6022.

Springing
The first twenty engines, 6000-6019, were fitted from new with equalising beams between the coupled wheel spring hangers. The beams were intended to help distribute the axle loading, but in practice they had negligible effect and, as from 1931, were removed so that each wheel was independently sprung. 6020-6029 were built without equalising beams.

Inside Valve Casing
The 1930 engines, 6020-6029, had modified covers for the inside valves. Later thirteen of the original series also acquired these covers; namely the twelve that received new half frames plus 6019. The original style of casing (in front of the smokebox saddle) on all engines had a curved top but, from 1948, that gradually gave way to square tops with tread plates. A further change came when the exhaust passages were later altered, the centre portion of the tread plate (above the valve covers) being raised to provide the necessary clearance.

Cabs
6000 was the first GWR locomotive to have a motor car-style windscreen wiper; it was fitted to the driver's lookout and when still fairly new, probably in December 1927. The same locomotive was also fitted with a small brass-rimmed hinged 'windscreen', on the driver's side. Such 'screens' were widely favoured as they helped to shield the driver's eyes when it was necessary to lean out of the cab, but the GWR did not favour the general use of such fitments, the corporate philosophy being that 'in normal circumstances it is not necessary for a driver to lean out of his cab when running forward'. During World War II the Kings had the side windows removed from the cabs, the resultant gaps being plated over; the windows were restored after the war. From March 1954, cab-roof ventilators were added.

Whistle Shields
6020-6029 had whistle shields from new. The shields were small trough-shaped fitments placed behind the whistles, that prevented steam from obscuring the view from the footplate. The first twenty

After the initial problems with the bogie springing which resulted in the derailment of 6003 at Midgham in 1927 one relatively minor, consequence was that one King bogie had a slotted front plate. It was fitted to 6004 - the first new King to be completed after the Midgham incident - and subsequently found its way on to at least another seven of the class over the years. These included 6014 KING HENRY VII, about to leave Platform 1 at Paddington on a Wolverhampton express in 1954. P. Kerslake/www.rail-online.co.uk

In January 1956, there were two failures of King bogies in quick succession. The Western Region was extremely concerned, and on 23 January the twenty-seven Kings which had had their bogie frames welded during repairs were promptly taken out of service. The bogies were repaired by welding additional strengthening strips to the frames; in the case of at least eleven engines the bogies were removed at running sheds and sent to Swindon for the necessary work to be done. 6013 KING HENRY VIII and 6028 KING GEORGE VI were at Old Oak on 2 February waiting for their repaired bogies to be returned from Swindon. P. Groom.

6026 KING JOHN at Old Oak Common with its front end supported on 'bottle' jacks. In addition, 6003, 6013, 6019, 6024, 6025 and 6028 were all reported as 'bogie-less' there on 28 January 1956. transporttreasury

The biggest and easily the worst, cosmetic change ever imposed on a King was the 'partial' streamlining applied to 6014 KING HENRY VII in early 1935. The transmogrification is well underway at Swindon in February, although the hideous bullet nose has yet to be added.

engines, 6000-6019, were soon brought into line.

Lamp Irons
Starting in 1932, the engines had their upper lamp irons removed from the top of the smokeboxes and re-sited on the smokebox doors. The reasons for this were twofold: firstly, in the new positions they were far easier to reach and, secondly, the currents of air around the smokebox door were far less than those above the smokebox and, consequently, the flame in the lamp would be less likely to be blown out. A side-effect of the re-siting of the irons was that the smokebox door footsteps (added to each engine soon after building principally to improve access to the upper iron) were rendered largely superfluous, and were eventually removed.

'Streamlining'
Streamlining — or the shape of vehicles to offer the minimum of resistance to their movement through the air — is becoming more and more insisted upon by all forms of transport. When any vehicle is in motion, there are certain resistances to be overcome. The most important at high speed being that due to the air. Fuel is the source of energy on all power driven vehicles; hence it is obvious that if these resistances can be reduced, the result will be an economy in fuel. With the advent of the aeroplane travelling at much higher speeds than had previously been attained, the influence of air resistance became very apparent. Study of natural forms, particularly those of fish and birds, established empirical laws upon

which the first streamline contours were based. These early designs were modified and improved as the result of exhaustive tests made in the 'wind tunnels' of the aeronautical section of the National Physical Laboratory and elsewhere. 'In the case of the aeroplane, the original need for the effort to economise fuel lay in the attempt to increase the range of flight - and the increased range became all the greater because of the increased speeds achieved by streamline-contouring.

When the question of reducing air resistance of a locomotive, with its attached train, is considered, the problem is vastly more difficult. The effect of the greatly increased length, and consequently the correspondingly increased side resistance due to flange friction, becomes of very high importance. Rigorous application of the principle of scientific streamlining becomes not only difficult but practically inexpedient, as the net reduction in a measure of fuel economy, and the recognition and application to locomotives of some of the salient features in the theory of scientific streamlining will produce beneficial results in a reduced fuel consumption for the duties performed. This is what is being attempted on the King Henry VII. By reducing head-on air resistance, in accordance with the established theory more energy is available for useful purposes, and less fuel will be required to perform the same amount of work as previously.

This was the official explanation for the biggest and easily the worst, cosmetic change ever imposed on a King – or any locomotive for that matter – for the partial (the official description!) streamlining applied to 6014 KING

HENRY VII in early 1935. Streamlining had become fashionable in both Europe and North America during the late 1920s and early 1930s. It was first applied to electric and diesel units, the simple box-like shapes of which were relatively easy to streamline, but it was much more challenging on a steam locomotive. The LNER 'Hush-Hush' 4-6-4 was the first British engine to have any form of streamlining but this was for technical rather than aesthetic reasons. Gresley then used it on his 1934 P2 2-8-2s and while his streamlined A4 Pacifics were in the development stage at that time, the first of these didn't appear until June 1935. It was believed that the LMS also had plans for streamlined locomotives, and in Britain's railway boardrooms the conviction of the day was that streamlining brought good publicity.

The Great Western's directors didn't want the company to be denied its share of the limelight, and so they instructed their Chief Mechanical Engineer to prepare drawings for the streamlining of one Castle and one King. The story runs that Collett was not amused by the prospect of desecrating such classic designs but, mindful maybe of the politics of 'something being seen to be done', he dutifully obeyed. The locomotives selected were 5005 MANORBIER CASTLE and 6014 KING HENRY VII. Unfortunately, official documents fail to shed any light on how the method of streamlining was decided, but it seems that Collett wanted as little to do with the matter as possible. One popular suggestion is that he simply smeared Plasticine over a model locomotive in his office, and subsequently informed the directors that the necessary modifications had been designed. Whatever the behind-the-scenes stories, the aesthetic outcome was disastrous: a bulbous hinged cover (officially described – with some optimism – as a bull nose) over the smokebox door, coverings over the front steam chests and in front of the outside cylinders and steam pipes, fairings behind the chimney and safety valves, a continuous splasher with a straight nameplate, a wedge-fronted cab, and cowling on the tender. It has often been suggested that Collett made the streamlining as ugly as possible so that it would be taken off before very long. If that is true, he wholly succeeded on one of those counts and partly succeeded on the other.

The streamlining was applied to 6014 during a works visit which lasted from 19 January to 11 March 1935, although the official photographs of the new creation are dated 6 March. It appears that the engine was already in the works for a General repair when the decision to streamline was taken; the repair sheet noted a cost of £691 for boiler repairs, £814 for the engine and £99 for the tender, but it is impossible to determine what proportions of those costs were incurred by the streamlining. For the record the tender involved was 2612. The streamlining was wholly for the sake of publicity and, to be fair, in that respect it certainly worked. Mechanically, though, it was a different matter. If an engine is going to derive

any benefit at all from streamlining, that benefit can be gained only when running into a headwind. As soon as the locomotive alters direction, the streamlining ceases to be any use whatsoever. Furthermore, the effect of a side wind on a lengthy train is likely to be several times that of a headwind.

Having had its so-called streamlining applied, 6014 was dispatched to Old Oak Common instead of its former home, Stafford Road. To make good the deficit at Stafford Road, 6026 KING JOHN was transferred there from Old Oak. The corporate logic behind the exchange was that the London shed was a more suitable home for such a high-profile engine, but there were those at Old Oak who, considering the extra work required to service the engine, would have preferred it to be at Penzance or Fishguard, were that physically possible.

Fortunately, 6014's full set of streamlining lasted for only five months. The coverings over and around the cylinders were regarded as a major hindrance to routine lubrication and were soon removed, along with the tender cowling, in August 1935. Collett justified the decision in the magazine *Locomotive* in December 1937: *Streamlining is really only effective for speeds of over 70mph, and then it largely depends on the direction of the wind. The Great Western main line suffers badly from side winds, and for that reason they only partially streamlined their locomotives, as any increase in the broad-side surface would be detrimental. They have found that even the fitting of a valance to the lower part of*

the carriage under the footboard is detrimental.

It is not intended at present to streamline any more GW locomotives for no saving has been detected, but in many cases the coal consumption and oil consumption have been increased. The boxing in of the motion retains the heat and makes the oil thinner so that it runs away more quickly, and it is not desirable to make different grades of mixtures for different engines.

However, the bull nose and the chimney and safety valve fairings were not taken off until December 1942/ January 1943, and during a works visit in August-October 1944 conventional splashers and nameplates were refitted. All that subsequently remained of the streamlining was the wedge-fronted cab (it was thought to reduce glare in certain lighting conditions), the special snifting valves and the bracket on the front face of the inside valve chest for the Reporting Number frame. These were retained until the engine's withdrawal.

Mechanical Lubricators
From late 1949, all engines of the class were fitted with mechanical lubricators for cylinders, valves and regulators. Initially, 23 had lubricators placed on the running plate immediately to the rear of the right-hand outside steam pipe, but this was found to hinder access to the inside cylinder motion and so the lubricators were re-sited ahead of the right-hand outside steam pipe. The original fitting of the lubricators was usually undertaken during reboilering;

6014 KING HENRY VII with all the bits attached, a bulbous hinged cover (officially described – with some optimism – as a bull nose) over the smokebox door, coverings over the front steam chests and in front of the outside cylinders and steam pipes, fairings behind the chimney and safety valves, a continuous splasher with a straight nameplate, a wedge-fronted cab, and cowling on the tender. It seems that Collett wanted as little to do with the matter as possible. One popular suggestion, borne out by the result, was that he simply smeared Plasticine over a model locomotive in his office, and subsequently informed the directors that the necessary modifications had been designed. It has often been said that he made the streamlining as ugly as possible so that it would be quickly taken off. If that is true, he wholly succeeded on one of those counts and partly succeeded on the other. The ensemble is completed by the circular GWR totem, another ill-fated and short-lived attempt to keep up with the fashion of the times.

In 1934 the GREAT WESTERN tender lettering separated by a coat of arms gave way to a circular totem formed by the letters 'GWR'. This was no doubt an attempt to modernise in line with prevailing fashion and was officially described as a roundel but popularly known as the 'shirt button' emblem. The tender of 6016 KING EDWARD V displays the roundel which was somewhat underwhelming. transporttreasury

the subsequent repositioning was, in some cases, not carried out until the engines were fitted with double chimneys.

Mechanical lubrication was a controversial innovation. Previously, GWR men had been happy with the sight-feed lubricators and considered that only the most inexperienced drivers could fail to realise when their engine needed a faster rate of lubrication. Almost inevitably, the pros and cons of mechanical lubrication occupied several column inches in the letters pages of contemporary railway magazines.

Speedometers
In 1932/33, several of the class were fitted with experimental type speedometers. The first was 6001 KING EDWARD VII, which had a BTH device fitted on 10/11 March 1932, removed on 1 April, refitted in mid-April, and re-adjusted on 18-21 May. The speedometer required an instrument box to be fitted between the cutaway and the window on the outside of the driver's side of the cab, requiring in turn a cab window that was narrower than usual – a feature retained by 6001 for the rest of its days.

The fitting of Jaeger speedometers to 6010 (2 September 1933), 6017 (18 September 1933) and 6023 (25 August 1933) is noted in the Swindon registers. Although other sources, backed up by photographic evidence, show that

similar experimental devices were also fitted to 6006, 6007, 6025 and 6028, the registers are silent on this. It is believed that the whole class had been fitted with standard speedometers by 1937.

Weights
As for their weights, things were, in fact, even more problematical than they appeared. It is seldom realised that, although the official engine weight was 89 tons, by the 1960s the engines actually weighed anything from 93 to 95 tons. A consequence of this was that the Kings' adhesive weight was at least 72 tons instead of the publicised 67½ tons - no wonder they were widely regarded as being extremely 'sure-footed'. The explanation lies in the sort of 'accumulative process' undergone during series production - published weights of any locomotive class related, on the whole, to the first engine which, in many cases, would have been treated to a little more care and attention than the 'production line' models which followed. Furthermore, the continuing process of modification and improvement usually added to the weight. In the case of the Kings, from about 1930 heavier section wheel centres were fitted; later, their bogie frames were stiffened; then, the replacement boilers incorporated heavier superheaters; later still double chimneys were fitted. Each stage might

have added only a relatively small amount to the total weight, but the cumulative effect was far from insignificant. The unreliability of published locomotive weights was emphasised by a magazine correspondent (*Trains Illustrated*, April 1963) who explained that he had personally observed 6023 being weighed in 1952. The real weights and their 'official' versions were:

	1952 weight	'official' weight
Bogie	21tons 4cwt	21tons 10cwt
Leading coupled axle	24tons 17cwt	22tons 10cwt
Centre coupled axle	24tons 17cwt	22tons 10cwt
Trailing coupled axle	25tons 0cwt	22tons 10cwt
TOTAL:	95tons 18cwt	89tons 0cwt
Available for adhesion	74tons 14cwt	67tons 10cwt

The correspondent was, however, at pains to point out that that was the most striking example he had encountered and, of course, that the situation was not unique to the Western Region.

Tenders
The King tenders were the standard Collett 4,000-gallon type, of which a total of 481 were built between September 1926 and July 1946. The Kings' individual tender numbers and subsequent changes are noted in the histories. The Lot numbers of the original tenders were:

Locomotives	Tender Lot	Costs (each)
6000-6014, 6016-6018	A113	£1,011-£1,163
6015/6019	A117	£1,011
6020-6029	A121	£1,003-£1,014
6007 (rebuild)	A144	

A few of the Kings were occasionally paired with one of the two 3,800-gallon coal-weighing tenders, 4127 (lined green) and 4128 (lined black), which were built to a Hawksworth design in 1952. At least five of the Kings are known to have run with one or other of these tenders – only short-term and, presumably, for experimental purposes or, alternatively, as an emergency 'spare' at the discretion of the shed staff. Unfortunately, the Swindon registers make no mention of this. Contemporary observation reports provide a few details. Unconfirmed sightings noted in the *Railway Observer* and *Trains Illustrated* include 6000 with tender 4127 on Paddington-Bristol workings in August 1952; 6004 and tender 4127 at Wolverhampton on 15 February 1953 (a blue-liveried engine with a green-liveried tender); 6003 with one of the two tenders at Paddington on 18 February 1953; 6005 and one of the two tenders at Paddington on 4 March 1953. At least three Stafford Road engines, including 6020, were noted with one of the tenders 'early in 1953'. Photographs and observations indicate that the green one, 4127, was by far the one most used. It also was in use for four years longer than its black partner. This suggests that their equipment differed and that on 4127 was better.

As a general note on the subject of the coal-weighing tenders, former Swindon official A.S. Peck stated that they were in regular use as spares. Old Oak had one on its books semi-permanently but, perversely, in between

outings it was normally to be found at Swindon. Both tenders were observed at Swindon Stock shed on 1 January 1956, but subsequent Stock Shed listings appear to make no mention of either of them. 4128 was condemned in August 1958 and 4127 in August 1962 - a popular move among fireman, no doubt, as the tenders were, apparently, very hard to work.

Another point which is evident from the registers is that, in common with various engines of other classes, a few of the Kings had their tenders changed after withdrawal, usable tenders being taken off and defective ones substituted. The exchange of tenders resulted in some angry letters from scrap dealers who had purchased an engine and tender from BR, the dealers complaining that they had not received the actual tender which they had bought. Peace was restored when BR pointed out that there was as much metal in a poor tender as there was in a good one.

Liveries
The Kings were originally painted in the GWR passenger livery of middle chrome green, lined on the cab, boiler and firebox bands and tender with ⅛in orange, ½in green, 1in black in the centre, ½in green and ⅛in orange. This was embellished with brass and copper fittings; the nameplates were the standard GWR pattern with brass letters riveted onto a 13in tall steel plate which had tubular brass beading. The handrails, incidentally, were of polished steel, whereas since 1916 other classes had normally had their handrails

painted green or black. The first six Kings, 6000-6005, were the last new GWR locomotives to be turned out with the garter coat of arms on the tenders, separating the words GREAT and WESTERN which were in standard GWR lettering. The garter coat of arms was allegedly dispensed with following an objection raised by a representative from the Royal College of Heralds. The College could not actually insist on its removal, but the GWR nevertheless dropped the symbol, presumably out of a sense of propriety, replacing it with the company coat of arms. Also dispensed with around the same time (1927) was the ermine from the old badge, the College no doubt having pointed out to the GWR that ermine was reserved for royalty.

Starting with 6006, the revised version of the lettering, with the coat of arms now minus the royal garter, was applied to the tenders. In 1934, this gave way to a circular totem formed by the letters 'GWR' - officially described as a roundel but popularly known as the 'shirt button' emblem. Before World War II, the Kings' cylinder covers and driving wheel bosses were kept bright, but thereafter they were painted black. In terms of livery that was a relatively small war-time sacrifice, as the Kings retained green liveries throughout the hostilities.

From spring 1942 until late 1945 all repaints were unlined but, even so, the perpetuation of any sort of green livery, lined or unlined, during the war was exclusive to the GWR, the three other major companies painting even their top-link classes black. The war-time

The war-time livery for King tenders included the company's coat of arms flanked by the letters 'G' and 'W' as on 6006 KING GEORGE I which has just passed Beaconsfield with a Birkenhead to Paddington express in 1947. C.R.L. Coles, Rail Archive Stephenson.

From spring 1942 until late 1945 all repaints were unlined but, even so, the perpetuation of any sort of green livery, lined or unlined, during the war was exclusive to the GWR, the three other major companies painting even their top-link classes black. 6008 KING JAMES II at Banbury on 3 May 1947 illustrates the unlined livery. www.rail-online.co.uk

livery for the Kings' tenders included the company's coat of arms flanked by the letters 'G' and 'W', most other engines simply having 'GWR' on their tenders or tanks.

After Nationalisation on 1 January 1948, the first livery change on the Kings was the inscribing of the tender sides with BRITISH RAILWAYS, albeit in the traditional GWR style of lettering. A temporary 'W' suffix was carried for a short time by 6000, 6003, 6017 and 6020; other locomotives with the same tender lettering included 6015, 6016 and 6018. The Kings were almost certainly the first complete Western Region class to be fitted with smokebox numberplates, the last being applied in February 1950; a few of the early smokebox plates had brass figures, but BR soon put a stop to that.

In an attempt to find a livery unlike anything used during the previous quarter-century, British Railways experimented with ultramarine with cream, red and grey lining (not dissimilar to the old Great Eastern livery) for its principal express locomotives, and this was applied to 6001 (June 1948), 6009 (May 1948), 6025 (June 1948) and 6026 (June 1948). The tenders of those four locomotives were lettered BRITISH RAILWAYS using unshaded cream characters.

However, the ultramarine livery (which was experimental) did not give satisfaction, and it was subsequently decided to substitute a light blue livery similar to the old Caledonian Railway livery. Lining was as follows: cab and tender ⅛in white, ½in blue, 1in black,

½in blue and ⅛in white, with a 4in outside radius where applicable; the cylinders had a ⅛in white line either side of 2¼in black; the boiler lagging bands were ⅛in white, ⅝in blue, 1in black, ⅝in blue and ⅛in white and the platform angles were blue with lining ⅛in white, above a ½in blue and below that ½in black. The livery was applied to a total of nine classes; five ex-LNER types, two LMS Pacific classes, the SR Merchant Navy Pacifics, and the Kings. The first to be repainted was 6000, re-liveried in June 1949. The blue did not wear well and was therefore short-lived, and the last King to change from green to blue (and, ultimately, the last to retain it) was 6014 in January 1952. It was superseded by the much more appropriate and suitable, lined middle chrome green, although the new version of the livery differed from the pre-1948 version in that the firebox bands and the cab lining was only waist high. Cab and tender panels were lined ⅛in orange, ½in green, 1in black, ½in green, ⅛in orange. Splashers were ⅛in orange, ⅝in green, 1in black, ⅝in green, ⅛in orange; the cylinders had a ⅛in orange either side of 2¼ in black; the boiler lagging bands were ⅛in orange, in green, 1in black, ⅛in green and in orange and the platform angles were unlined. Starting in March 1952, the Kings were rapidly restored to green (after the stock of blue paint was used up) as they passed through

the works, the last to see the return of the new green livery being 6014 in February 1954.

The dates on which each locomotive had its livery changed are shown in the accompanying table In common with all other locomotives, the Kings were inscribed with the BR emblem of the day. From 1949, the 'lion and wheel' (aka the 'ferret and dartboard') emblem replaced the BRITISH RAILWAYS lettering on the tenders, and from March 1957 the second style of BR crest was applied.

The Kings were placed in British Railways highest, express passenger, power classification which was initially '7P', but was changed to '8P' from 1 January 1951.

	BR Blue		BR green
	first	second	
6000 KING GEORGE V		6/49	4/52
6001 KING EDWARD VII	6/48	12/49	1/53
6002 KING WILLIAM IV		10/49	3/52
6003 KING GEORGE IV		4/50	10/52
6004 KING GEORGE III		9/50	9/53
6005 KING GEORGE II		2/50	1/53
6006 KING GEORGE I		3/50	4/53
6007 KING WLLIAM III		1/50	10/52
6008 KING JAMES II		11/49	1/53
6009 KING CHARLES II	5/48	11/49	3/53
6010 KING CHARLES I		6/50	2/53
6011 KING JAMES I		7/49	12/52
6012 KING EDWARD VI		5/50	4/53
6013 KING HENRY VIII		6/50	3/53
6014 KING HENRY VII		8/50	2/54
6015 KING RICHARD III		10/49	10/52
6016 KING EDWARD V		12/49	2/53
6017 KING EDWARD IV		5/50	8/52
6018 KING HENRY VI		12/50	4/52
6019 KING HENRY V		9/49	11/52
6020 KING HENRY IV		7/49	3/52
6021 KING RICHARD II		11/51	5/53
6022 KING EDWARD III		12/49	6/53
6023 KING EDWARD II		8/50	3/52
6024 KING EDWARD I		11/50	9/53
6025 KING HENRY III	6/48	8/50	1/54
6026 KING JOHN	6/48	11/49	6/52
6027 KING RICHARD I		5/50	6/53
6028 KING GEORGE VI		11/50	11/53
6029 KING EDWARD VIII		6/50	5/52

After Nationalisation on 1 January 1948, the first livery change on the Kings was the inscribing of the tender sides with BRITISH RAILWAYS, albeit in the traditional GWR style of lettering. 6016 KING EDWARD V is in lined green, but without a smokebox numberplate.

Right. The newly formed British Railways experimented with ultramarine with cream, red and grey lining (not dissimilar to the old Great Eastern livery) for its principal express locomotives, and this was applied to 6001, 6009, 6025 and 6026. The tenders of those four locomotives were lettered BRITISH RAILWAYS in full in unshaded cream characters. 6009 KING CHARLES II at Leamington Spa on 22 August 1948 had been repainted in May 1948. In June BRITISH RAILWAYS on one side of its tender was temporarily painted out and a hand painted emblem applied for exhibition purposes instead. Some twelve months later this was adopted as the standard 'lion and wheel'.

Below. The ultramarine livery was not standardised, and was replaced by a light blue livery similar to the old Caledonian Railway livery. Lining was as follows: cab and tender $\frac{1}{8}$in white, $\frac{1}{2}$in blue, 1in black, $\frac{1}{2}$in blue and $\frac{1}{8}$in white, with a 4in outside radius where applicable; the cylinders had a $\frac{1}{8}$in white line either side of 2¼in black; the boiler lagging bands were $\frac{1}{8}$in white, $\frac{5}{8}$in blue, 1in black, $\frac{5}{8}$in blue and $\frac{1}{8}$in white and the platform angles were blue with lining $\frac{1}{8}$in white, above a $\frac{1}{2}$in blue and below that $\frac{1}{2}$in black. The first King to be repainted was 6000 KING GEORGE V, re-liveried in June 1949, and illustrating the 'lion and wheel' (aka the 'ferret and dartboard') emblem used on the tender. The blue did not wear well and was therefore short-lived. Note the perpetuation of the GWR shed code BRD (Bristol Bath Road) on the footplate angle.

Below right. The light blue livery was replaced by the much more appropriate and suitable dark green, lined with orange and black, although the new version of the livery differed from the pre-1949 version in that the firebox bands and the cab side windows were not lined. Starting in March 1952, the Kings were rapidly restored to green as they passed through the works, the last to receive the new green livery being 6014 in February 1954. The final livery carried by all of the class as illustrated by 6019 KING HENRY V, applied to repaints from March 1957, and had the later BR crest instead of the earlier 'lion on a wheel' emblem.

6014 KING HENRY VII on the 4.10pm Paddington-Birkenhead near Beaconsfield in 1961. It was withdrawn in September 1962 and cut up at Cox & Danks of Langley Green in March 1963. The reporting number frame makes use of the fitting provided in its semi-streamlined era. www.rail-online.co.uk

5. The Record

The following Engine Histories have been collated from the official Swindon Engine History sheets. As pointed out in earlier volumes of this series these, while containing much useful and even fascinating information, should be regarded as a guide to what happened to the engines, not an unimpeachable document to be afforded the status of gospel. It seems to be stating the obvious that they only show what was written on them at the time, but the temptation to read and interpret too much should be resisted. Even so, the Histories are a marvellous, fascinating, invaluable record of what happened, but they are often infuriatingly silent on events that we enthusiasts half a century or more later consider of vital interest and importance. They were filled in, by hand, by clerks and naturally enough contain errors of omission and commission. A few words of explanation regarding the presentation of the histories are in order.

Shed allocations: The Swindon allocation register for 1933 has long since been missing. The allocations for that year have, therefore, been deduced from works and repair records, which means that they are accurate to the month rather than the exact day on which a move was made to the next depot.

Places of repair: As a general guide, 'Factory' denotes works (such as Swindon and Newton Abbot etc), while 'Shops' denotes workshops at a running shed. The Swindon Histories were sometimes confusing when it came to the categories of 'Factory' and 'Shop'. For example, they occasionally included references to 'Bath Road Factory' but, of course, those entries referred to the running shed workshops since Bath Road had no 'locomotive works' in the accepted sense (at least, not since Bristol & Exeter Railway days!). Where neither 'Factory' nor 'Shop' were quoted in the original GWR documents, it is assumed that the repair in question was undertaken in the running shed itself.

Types of repairs: The Histories use the official repair code abbreviations which were in effect at the time. After 1928 these were: G - General; H - Heavy; I - Intermediate; L - Light; R - Running. After Nationalisation, British Railways adopted LMS-style repair codes and these came into use on the Western Region in December 1948. They were: HC - Heavy Casual; HG - Heavy General; HI - Heavy Intermediate. LC - Light Casual; LI - Light Intermediate; U - Unclassified.

According to the classification prescribed by the Board of Trade a Heavy repair was any one during which an engine was reboilered or had its boiler removed from the frames. It was also when any two of the following were carried out:

Fitting new tyres to four or more wheels.
Fitting new cylinders.
Fitting new axles.
Re-tubing or otherwise repairing the boiler whilst still in the frames with not less than fifty firebox stays renewed.
Both turning wheels and refitting axleboxes.
Stripping and renewing both motion and brake gear.

Intriguingly, Light repairs often involved major work such as fitting new axles, replacing cylinders, partially re-tubing or patching the boiler in situ, or refurbishing the motion, axleboxes, frames, etc. As long as only one of these items was involved, however, the repair was still regarded as Light.

'Wait': Many routine overhauls to locomotives were scheduled in advance, and a locomotive was often held at its running shed for the few days before the date of the works visit. Such instances are identified in the Histories by the word 'wait'. The word 'wait' also cropped up occasionally when an engine failed and had to be taken to the nearest running shed to await entry to Swindon Works. The period a locomotive spent waiting to enter the works was used for administrative purposes - once the word 'wait' had been entered against a

6025 KING HENRY III and 6024 KING EDWARD I under repair in Swindon 'A' shop alongside the other engine to have the misfortune to be "streamlined", 5005 MANORBIER CASTLE, in 1939. Both Kings were in for Intermediate repairs which were completed during June. C.R.L. Coles/Rail Archive Stephenson

locomotive it came under the jurisdiction of Swindon Works, even if it were physically at Laira, Old Oak or wherever. It was considered acceptable for up to 5% of GWR stock to be under the works' jurisdiction simultaneously, but some serious explaining had to be done by the Swindon management if more than 5% was booked against the works at any one time. The Histories which follow exclude these 'wait' periods at the sheds for repairs carried out at Swindon Works.

Swindon/Swindon Stock: Some GWR locomotives arriving at Swindon for non-urgent repairs were recorded as entering 'Swindon Factory Pool'. That said, in the case of the Kings a prompt repair and an early return to traffic were usually essential, and so they rarely spent time languishing in 'Swindon F.Pool' (as it was written).
When a repair at Swindon Works had been completed, the engine usually spent a couple of days or so at Swindon Stock shed (a building almost alongside the running shed) before being dispatched to its designated home. As with the 'wait' periods, the histories omit these for the sake of clarity.

Boilers: An asterisk (*) denotes that the boiler was brand new.

Livery changes and modifications: the dates of these changes, which are those at the completion of the relevant repair, have been deduced from photographs, dates of works visits and information in the original *Peto's Register* – they were not recorded in the Engine History sheets.

The fitting of ATC was carried out within a very short time of each engine entering service and are therefore not regarded here as modifications.

Allocations

Five engines were allocated to Old Oak Common for over thirty years; 6009 KING CHARLES II throughout, 6003 up to September 1960, 6007 and 6013 until 1959 and 6015 until June 1962, whereas 6001 KING EDWARD VII was reallocated thirteen times. The other Old Oak Kings, and the Laira and Newton Abbot engines each had a handful of moves. The Stafford Road allocation was quite stable with 6005, 6006 and 6008 there from 1930 until withdrawal.

Exeter shed had 6000, 6002 and 6004 on its books for brief spells between 1939 and 1942. Bristol Bath Road only had 6011, 6017 and 6026 between 1939 and 1943, and then 6000, 6018, 6019 at the end of the decade. Cardiff Canton gained 6003, 6004, 6018, 6019, 6023 and 6028 in September 1960.

Mileages and Availability

As will be seen from the registers, the highest mileage achieved by a King was the 1,950,462 miles credited to 6013 KING HENRY VIII. The lowest was the 1,511,174 miles of the earliest withdrawal, 6006 KING GEORGE I.

The average annual mileage from building to withdrawal was 53,284 with only six engines achieving below 50,000 p.a. Two of these, 6005

and 6006, had been based at Stafford Road from August 1930 onwards. Surprisingly, the engine with the highest annual average was the last built, 6029, which achieved 58,292 miles p.a.; 6013 and 6027 also exceeded 57,000 miles p.a. Pre-war, the average was slightly higher at 58,429 p.a. but this masked some significant variations. Two engines managed less than 50,000 miles pa, with 6018 the lowest at 48,307 and 6005 on 49,282, and 13 reached 60,000 or higher, led by 6027 with 68,854. This compares favourably with the mileages achieved by the principal express classes on the LMS and LNER, which had the advantage of higher average distances run per train worked. The LMS Princess Royals had an overall annual average of 57,266 (76,505 from 1936-9), the Gresley A1/A3s had 52,678 (67,631 in 1936-9) – both classes declined significantly after the war. The LMS Coronations had an annual average of around 68,000 miles p.a. and the LNER A4s around 65,000 miles p.a.

After nationalisation, British Railways collected availability and mileage statistics across all Regions and these showed the Kings well behind the Coronation and A4 Pacifics, although the figures for the Princess Royals and A3s were much closer.

Class	1950		1954		1957	
	Miles	%	Miles	%	Miles	%
King	52,978	61%	51,010	56%	50,328	55%
LMS Coronation	69,649	70%	74,333	72%	74,144	72%
LNER A4	56,641	69%	62,841	70%	65,575	72%
SR Merchant Navy	45,833	56%	46,128	57%	58,575	64%

6018 KING HENRY VI outside 'A' Shop at Swindon in an undated picture. Heavy repairs took place approximately every three years and 6018 was there in autumn 1959 and at the end of 1961/early 1962. It would make one final visit in July 1963 following its run on the last S.L.S. Special on 28 April. 6018 came very close to being preserved when the Butlin's Holiday Camp company was purchasing steam locomotives for display. It was sent to Swindon for 'repairs' in preparation for a move to the Minehead camp but the sale fell through, and Butlin's bought one of the Stanier Coronation Pacifics instead. www.rail-online.co.uk

6002 KING WILLIAM IV, freshly repainted outside the Works on 3 June 1962, had been at Swindon since 12 March and went into the shops on 26 March for a Heavy Casual, the last one completed on a King. It did not return to work until 15 June when it was transferred from Old Oak's books to Stafford Road. The records show that it worked for less than a week before it underwent an Unclassified repair at its new home shed, which lasted until 9 August. 6002 then went back into service for a few weeks before being condemned on 21 September with a final mileage of 1,891,952. www.rail-online.co.uk

Old Oak Common's 6009 KING CHARLES II undergoing a Light Casual in Swindon 'A' Shop on 3 June 1962, just three months before being withdrawn from service. It was one of four Kings that received repairs at Swindon during the four months following an Assistant Running & Maintenance Officers meeting in mid-March when the Western Region's plans for further overhauls on Kings were discussed. www.rail-online.co.uk

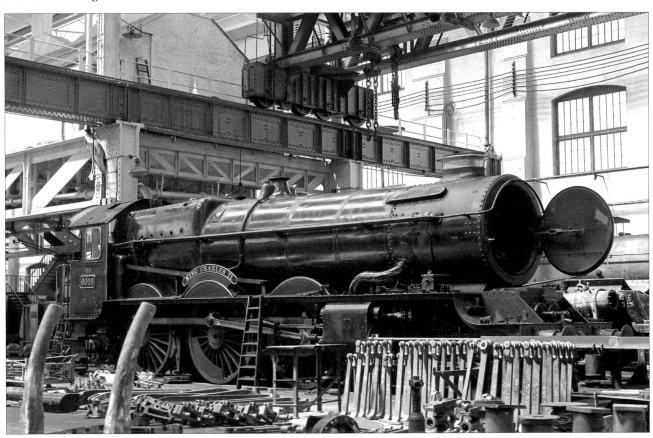

6000 KING GEORGE V

To stock 29 June 1927

Modifications
WB boiler	10/4/52
Double chimney	4/12/56
New front frames, inside cylinders	4/12/56

Livery changes
BR standard blue	27/6/49
BR green	10/4/52

Allocations
30/6/27	Old Oak Common
2/8/27	USA
12/12/27	Old Oak Common
9/11/39	Exeter
3/40	Newton Abbot
4/40	Exeter
14/6/41	Laira
9/41	Exeter
2/42	Laira
30/12/48	Bath Road
4/10/52	Old Oak Common

Withdrawn 3/12/62

Repairs
28/11/27-12/12/27**L**	Swindon Factory
7/2/28-16/2/28**L**	Swindon Factory
21/2/28-24/2/28**L**	Swindon Factory
5/6/28-28/6/28**L**	Swindon Factory
21/2/29-17/5/29**I**	Swindon Factory
12/6/29-20/6/29**L**	Swindon Factory
5/10/29-7/11/29**L**	Swindon Factory
2/12/29-7/12/29**R**	Swindon Factory
18/3/30-12/4/30**L**	Swindon Factory
28/10/30-23/12/30**G**	Swindon Factory
22/7/31-23/7/31**R**	Swindon Factory
1/4/32-5/5/32**G**	Swindon Factory
13/2/33-30/3/33**I**	Swindon Factory
21/11/33-6/12/33**R**	Old Oak Common Shops
9/4/34-29/6/34**G**	Swindon Factory
23/7/34-31/7/34**L**	Swindon Factory
11/1/35-15/1/35**L**	Swindon Factory
8/5/35-28/6/35**I**	Swindon Factory
26/9/35-28/9/35**L**	Swindon Factory
12/6/36-10/7/36**I**	Swindon Factory
2/12/36-16/12/36**L**	Old Oak Common Shops
9/1/37-12/2/37**L**	Swindon Factory
1/3/37-11/3/37**R**	Swindon Factory
20/4/37-5/5/37**R**	Old Oak Common Shops
29/11/37-20/1/38**G**	Swindon Factory
9/5/38-13/5/38**L**	Swindon Factory
20/5/38-16/6/38**R**	Old Oak Common Shops
5/8/38-16/8/38**L**	Swindon Factory
2/2/39-22/3/39**I**	Swindon Factory
27/10/39-9/11/39**L**	Newton Abbot Factory
23/12/39-19/2/40**I**	Swindon Factory
22/3/41-6/6/41**G**	Swindon Factory
7/4/42-19/5/42**L**	Swindon Factory
31/8/42-17/9/42**R**	Laira Shops
8/10/42-21/11/42**I**	Swindon Factory
19/3/43-22/4/43**L**	Swindon Factory
14/6/43-5/7/43**R**	Laira Shops
20/10/43-18/11/43**R**	Old Oak Common
26/11/43-7/1/44**R**	Laira Shops
2/2/44-24/2/44**L**	Swindon Factory
27/4/44-16/5/44**R**	Laira Shops
20/6/44-5/8/44**I**	Swindon Factory
4/10/44-24/10/44**R**	Laira Shops
1/1/45-2/2/45**R**	Laira Shops
9/4/45-27/4/45**R**	Laira Shops
9/6/45-25/6/45**R**	Laira Shops
12/7/45-31/8/45**L**	Swindon Factory
16/10/45-26/11/45**L**	Swindon Factory
17/1/46-9/2/46**R**	Laira Shops
8/3/46-18/4/46**G**	Swindon Factory
15/5/46-31/5/46**R**	Laira Shops
16/9/46-5/10/46**R**	Laira Shops
7/11/46-28/11/46**R**	Laira Shops
12/2/47-21/3/47**L**	Swindon Factory
20/6/47-8/8/47**L**	Swindon Factory
10/9/47-10/9/47**L**	Newton Abbot Factory
26/1/48-1/3/48**I**	Swindon Factory
16/3/48-24/3/48**R**	Laira Shops
17/4/48-5/5/48**R**	Laira Shops
8/12/48-30/12/48**R**	Old Oak Common
12/5/49-20/6/49**HG**	Swindon Factory
23/6/49-27/6/49**HG**	Swindon Factory
9/8/49-28/8/49**LC**	Old Oak Common Shops
20/10/49-6/11/49**U**	Bath Road Shops
25/11/49-21/12/49**LC**	Swindon Factory
16/2/50-2/3/50**U**	Swindon Factory
2/8/50-16/8/50**U**	Bath Road Shops
28/11/50-5/1/51**HI**	Swindon Factory
7/8/51-21/8/51**U**	Swindon Factory
15/11/51-21/12/51**U**	Shrewsbury LMR
5/3/52-10/4/52**HG**	Swindon Factory
20/2/53-27/4/53**LC**	Swindon Factory
13/10/53-2/11/53**U**	Taunton Shops
5/2/54-2/3/54**U**	Bath Road Shops
12/3/54-26/4/54**HI**	Swindon Factory
30/12/54-27/1/55**LC**	Laira Shops
9/2/55-25/2/55**U**	Old Oak Common Shops
6/8/55-13/9/55**HG**	Swindon Factory
30/1/56-12/2/56**LC**	Laira Shops
25/2/56-29/3/56**LC**	Swindon Factory
28/6/56-4/8/56**U**	Taunton Shops
17/10/56-4/12/56**HI**	Swindon Factory
12/7/57-25/7/57**U**	Old Oak Common Shops
28/3/58-24/6/58**HG**	Swindon Factory
5/7/59-23/7/59**U**	Old Oak Common Shops
8/10/59-4/12/59**HI**	Swindon Factory
16/12/59-23/12/59**HI**	Swindon Factory
7/9/60-26/9/60**U**	Old Oak Common Shops
3/1/61-3/2/61**U**	Old Oak Common Shops
5/6/61-22/8/61**LI**	Swindon Factory
11/9/61-22/9/61**U**	Old Oak Common Shops
21/6/62-18/7/62**U**	Swindon Factory

Boilers and mileages
First	4662*	
23/12/30	4663	161,083
5/5/32	4666	250,145
30/3/33		316,938
29/6/34	4680	394,172
28/6/35		457,071
10/7/36		535,276
20/1/38	4686	632,713
22/3/39		705,343
19/2/40		767,980
6/6/41	4675	841,970
21/11/42		924,818
5/8/44		1,000,678
18/4/46	4678	1,078,179
1/3/48		1,160,947
27/6/49	4677	1,222,797
5/1/51	4668	1,293,688
10/4/52	8600*	1,357,573
26/4/54		1,448,421
13/9/55	8624	1,532,795
4/12/56		1,596,025
24/6/58	8610	1,686,164
4/12/59	8616	1,763,428
22/8/61		1,850,242
Final mileage		1,910,424

Below. 6000 KING GEORGE V passes Taunton with the 11.0am Paddington to Penzance express in 1928. F.R. Hebron, Rail Archive Stephenson

Bottom. On a very quiet Sunday in around 1954, 6000 KING GEORGE V awaits departure from Platform 2 at Paddington on an unidentified express. An Old Oak Common engine at this date, 6000 had previously been at Bristol Bath Road from December 1948 until October 1952, along with 6018 and 6019. It had returned to green livery in April 1952 after enduring three years in BR light blue. P. Kerslake, www.rail-online.co.uk

Due into Swindon at 10.41am, 6000 KING GEORGE V on the 9.5am from Paddington to Bristol is a minute late as it slows for the station stop. It had replacement front frames incorporating a new inside cylinder block, during a Heavy Intermediate overhaul at in late 1956, as shown by the strengthened lifting holes in the sides of the front frames, just visible here, together with the raised top to the inside valve chest. www.rail-online.co.uk

There was one King which needed no further identification because of the bell on the front platform fitted for its visit to the United States in 1927. 6000 KING GEORGE V in the classic GWR scene along the sea wall at Teignmouth and approaches the station with the 8.50am Saturdays Only Paddington to Paignton train in 1956. 6000 had not yet received its replacement inside cylinder block and associated new front frames which were fitted to fourteen Kings between September 1954 and June 1958. KING GEORGE V was possibly dealt with during its Heavy Intermediate Overhaul in October 1956 but more likely during its subsequent Heavy General Overhaul in March 1958. www.rail-online.co.uk

At West Bromwich in 1958, 6000 KING GEORGE V heads 'The Inter-City', the 4.35pm from Wolverhampton to Paddington, with a uniform train of the revived 'chocolate and cream' liveried coaches which were introduced on the Western Region named trains in 1956. M. Mensing

43xx 2-6-0 6324 is in the bay platform at Reading with a parcels train but the platform-enders have eyes only for 6000 KING GEORGE V. It was in its penultimate year in service, still allocated to Old Oak Common from where it would be withdrawn the following year, in December 1962. www.rail-online.co.uk

6001 KING EDWARD VII

To stock July 1927

Modifications
WB boiler	9/3/53
Double chimney	26/6/56

Livery changes
BR dark blue	21/6/48
BR standard blue	23/12/49
BR green	13/1/53

Allocations
9/7/27	Old Oak Common
9/10/54	Stafford Road

Withdrawn   4/9/62
Sold as scrap to Cox & Danks of Langley Green 17/12/62

Repairs

22/8/27-23/8/27**L**	Swindon Factory
16/9/27-23/9/27**L**	Swindon Factory
5/3/28-28/3/28**L**	Swindon Factory
6/6/28-2/7/28**L**	Swindon Factory
28/8/28-13/9/28**L**	Swindon Factory
18/1/29-23/2/29**L**	Swindon Factory
1/5/29-14/5/29**L**	Swindon Factory
22/7/29-27/7/29**R**	Swindon Factory
1/8/29-2/8/29**L**	Swindon Factory
11/2/30-28/2/30**L**	Swindon Factory
10/3/30-24/5/30**H**	Swindon Factory
15/8/30-3/9/30**R**	Exeter
16/11/30-28/11/30**R**	Old Oak Common Shops
10/1/31-9/2/31**L**	Swindon Factory
11/4/31-4/5/31**L**	Swindon Factory
27/5/31-5/6/31**L**	Swindon Factory
6/1/32-29/2/32**G**	Swindon Factory
7/11/32-25/11/32**R**	Old Oak Common Shops
18/1/33-10/3/33**I**	Swindon Factory
13/11/33-25/11/33**R**	Old Oak Common Shops
5/12/33-20/12/33**R**	Old Oak Common Shops
17/1/34-13/3/34**G**	Swindon Factory
7/4/34-9/4/34**Expt**	Swindon Factory
11/6/34-20/6/34**L**	Swindon Factory
27/2/35-23/4/35**I**	Swindon Factory
1/6/35-14/6/35**L**	Swindon Factory
28/4/36-7/7/36**G**	Swindon Factory
13/8/36-21/8/36**L**	Swindon Factory
27/10/36-7/11/36**L**	Swindon Factory
8/9/37-30/9/37**R**	Old Oak Common Shops
1/11/37-10/12/37**I**	Swindon Factory
22/8/38-9/9/38**L**	Stafford Road Factory
22/11/38-28/11/38**L**	Stafford Road Factory
29/11/38-17/1/39**G**	Swindon Factory
30/3/39-6/5/39**L**	Swindon Factory
2/10/39-25/10/39**R**	Old Oak Common Shops
28/12/39-11/1/40**R**	Old Oak Common Shops
3/2/40-20/3/40**I**	Swindon Factory
20/3/41-6/5/41**I**	Swindon Factory
22/7/41-25/8/41**R**	Taunton Shops
13/10/41-29/10/41**R**	Swindon Factory
13/7/42-1/9/42**G**	Swindon Factory
23/3/43-3/5/43**L**	Swindon Factory
29/7/43-12/8/43**L**	Stafford Road Factory
15/12/43-21/1/44**I**	Swindon Factory
19/3/44-29/4/44**R**	Old Oak Common Shops
24/5/44-1/7/44**L**	Old Oak Common Shops
11/8/44-23/8/44**R**	Reading Shops
5/2/45-21/2/45**R**	Old Oak Common
28/3/45-21/4/45**R**	Old Oak Common Shops
24/7/45-29/8/45**R**	Old Oak Common
13/12/45-19/1/46**G**	Swindon Factory
18/7/46-2/8/46**R**	Old Oak Common Shops
6/10/46-31/10/46**R**	Reading Shops
12/11/46-2/12/46**R**	Old Oak Common
25/2/47-29/3/47**I**	Swindon Factory
31/10/47-23/11/47**R**	Old Oak Common
5/5/48-21/6/48**G**	Swindon Factory
10/4/49-5/5/49**U**	Reading Shops
25/5/49-1/7/49**U**	Laira Shops
21/7/49-12/8/49**U**	Old Oak Common
25/9/49-12/10/49**U**	Old Oak Common Shops
22/11/49-23/12/49**HG**	Swindon Factory
9/3/50-23/3/50**U**	Old Oak Common
23/10/50-2/12/50**U**	Taunton Shops
2/2/51-13/3/51**HG**	Swindon Factory
5/4/51-18/4/51**HG**	Swindon Factory
9/11/51-13/12/51**U**	Bath Road Shops
27/12/51-14/1/52**U**	Old Oak Common Shops
24/1/52-12/2/52**U**	Taunton Shops
16/4/52-8/5/52**U**	Old Oak Common Shops
10/7/52-28/7/52**U**	Old Oak Common Shops
20/8/52-28/8/52**U**	Stafford Road Factory
1/9/52-18/9/52**U**	Stafford Road Factory
13/11/52-13/1/53**U**	Laira Shops
26/1/53-9/3/53**HG**	Swindon Factory
18/1/54-5/2/54**U**	Old Oak Common Shops
10/8/54-29/9/54**HI**	Swindon Factory
31/12/54-31/1/55**U**	Stafford Road
14/3/55-25/3/55**LC**	Stafford Road Factory
20/5/55-25/5/55**U**	Stafford Road
26/9/55-20/10/55**U**	Stafford Road
19/11/55-26/2/56**HG**	Swindon Factory
30/6/56-14/9/56**LC**	Swindon Factory
9/7/57-23/7/57**U**	Stafford Road Factory
21/8/57-9/9/57**U**	Stafford Road
17/10/57-3/12/57**LI**	Swindon Factory
3/3/58-14/5/58**LC**	Swindon Factory
3/6/58-26/6/58**LC**	Stafford Road Factory
7/9/59-13/11/59**LI**	Swindon Factory
25/4/60-11/5/60**U**	Stafford Road
1/10/60-25/10/60**U**	Stafford Road
27/3/61-25/5/61**LI**	Swindon Factory
8/9/61-11/10/61**U**	Stafford Road
18/3/62-14/4/62**U**	Stafford Road

Boilers and mileages

First	4663*	
24/5/30	4680	149,916
29/2/32	4667	245,536
10/3/33		312,363
13/3/34	4689	373,315
23/4/35		445,779
7/7/36	4671	523,615
10/12/37		615,971
17/1/39	4681	694,050
20/3/40		768,219
6/5/41		851,048
1/9/42	4664	935,629
21/1/44		1,021,691
19/1/46	4682	1,122,133
29/3/47	4694	1,190,496
21/6/48	4674	1,263,590
23/12/49	4669	1,336,862
12/3/51	4691	1,418,165
9/3/53	8608*	1,510,364
29/9/54		1,580,147
24/2/56	8627	1,629,809
13/11/59		1,796,436
Final mileage		1,940,044

Tenders			
First	2387	23/12/49	2710
23/2/29	2399	12/3/51	2728
14/5/29	2388	30/1/54	4015
10/30	2400	29/9/54	2695
23/4/35	2609	24/2/56	2829
17/1/39	2548	14/9/57	2742
6/5/39	2434	22/2/58	2556
20/3/40	2554	14/5/58	2742
6/5/41	2704	28/6/58	2646
1/9/42	2665	13/11/59	2809
7/11/42	2629	25/5/61	2838
19/1/46	2800		
21/6/48	2772		

Below. 6001 KING EDWARD VII waits at Banbury with an express for Paddington in around 1935. It had been fitted with a BTH speedometer in 1932 and this required an instrument box to be fitted between the cutaway and the window on the outside of the driver's side of the cab, requiring in turn a cab window that was narrower than usual - a feature retained by 6001 for the rest of its days. The BTH speedometer was soon taken off and was replaced by a standard GWR type by 1937. J.N. Hall, Rail Archive Stephenson

Bottom. 6001 KING EDWARD VII displays signs of post-war general neglect and the lack of cleaners at Old Oak Common Depot at this period. It was 18 months since its last General repair when it received the austerity style of tender insignia, and would have to wait until May 1948 for its next visit to Swindon. Beneath the layers of grime can be seen the original rounded inside valve chest cover and the first design of front brass axlebox cover together with the original style of main steam pipe which remained in use until the mid 'fifties. 6001 was allocated from new to Old Oak in July 1927 and remained there until October 1954 when it moved to Wolverhampton Stafford Road. www.rail-online.co.uk

Above. Old Oak's 6001 KING EDWARD VII at the summit of the 1 in 42 climb of Hemerdon Bank, the view not spoiled as was often the case by a grubby Manor or similar coupled ahead as a pilot over the banks to Newton Abbot. 6001's seven coach load is well within the ten coach maximum for an unassisted 'King' even with a heavy restaurant car, second from the engine. The train is the 2pm Sunday working to Paddington on 7 March 1954. 6001 was transferred from Old Oak to Stafford Road in October of that year. P. Kerslake, www.rail-online.co.uk

Left. 6001 KING EDWARD VII on 19th March 1961 at Stafford Road shows the narrow cabside window which dated from 1932 when it was experimentally equipped with a BTH speedometer which required an instrument box to be fitted between the cutaway and the window on the outside of the driver's side of the cab. the bracket for that later design also visible here above the coupling rod and below the running plate. This close up view also shows clearly the blanking plate and bolts where that equipment had been located; the bracket for the speedometer which was subsequently fitted to all of the class is also visible here above the coupling rod and below the running plate. www.rail-online.co.uk

6001 KING EDWARD VII on 19 March 1961 at its home shed of Wolverhampton Stafford Road. It was allocated there from late-1954 until withdrawn along with the other remaining members of the class based there in September 1962. 6001 is preparing to move off shed to work train 'A91', the 3.35pm from Wolverhampton to Paddington. www.rail-online.co.uk

6001 KING EDWARD VII coasts into Banbury on 24 May 1962. www.rail-online.co.uk

125

6002 KING WILLIAM IV

To stock July 1927

Modifications
WB boiler	1/3/56
Double chimney	1/3/56
New front frames, inside cylinders	1/3/56

Livery changes
BR standard blue	21/10/49
BR green	27/3/52

Allocations
22/7/27	Laira
11/1/38	Newton Abbot
5/38	Laira
11/39	Exeter
5/6/40	Laira
7/40	Exeter
8/40	Laira
26/9/41	Exeter
28/1/42	Laira
12/48	Stafford Road
12/8/50	Old Oak Common
22/6/59	Laira
13/9/60	Old Oak Common
15/6/62	Stafford Road

Withdrawn 21/9/62
Sold as scrap to Cox & Danks of Langley Green 28/1/63

Repairs
25/8/27-26/8/27L	Swindon Factory
30/9/27-5/10/27L	Swindon Factory
14/11/28-10/12/28L	Swindon Factory
15/2/29-25/2/29R	Newton Abbot Factory
9/4/29-16/4/29L	Laira Shops
18/4/29-13/6/29H	Swindon Factory
11/12/29-20/12/29L	Laira Shops
19/3/30-28/3/30L	Laira Shops
7/5/30-23/6/30L	Swindon Factory
3/12/30-18/12/30R	Newton Abbot Factory
4/3/31-23/4/31G	Swindon Factory
5/5/31-22/5/31R	Swindon Factory
4/4/32-29/4/32L	Swindon Factory
14/6/32-21/6/32L	Swindon Factory
3/8/32-25/8/32R	Laira Shops
17/10/32-6/12/32I	Swindon Factory
31/3/33-1/3/33L	Swindon Factory
20/7/33-3/8/33R	Laira Shops
12/1/34-29/1/34R	Laira Shops
7/2/34-10/4/34G	Swindon Factory
8/10/34-6/11/34L	Swindon Factory
14/11/34-27/11/34R	Newton Abbot Factory
21/1/35-6/2/35R	Laira Shops
8/5/35-25/6/35I	Swindon Factory
7/11/35-25/11/35R	Laira Shops
21/7/36-24/7/36L	Swindon Factory
4/8/36-28/8/36R	Old Oak Common Shops
22/9/36-2/11/36G	Swindon Factory
9/9/37-24/9/37R	Laira Shops
13/11/37-7/1/38I	Swindon Factory
7/3/38-17/3/38L	Swindon Factory
7/9/38-8/10/38L	Swindon Factory
8/3/39-28/4/39I	Swindon Factory
5/7/39-13/7/39L	Swindon Factory
7/2/40-9/3/40L	Old Oak Common Shops
13/4/40-28/5/40I	Swindon Factory
8/4/41-22/4/41R	Laira Shops
23/6/41-19/9/41G	Swindon Factory
9/1/42-25/1/42L	Exeter Shops
6/5/42-4/6/42L	Swindon Factory
27/7/42-28/8/42L	Swindon Factory
16/11/42-1/12/42R	Laira Shops
3/5/43-8/6/43I	Swindon Factory
27/9/43-23/10/43L	Swindon Factory
8/3/44-21/4/44L	Swindon Factory
24/10/44-19/12/44I	Swindon Factory
20/2/45-12/3/45R	Laira Shops
24/3/45-18/4/45L	Swindon Factory
9/11/45-11/12/45L	Swindon Factory
8/2/46-9/3/46L	Swindon Factory
22/3/46-13/4/46R	Laira Shops
15/5/46-22/6/46G	Swindon Factory
1/7/46-26/7/46R	Laira Shops
28/10/46-15/11/46R	Laira Shops
20/1/47-9/2/47R	Laira Shops
7/4/47-23/4/47R	Laira Shops
15/5/47-18/5/47R	Laira Shops
27/8/47-27/9/47R	Laira Shops
18/11/47-1/1/48I	Swindon Factory
4/3/48-18/3/48R	Laira Shops
17/1/49-27/1/49LC	Stafford Road Factory
16/4/49-26/4/49LC	Stafford Road
13/9/49-21/10/49HG	Swindon Factory
6/9/50-25/9/50U	Old Oak Common Shops
13/3/51-23/4/51HI	Swindon Factory
29/10/51-23/11/51LC	Swindon Factory
20/2/52-27/3/52HC	Swindon Factory
27/11/52-2/1/53HI	Swindon Factory
23/1/53-10/2/53U	Swindon Factory
8/10/53-10/12/53LC	Swindon Factory
31/12/53-4/1/54U	Leamington Shops
2/4/54-20/5/54HC	Swindon Factory
9/8/54-2/9/54U	Taunton Shops
5/11/54-16/12/54HI	Swindon Factory
17/6/55-28/7/55LC	Swindon Factory
8/9/55-6/10/55LC	Swindon Factory
3/11/55-1/3/56HG	Swindon Factory
23/5/56-26/5/56U	Swindon Factory
12/2/57-6/3/57U	Old Oak Common
15/4/57-16/5/57U	Laira Shops
20/9/57-14/11/57HI	Swindon Factory
18/11/57-4/12/57U	Swindon Factory
6/6/58-3/7/58LC	Swindon Factory
24/4/59-22/6/59HG	Swindon Factory
6/4/60-22/4/60U	Laira Shops
11/8/60-4/9/60U	Laira Shops
26/9/60-30/9/60U	Stafford Road
15/11/60-8/12/60U	Old Oak Common
10/12/60-2/2/61LI	Swindon Factory
18/5/61-2/6/61U	Old Oak Common Shops
16/9/61-21/10/61U	Stafford Road
14/11/61-4/12/61U	Old Oak Common Shops
12/3/62-20/6/62HC	Swindon
20/6/62-9/8/62U	Stafford Road

Boilers and mileages
First	4664*	
13/6/29		100,583
23/4/31	4678	211,757
6/12/32		295,963
10/4/34	4667	360,747
25/6/35		432,082
2/11/36	4678	521,571
7/1/38		607,901
28/4/39		682,146
28/5/40		747,156
19/9/41	4676	830,177
8/6/43		934,205
19/12/44		1,015,460
22/6/46	4693	1,088,623
1/1/48	4663	1,171,565
21/10/49	4665	1,267,256
23/4/51	4693	1,342,339
27/3/52	4671	1,389,101
2/1/53	4690	1,432,483
20/5/54	4691	1,492,051
16/12/54	4661	1,518,485
1/3/56	8626	1,565,334
14/11/57		1,659,451
22/6/59	8607	1,746,876
2/2/61		1,836,406
Final mileage		1,891,952

Tenders			
First	2388	20/5/54	2710
25/2/29	2403	9/10/54	2905
23/6/30	2398	1/3/56	2838
12/11/37	2391	14/11/57	2786
28/4/39	2442	18/4/59	2613
28/5/40	2743	22/6/59	2386
19/9/41	2642	30/12/61	2728
4/6/42	2790	15/6/62	2841
8/6/43	2776	11/8/62	2818
19/12/44	2742		
23/11/51	2694		
2/1/53	2763		

An early 1939 picture of 6002 KING WILLIAM IV which shows some of the original features of the Kings which were to be altered in the subsequent years. It has the 1930s shirt button emblem on the tender, but most noticeable is the smooth casing over the inside valve chest, which must have been a trap for unwary shed staff and footplatemen with their heavy duty boots, especially in the wet when it would have been slippery, especially without the treadplate added in later years. The original style of outside steampipes seen here lasted until 1953 when a new design was fitted, reducing the tendency for fractures to occur in this original design as the result of movement and flexing between the outside cylinders and frames. Although the top lamp bracket is now on the smokebox door, 6002 still has the footstep in place from when the bracket was mounted on the top of the smokebox, and the engine has the original design of brass axlebox covers to the leading bogie axle. www.rail-online.co.uk

6002 KING WILLIAM IV was ex-works on a 'running-in' local stopper at Bath on 3 March 1956. It is in final condition, newly fitted with double chimney and high superheat boiler, and it also received new front frames and a replacement inside cylinder during the same works visit. 6002 has mechanical lubrication and a self-cleaning smokebox. It had spent the decade up to nationalisation alternating between Laira, Newton Abbot and Exeter sheds before allocation for almost the whole of the 1950s to Old Oak. www.rail-online.co.uk

6002 KING WILLIAM IV has just emerged from Hockley No.1 Tunnel and arrives at Birmingham Snow Hill with an Up express on 20 July 1958. It is in the final BR livery with the post-1956 crest on the tender. The factory of Taylor & Challen Ltd. which made industrial presses, appears in the background of many pictures taken at Snow Hill. The company's name was on a large panel of ceramic tiles in slightly scrolled Edwardian lettering which is still visible below the later signage. www.rail-online.co.uk

On 27th June 1959, Old Oak Common's 6002 KING WILLIAM IV brings the Paddington bound 'Cornish Riviera Express' out from Kennaway Tunnel and past Marine Parade on the approach to Dawlish station. www.rail-online.co.uk

6002 KING WILLIAM IV on 9 July 1961 with the 11.10am Paddington-Birkenhead express at Leamington. It had the unusual distinction of having spent time allocated to no less than five GWR/Western Region sheds during its working life, including time at Exeter and Newton Abbot as well as the more customary King locations at Stafford Road, Old Oak Common and Laira. www.rail-online.co.uk

Remarkably, 6002 was given a Heavy Overhaul at Swindon Works as late as February 1962 at a time when other members of the class were being withdrawn, but despite that late overhaul KING WILLIAM IV was withdrawn from service just seven months later in September 1962, the engine being disposed of by Cox and Danks of Langley Green in early 1963. 6002 was passing Old Oak Junction with the 7.35am from Birkenhead on 21 August 1962. It had been transferred to Stafford Road shed from Old Oak after completion of the overhaul in June 1962. www.rail-online.co.uk

6003 KING GEORGE IV

To stock July 1927

Modifications
WB boiler   28/10/52
Double chimney   4/4/57

Livery changes
BR standard blue 13/4/50
BR green   28/10/52

Allocations
22/7/27   Old Oak Common
13/9/60   Canton
15/2/62   Old Oak Common

Withdrawn   25/6/62
Swindon Factory   17/7/62
Cut up at Swindon   8/9/62 (w/e)

Repairs
10/8/27-18/8/27**L**	Swindon Factory
24/8/27-25/8/27**L**	Old Oak Common Shops
5/10/27-13/10/27**L**	Swindon Factory
16/2/28-21/2/28**L**	Swindon Factory
11/6/28-23/6/28**L**	Swindon Factory
6/7/28-10/7/28**L**	Swindon Factory
22/9/28-13/10/28**L**	Swindon Factory
8/12/28-26/1/29**L**	Swindon Factory
11/4/29-16/4/29**R**	Swindon Factory
23/5/29-27/6/29**H**	Swindon Factory
20/2/30-28/4/30**H**	Swindon Factory
25/7/30-22/8/30**L**	Swindon Factory
15/1/31-16/2/31**L**	Swindon Factory
3/6/31-4/6/31**L**	Swindon Factory
25/11/31-29/1/32**I**	Swindon Factory
13/6/32-14/6/32**L**	Swindon Factory
27/10/32-16/11/32**R**	Laira Shops
25/1/33-21/3/33**G**	Swindon Factory
30/1/34-21/3/34**I**	Swindon Factory
3/12/34-27/12/34**L**	Swindon Factory
13/2/35-13/4/35**I**	Swindon Factory
4/3/36-23/3/36**L**	Swindon Factory
6/4/36-16/5/36**G**	Swindon Factory
2/3/37-22/3/37**R**	Old Oak Common Shops
6/4/37-26/5/37**I**	Swindon Factory
30/8/37-23/9/37**R**	Old Oak Common Shops
31/3/38-17/2/38**L**	Swindon Factory
7/5/38-1/7/38**I**	Swindon Factory
4/8/38-16/8/38**L**	Swindon Factory
28/1/39-13/2/39**L**	Swindon Factory
22/5/39-6/7/39**G**	Swindon Factory
22/12/39-12/1/40**L**	Swindon Factory
6/9/40-21/10/40**I**	Swindon Factory
7/7/41-25/7/41**R**	Old Oak Common Shops
13/10/41-2/12/41**I**	Swindon Factory
30/4/42-23/5/42**R**	Old Oak Common Shops
26/1/43-20/3/43**G**	Swindon Factory
22/2/44-31/3/44**L**	Swindon Factory
4/7/44-1/8/44**R**	Old Oak Common Shops
27/10/44-31/10/44**R**	Old Oak Common Shops
24/3/45-12/5/45**I**	Swindon Factory
28/1/46-1/3/46**L**	Swindon Factory
6/8/46-22/8/46**R**	Laira Shops
22/9/46-12/10/46**R**	Reading Shops
12/10/46-18/11/46**G**	Swindon Factory
25/11/46-6/12/46**R**	Laira Shops
16/3/47-30/4/47**R**	Old Oak Common Shops
24/6/47-8/7/47**R**	Old Oak Common
9/10/47-23/10/47**R**	Old Oak Common Shops
30/1/48-10/3/48**I**	Swindon Factory
18/8/48-9/5/48**R**	Old Oak Common Shops
26/6/48-13/7/48**R**	Taunton Shops
15/8/48-13/9/48**L**	Old Oak Common Shops
12/11/48-26/11/48**R**	Old Oak Common Shops
14/1/49-19/1/49**U**	Taunton Shops
27/1/49-24/2/49**U**	Old Oak Common Shops
19/7/49-17/8/49**LC**	Swindon Factory
31/10/49-2/12/49**LC**	Swindon Factory
16/1/50-16/2/50**U**	Taunton Shops
2/3/50-13/4/50**HG**	Swindon Factory
21/2/51-3/4/51**HI**	Swindon Factory
4/9/51-2/10/51**U**	Taunton Shops
10/10/51-5/11/51**U**	Old Oak Common Shops
30/11/51-6/12/51**U**	Laira Shops
1/2/52-5/3/52**LC**	Swindon Factory
12/9/52-28/10/52**HG**	Swindon Factory
6/11/52-1/12/52**U**	Reading Shops
9/9/53-25/9/53**U**	Old Oak Common Shops
4/12/53-2/2/54**HI**	Swindon Factory
6/9/54-7/10/54**U**	Old Oak Common Shops
19/2/55-24/3/55**U**	Laira Shops
14/4/55-19/5/55**HI**	Swindon Factory
15/6/55-20/7/55**U**	Laira Shops
28/9/55-13/10/55**U**	Old Oak Common
20/1/56-10/2/56**LC**	Old Oak Common Shops
6/4/56-17/5/56**LC**	Swindon Factory
28/5/56-2/7/56**U**	Taunton Shops
18/9/56-18/10/56**U**	Old Oak Common Shops
25/11/56-20/12/56**U**	Old Oak Common Shops
1/2/57-4/4/57**HI**	Swindon Factory
9/10/57-29/10/57**U**	Old Oak Common Shops
3/5/58-30/7/58**HI**	Swindon Factory
7/10/59-22/10/59**U**	Old Oak Common
18/12/59-30/3/60**HG**	Swindon Factory
1/2/61-19/5/61**LC**	Swindon Factory
28/10/61-12/11/61**U**	Swindon
17/1/62-15/2/62**LC**	Old Oak Common Shops

Boilers and mileages
First	4665*	
27/6/29		106,236
28/4/30	4682	152,100
29/1/32		252,039
21/3/33	4671	321,058
21/3/34		384,855
13/4/35		451,971
16/5/36	4684	519,995
26/5/37		591,551
1/7/38		666,202
6/7/39	4691	727,569
21/10/40		813,900
2/12/41		896,868
20/3/43	4680	981,894
12/5/45		1,101,381
18/11/46	4676	1,195,108
10/3/48	4664	1,251,678
13/4/50	4674	1,330,692
3/4/51		1,391,543
28/10/52	8604*	1,469,386
2/2/54		1,527,590
19/5/55	8614	1,594,701
4/4/57	4699	1,673,746
30/7/58	8619	1,745,987
30/3/60	8602	1,828,621
Final mileage		1,920,479

Below. 6003 KING GEORGE IV at Laira shed in around 1929. It was built in July 1927 and spent over thirty years allocated to Old Oak Common. P.F. Cooke, Rail Archive Stephenson.

Bottom. From spring 1942 until late 1945 all repaints were unlined but, even so, the perpetuation of any sort of green livery, lined or unlined, during the war was exclusive to the GWR, the three other major companies painting even their top-link classes black. The wartime livery for the Kings' tenders included the company's coat of arms flanked by the letters 'G' and 'W', as shown on 6003 KING GEORGE IV at Leamington Spa in August 1945. www.rail-online.co.uk

Three years after the previous picture, and now in early British Railways livery, 6003 KING GEORGE IV at Leamington Spa on 27 March of 1948, less than three weeks after completing an Intermediate repair when it regained lined green. The tender sides were inscribed with BRITISH RAILWAYS, albeit in the traditional GWR style of lettering. It was one of four Kings given a temporary 'W' suffix, as can just be discerned, below the cab number plates and does not yet have a smokebox number plate. 6003 retains the original GWR pattern of rounded inside valve chest casing although a squared design with a treaded top plate was being fitted as a replacement from about this time as the engines went through Swindon Works. www.rail-online.co.uk

6003 KING GEORGE IV passes through Bathampton on 15 October 1955 with the Down 'Merchant Venturer', the 11.15am from Paddington due into Temple Meads at 1.28pm, with just one intermediate stop en route at Bath Spa. Its return working was probably on the afternoon 'Bristolian' back home to London after a brief stop-over on Bath Road shed. On 30 April 1954 6003 had been used on a test run from Paddington to Bristol and back to evaluate the practicalities of the proposed accelerated 'Bristolian' service to begin on 14 June 1954 and achieved a maximum speed of over 90 mph on both the outward and return runs that day. 6003 had been through Swindon Works for a month long Heavy Intermediate overhaul commencing in April 1955, but did not receive replacement front frames during that visit as this picture shows the original inside valve spindle covers and no strengthening pieces fitted inside the lifting holes within the front frames. www.rail-online.co.uk

Old Oak Common's 6003 KING GEORGE IV heads the queue on Laira shed's coaling line in this 1956 picture after working an express down to Plymouth from Paddington. One of the shed staff is removing the Reporting Number in its frame in order to gain access to the smokebox and clear the accumulated build-up of ash with the steam lance that is leaning against the wall and which will be attached to the valve visible on the side of 6003's smokebox front. P. Kerslake, www.rail-online.co.uk

6003 KING GEORGE IV is clearly fresh from Swindon Works in this late 1950s picture at Bristol Bath Road. 6003 spent the whole of its working life from 1927 allocated to Old Oak, spending about 18 months at Cardiff Canton before returning to the London shed in February 1962 when new Hymeks took over their passenger work. The decision to transfer a number of Kings to Canton in late 1960 was made in an effort to find suitable work for those engines at a time when many of their previous main line duties had been taken over by the influx of new diesels. What the shedmasters at Cardiff thought of their newly acquired engines has not been publicly recorded, and several of them, including 6003, were kept 'in store' at Canton, with their chimneys sheeted over. A number did, however, appear on the top link passenger express workings between Cardiff and Paddington, including the tightly timed 'Red Dragon', and they also worked the heavily loaded milk trains from West Wales to Kensington. www.rail-online.co.uk

6004 KING GEORGE III

To stock July 1927

Modifications
WB boiler	9/9/53
New front frames, inside cylinders	19/5/55
Double chimney	21/11/56

Livery changes
BR standard blue	22/9/50
BR green	9/9/53

Allocations
25/8/27	Laira
10/41	Exeter
1/42	Laira
12/48	Stafford Road
27/3/54	Laira
18/12/59	Old Oak Common
13/9/60	Canton

Withdrawn 19/9/62
Cut up at Swindon 3/11/62

Repairs
27/8/27-1/9/27**L**	Swindon Factory
20/9/27-22/9/27**L**	Swindon Factory
21/11/27-28/11/27**R**	Laira Shops
9/4/28-29/5/28**L**	Swindon Factory
11/8/28-22/8/28**L**	Swindon Factory
28/11/28-29/12/28**L**	Swindon Factory
6/2/29-19/2/29**R**	Laira Shops
17/4/29-21/6/29**H**	Swindon Factory
29/10/29-18/11/29**L**	Swindon Factory
28/3/30-3/4/30**L**	Laira Shops
5/4/30-14/4/30**L**	Swindon Factory
30/6/30-12/7/30**R**	Swindon Factory
14/8/30-15/8/30**L**	Swindon Factory
12/11/30-12/12/30**L**	Laira Shops
30/12/30-9/1/31**L**	Newton Abbot Factory
2/2/31-10/3/31**L**	Swindon Factory
15/4/31-8/6/31**I**	Swindon Factory
2/9/31-10/9/31**L**	Swindon Factory
31/12/31-11/2/32**G**	Swindon Factory
12/4/32-30/4/32**R**	Laira Shops
9/6/32-7/7/32**R**	Laira Shops
23/3/33-27/3/33**L**	Swindon Factory
2/5/33-3/7/33**I**	Swindon Factory
14/5/34-6/7/34**I**	Swindon Factory
24/9/34-5/10/34**L**	Swindon Factory
20/7/35-1/8/35**L**	Swindon Factory
3/10/35-18/11/35**G**	Swindon Factory
5/12/35-18/12/35**L**	Swindon Factory
18/4/36-4/5/36**R**	Laira Shops
26/9/36-14/10/36**R**	Laira Shops
16/2/37-2/4/37**I**	Swindon Factory
28/4/37-13/5/37**L**	Swindon Factory
21/9/37-2/10/37**L**	Swindon Factory
11/11/37-3/12/37**L**	Swindon Factory
6/1/38-22/1/38**R**	Laira Shops
1/4/38-18/4/38**R**	Laira Shops
28/6/38-30/8/38**I**	Swindon Factory
2/3/39-5/4/39**L**	Swindon Factory
13/6/39-13/7/39**L**	Swindon Factory
5/12/39-30/1/40**I**	Swindon Factory
12/4/40-6/5/40**L**	Swindon Factory
18/7/40-13/8/40**L**	Swindon Factory
3/4/41-17/6/41**G**	Swindon Factory
19/3/42-5/4/42**R**	Old Oak Common Shops
14/4/42-1/5/42**R**	Laira Shops
16/9/42-6/11/42**I**	Swindon Factory
27/11/42-30/11/42**R**	Laira Shops
8/1/43-28/1/43**R**	Taunton Shops
5/7/43-15/7/43**R**	Laira Shops
6/9/43-25/9/43**R**	Laira Shops
8/2/44-14/3/44**I**	Swindon Factory
5/9/44-14/10/44**L**	Swindon Factory
24/12/44-29/1/45**R**	Laira Shops
18/4/45-2/5/45**R**	Laira Shops
3/7/45-20/7/45**R**	Laira Shops
1/8/45-28/9/45**G**	Swindon Factory
8/4/46-30/4/46**R**	Laira Shops
7/10/46-1/11/46**R**	Laira Shops
2/11/46-14/12/46**I**	Swindon Factory
20/2/47-11/3/47**R**	Laira Shops
8/5/47-24/5/47**R**	Laira Shops
22/9/47-8/10/47**R**	Laira Shops
19/11/47-5/12/47**R**	Laira Shops
31/12/47-21/2/48**R**	Reading Shops
18/3/48-8/4/48**R**	Laira Shops
26/4/48-29/4/48**Tender**	Newton Abbot Factory
6/10/48-12/11/48**I**	Swindon Factory
21/6/49-5/7/49**U**	Stafford Road
25/8/49-23/9/49**HC**	Swindon Factory
21/8/50-22/9/50**HG**	Swindon Factory
24/7/51-13/9/51**LC**	Stafford Road
4/10/51-12/10/51**U**	Stafford Road
7/1/52-12/2/52**HI**	Swindon Factory
31/10/52-11/11/52**U**	Stafford Road
9/12/52-23/1/53**HC**	Swindon Factory
23/7/53-9/9/53**HG**	Swindon Factory
1/4/54-3/5/54**U**	Laira Shops
12/8/54-8/9/54**LC**	Swindon Factory
31/12/54-6/1/55**U**	Laira Shops
20/1/55-1/2/55**U**	Laira Shops
23/2/55-19/5/55**HG**	Swindon Factory
19/7/55-29/8/55**LC**	Swindon Factory
19/1/56-23/2/56**LC**	Laira Shops
22/6/56-12/7/56**U**	Taunton Shops
11/10/56-21/11/56**HI**	Swindon Factory
21/2/57-22/2/57**U**	Laira Shops
11/6/57-21/6/57**U**	Laira Shops
10/7/57-30/7/57**U**	Laira Shops
5/11/57-16/11/57**LC**	Newton Abbot Factory
10/3/58-24/4/58**HG**	Swindon Factory
11/9/58-29/9/58**U**	Laira Shops
7/10/58-24/10/58**U**	Laira Shops
30/1/59-13/2/59**U**	Newton Abbot Factory
5/6/59-3/7/59**U**	Bath Road Shops
20/10/59-18/12/59**HI**	Swindon Factory
7/6/60-29/7/60**LC**	Swindon Factory
15/8/60-30/8/60**U**	Old Oak Common
16/1/61-2/2/61**U**	Canton Shops
5/4/61-3/8/61**HC**	Swindon Factory

Boilers and mileages
First	4666	
21/6/29		97,573
8/6/31		207,659
11/2/32	4669	242,026
3/7/33		318,473
6/7/34		376,904
18/11/35	4682	465,903
2/4/37		544,360
30/8/38		627,276
30/1/40		713,445
17/6/41	4688	790,873
6/11/42		877,942
14/3/44		962,721
28/9/45	4674	1,049,240
14/12/46	4661	1,125,654
12/11/48		1,222,949
23/9/49	4675	1,261,993
22/9/50	4685	1,309,779
12/2/52	4694	1,375,860
23/1/53	4663	1,426,160
9/9/53	8612 *	1,452,811
19/5/55	8623	1,533,852
21/11/56		1,621,595
24/4/58	4696	1,727,016
18/12/59	8620	1,820,789
3/8/61	8624	1,871,922

Final mileage   1,917,258

Tenders			
First	2391	14/3/44	2788
19/2/29	2401	14/10/44	2743
21/6/29	2391	2/11/46	2759
14/4/30	2413	12/11/48	2629
12/7/30	2392	8/9/54	2612
10/3/31	2393	19/5/56	2398
8/6/31	2425	21/11/56	2870
11/2/32	2399	10/8/57	2913
19/11/32	2434	24/4/58	2868
6/7/34	2440	6/9/58	2789
5/4/39	2609	18/12/59	2875
17/6/41	2707	22/4/61	2846
6/11/42	2695	3/8/61	2813

Below. 6004 KING GEORGE III in the early 1930s at Old Oak Common. It still has the royal garter coat of arms on the tender which was discontinued following an objection raised by a representative from the Royal College of Heralds. 6004 entered traffic in July 1927 and, as one of the even numbered engines, was allocated to Laira.

Bottom. 6004 KING GEORGE III still has the war-time simplified GW lettering on the tender. This picture at Leamington Spa was probably taken shortly after 6004 was transferred from Laira to Stafford Road in December 1948. www.rail-online.co.uk

135

An immaculate 6004 KING GEORGE III sets off from Plymouth with the 8.30am to Paddington, past the site of the old Mutley station and with the Royal Eye Hospital in the background, probably during 1956. 6004 came to Laira in March 1954 from Wolverhampton Stafford Road in exchange for Laira's 6014, the last blue King, which was then used on the Paddington to Wolverhampton main line for water softening tests following overhaul at Swindon. P. Kerslake, www.rail-online.co.uk

Arriving at Plymouth North Road on the 'Cornish Riviera Limited' with newly repainted 'chocolate & cream' stock and a new style of headboard, Laira's 6004 KING GEORGE III with the Down train on 30 July 1956. 6004 had by then received new front frames and cylinder block, as this shot clearly shows the modified top to the inside cylinder block and strengthened lifting holes in the front frames, together with the later style of inside valve spindle covers. This work was carried out at Swindon between September 1954 and June 1958 as many of the Kings were suffering from cracked mainframes, requiring substantial remedial work. www.rail-online.co.uk

6004 KING GEORGE III passing Sprey Point on the sea wall at Teignmouth with the 'Cornish Riviera Limited' on a rather dull and murky day in 1956. In days past there was a cafe here at Sprey Point, which lasted until the end of the war, but today there is just a ganger's hut. www.rail-online.co.uk

6004 KING GEORGE III ready to depart from Paddington with 'The Inter-City' to Wolverhampton on 16 August 1961. The train carried the name from September 1950 until 1965, after which it was adopted by British Rail as the brand name for all of its express services and subsequently has been used throughout Europe for similar long-distance passenger trains. 6004 had been allocated to Cardiff Canton since September 1960, when it was transferred from Old Oak Common. www.rail-online.co.uk

6005 KING GEORGE II

To stock July 1927

Modifications
WB boiler	16/1/53
New front frames, inside cylinders	4/2/55
Double chimney	16/7/56

Livery changes
BR standard blue	22/2/50
BR green	16/1/53

Allocations
6/8/27	Old Oak Common
30/8/30	Stafford Road
3/5/34	Old Oak Common
2/6/34	Stafford Road
7/9/62	Old Oak Common

Withdrawn 20/11/62
Sold as scrap to J.Cashmore of Great Bridge   17/10/63

Repairs
23/8/27-24/8/27**L**	Swindon Factory
21/9/27-27/9/27**L**	Old Oak Common Shops
5/1/28-3/2/28**L**	Swindon Factory
1/5/28-30/5/28**L**	Swindon Factory
4/6/28-20/6/28**L**	Swindon Factory
3/1/29-20/3/29**L**	Swindon Factory
1/6/29-20/6/29**L**	Swindon Factory
17/10/29-6/12/29**L**	Swindon Factory
9/12/29-16/1/30**L**	Swindon Factory
28/4/30-30/6/30**H**	Swindon Factory
4/10/30-10/10/30**R**	Swindon Shops
20/10/30-27/10/30**L**	Swindon Shops
17/12/30-18/12/30**R**	Swindon Shops
9/1/31-30/3/31**Expt**	Swindon Factory
7/7/31-11/9/31**G**	Swindon Factory
18/7/32-9/8/32**L**	Swindon Factory
25/1/33-23/3/33**I**	Swindon Factory
7/8/33-11/8/33**L**	Stafford Road Factory
6/9/33-9/9/33**R**	Stafford Road Factory
4/11/33-22/12/33**G**	Swindon Factory
19/11/34-11/12/34**L**	Stafford Road Factory
1/1/35-22/2/35**I**	Swindon Factory
2/9/35-13/9/35**L**	Stafford Road Factory
7/2/36-20/3/36**G**	Swindon Factory
28/6/37-26/8/37**I**	Swindon Factory
5/9/38-25/10/38**G**	Swindon Factory
3/11/39-9/12/39**I**	Swindon Factory
8/11/40-19/12/40**L**	Swindon Factory
27/1/41-12/3/41**L**	Swindon Factory
22/11/41-8/1/42**L**	Swindon Factory
28/1/42-7/2/42**L**	Stafford Road Factory
25/7/42-17/8/42**R**	Stafford Road Factory
1/9/42-22/9/42**L**	Swindon Factory
23/3/43-11/5/43**L**	Swindon Factory
8/2/44-25/3/44**G**	Swindon Factory
30/9/44-19/10/44**R**	Stafford Road Factory
18/2/45-13/3/45**R**	Stafford Road Factory
31/5/45-17/7/45**I**	Swindon Factory
9/4/46-14/5/46**L**	Swindon Factory
24/6/46-23/7/46**L**	Swindon Factory
29/10/46-15/11/46**R**	Stafford Road Factory
25/1/47-14/2/47**R**	Stafford Road Factory
21/3/47-28/4/47**G**	Swindon Factory
5/4/48-19/4/48**R**	Stafford Road Factory
7/9/48-14/10/48**I**	Swindon Factory
11/9/49-29/9/49**U**	Old Oak Common Shops
17/1/50-22/2/50**HG**	Swindon Factory
15/5/51-5/7/51**HG**	Swindon Factory
3/8/51-21/8/51**U**	Old Oak Common Shops
22/5/52-11/6/52**U**	Old Oak Common Shops
3/9/52-25/9/52**U**	Old Oak Common Shops
2/12/52-16/1/53**HG**	Swindon Factory
14/3/53-23/3/53**U**	Stafford Road
28/9/53-30/10/53**U**	Stafford Road Factory
27/1/54-24/2/54**U**	Old Oak Common Shops
27/4/54-23/6/54**LC**	Swindon Factory
21/10/54-4/2/55**HG**	Swindon Factory
4/3/55-15/3/55**LC**	Swindon Factory
30/1/56-18/2/56**LC**	Stafford Road Factory
2/6/56-16/7/56**HI**	Swindon Factory
6/11/56-27/11/56**U**	Stafford Road
12/3/57-27/3/57**U**	Stafford Road
14/11/57-2/12/57**U**	Shrewsbury Shops
6/3/58-21/4/58**LI**	Swindon Factory
21/6/58-3/9/58**LC**	Swindon Factory
26/1/59-17/2/59**U**	Stafford Road
19/3/59-28/5/59**LI**	Swindon Factory
29/10/59-18/11/59**U**	Stafford Road
12/2/60-9/3/60**U**	Stafford Road
30/5/60-25/8/60**HG**	Swindon Factory
26/12/60-20/1/61**U**	Stafford Road
9/5/61-19/6/61**U**	Stafford Road
22/12/61-24/1/62**U**	Stafford Road
28/3/62-28/5/62**LI**	Swindon Factory

Boilers and mileages
First	4661*	
30/6/30		135,072
11/9/31	4673	173,295
23/3/33		236,477
22/12/33	4684	275,895
22/2/35		335,671
20/3/36	4690	396,215
26/8/37		476,784
25/10/38	4676	547,187
9/12/39		608,672
12/3/41	4674	665,378
8/1/42		699,113
11/5/43	4670	761,017
25/3/44	4661	796,949
17/7/45		858,513
14/5/46	4668	902,032
28/4/47	4688	941,914
14/10/48	4681	1,020,088
22/2/50	4687	1,091,801
5/7/51	4663	1,161,946
16/1/53	8606*	1,233,518
4/2/55	8620*	1,309,292
16/7/56	8615	1,376,773
28/5/59		1,512,075
25/8/60	8601	1,571,562
28/5/62		1,655,227

Final mileage 1,679,275

Tenders
First	2390
20/3/29	2393
20/6/29	2384
11/9/31	2440
3/34	2394
2/36	2401
9/12/39	2548
12/3/41	2643
8/1/42	2788
25/3/44	2642
14/5/46	2790
14/10/48	2743
5/7/51	2763
16/1/53	2694
23/6/54	2763
4/2/55	2913
16/7/56	2556
22/2/58	2742
21/4/58	2556
28/5/62	2787

Two bowler hatted gentlemen pose in front of 6005 KING GEORGE II in the late 1920s. This was the last of the 1927 built engines, entering traffic at the end of July and allocated to Old Oak for its first three years, and its tender has the original garter coat of arms between the company name.

6005 KING GEORGE II waiting at Leamington Spa in 1935, shows two changes since it was built in 1927. Firstly, the fitting of a speedometer operating from the rear crankpin and secondly, the tender has the circular totem formed by the letters 'GWR' - officially described as a roundel but popularly known as the 'shirt button' emblem. 6005 spent virtually the whole of its working life as a Stafford Road locomotive apart from its initial three years at Old Oak Common. It still has the original design of rounded casing over the inside valve chest and the inside valve spindle covers fitted to the first twenty Kings. www.rail-online.co.uk

On the 8.55am Birkenhead-Paddington, 6005 KING GEORGE II passes through Tyseley in 1959. The GWR signage for its 'Express Goods Services - One Day Transits', although painted out, is still visible on the warehouse in the background. www.rail-online.co.uk

6005 KING GEORGE II with the up 11.45am Birkenhead-Paddington at Wednesbury, 16 June 1959. This train was still referred to locally as the 'Zulu', a name dating back to the 19th Century when it was called the 'Northern Zulu', or 'Afghan', the broad gauge 'Zulu' being the 3.0pm Paddington-Plymouth and the 11.15am Penzance-Paddington.

6005 KING GEORGE II on the 8.55am Birkenhead-Paddington, probably in 1960, with coal piled high in the tender to allow a quick turnaround at Ranelagh Bridge without the need to go to Old Oak Common to top up the tender for the return working,It has the bogie with a slotted front cross-stay, originally fitted to 6004 - the first new King to be completed after the Midgham incident in 1927 and noted with several other engines over the years. 6005 had completed a Heavy Overhaul in August 1960, its last before withdrawal. As can be seen from the strengthened lifting holes in the front frames, it was one of the class to have new front frames in the mid-1950s. www.rail-online.co.uk

Stafford Road's 6005 KING GEORGE II near Beaconsfield with the 1.10pm Paddington-Birkenhead showing the modified covers to the inside valve spindles and the strengthening plate welded to each side of the lifting holes at the front end, one of which shows clearly here. The slotted bogie in the previous picture has been replaced by the standard type. KING GEORGE II was transferred to Old Oak Common in September 1962 and was withdrawn two months later. www.rail-online.co.uk

6006 KING GEORGE I

To stock February 1928

Modifications
WB boiler	23/4/53
Double chimney	27/6/56

Livery changes
BR standard blue	22/3/50
BR green	23/4/53

Allocations
8/3/28	Laira
12/4/30	Old Oak Common
10/5/30	Laira
25/7/30	Old Oak Common
30/8/30	Stafford Road

Withdrawn
	15/2/62
Swindon Factory	26/2/62
Cut up at Swindon	21/4/62

Repairs
4/6/28-11/6/28**L**	Swindon Factory
10/12/2-21/1/29**L**	Swindon Factory
24/4/29-22/6/29**L**	Swindon Factory
29/11/29-11/12/29**L**	Laira Shops
3/3/30-8/4/30**L**	Swindon Factory
26/5/30-16/7/30**H**	Swindon Factory
25/8/31-6/11/31**G**	Swindon Factory
22/7/32-12/8/32**L**	Swindon Factory
14/11/32-21/12/32**L**	Swindon Factory
19/4/33-29/6/33**G**	Swindon Factory
5/3/34-29/3/34**L**	Stafford Road Factory
9/5/34-4/7/34**I**	Swindon Factory
5/2/35-21/2/35**L**	Swindon Factory
9/10/35-21/11/35**G**	Swindon Factory
20/10/36-1/12/36**L**	Swindon Factory
3/9/37-23/10/37**G**	Swindon Factory
23/12/38-11/2/39**I**	Swindon Factory
4/4/39-24/4/39**L**	Swindon Factory
15/2/40-16/3/40**L**	Swindon Factory
13/5/40-16/5/40**L**	Stafford Road Factory
24/10/40-7/12/40**I**	Swindon Factory
2/8/41-3/9/41**L**	Swindon Factory
31/5/42-5/6/42**R**	Stafford Road Factory
11/8/42-2/10/42**I**	Swindon Factory
13/4/43-23/7/43**L**	Swindon Factory
5/1/44-5/2/44**R**	Swindon Factory
2/3/44-3/4/44**L**	Swindon Factory
19/4/44-6/5/44**R**	Stafford Road
6/8/44-28/9/44**R**	Old Oak Common Shops
17/11/44-8/1/45**G**	Swindon Factory
23/10/45-13/12/45**L**	Swindon Factory
27/1/46-10/2/46**R**	Stafford Road Factory
13/9/46-1/10/46**R**	Old Oak Common
7/11/46-19/12/46**I**	Swindon Factory
15/5/47-3/6/47**R**	Old Oak Common
11/12/47-21/1/48**L**	Swindon Factory
16/3/48-24/3/48**R**	Stafford Road Factory
27/4/48-20/5/48**R**	Old Oak Common Shops
22/9/48-29/10/48**I**	Swindon Factory
28/8/49-26/9/49**LC**	Stafford Road
13/2/50-22/3/50**HG**	Swindon Factory
12/4/51-10/5/51**U**	Old Oak Common Shops
12/6/51-13/8/51**HI**	Swindon Factory
4/6/52-3/7/52**HC**	Swindon Factory
9/9/52-1/10/52**U**	Stafford Road
24/2/53-23/4/53**HG**	Swindon Factory
23/11/53-28/12/53**LC**	Swindon Factory
20/8/54-15/10/54**HC**	Swindon Factory
4/1/55-25/1/55**U**	Old Oak Common Shops
10/2/55-5/4/55**HI**	Swindon Factory
12/11/55-26/11/55**U**	Banbury Shops
31/1/56-16/2/56**LC**	Old Oak Common Shops
10/5/56-27/6/56**HG**	Swindon Factory
1/5/57-18/5/57**U**	Stafford Road
15/6/57-1/7/57**U**	Stafford Road
5/10/57-21/10/57**U**	Stafford Road
12/11/57-29/11/57**U**	Old Oak Common Shops
15/1/58-24/2/58**LI**	Swindon Factory
17/7/58-6/8/58**U**	Stafford Road
6/10/58-24/10/58**U**	Old Oak Common Shops
1/11/58-20/11/58**U**	Stafford Road
24/2/59-20/3/59**U**	Stafford Road
21/4/59-25/5/59**U**	Stafford Road
23/11/59-5/2/60**LI**	Swindon Factory
1/7/60-14/7/60**LC**	Stafford Road Factory
29/8/60-27/9/60**U**	Stafford Road
3/11/60-23/11/60**U**	Tyseley Shops
16/12/60-1/4/61**U**	Stafford Road Factory
1/4/61-21/4/61**U**	Stafford Road
14/8/61-26/9/61**U**	Tyseley Shops
21/11/61-10/12/61**U**	Stafford Road

Boilers and mileages
First	4667*	
16/7/30		120,535
6/11/31	4661	191,283
29/3/34	4690	271,533
4/7/34		327,644
21/11/35	4686	410,824
23/10/37	4661	522,139
11/2/39		596,527
16/3/40	4684	651,349
7/12/40		684,465
2/10/42		771,151
23/7/43	4674	799,456
8/1/45	4682	849,508
13/12/45	4689	886,322
19/12/46		928,277
21/1/48	4685	972,701
29/10/48		1,006,149
22/3/50	4681	1,073,356
13/8/51	4692	1,135,686
3/7/52	4675	1,186,201
23/4/53	8609*	1,222,955
5/4/55	8607	1,299,182
27/6/56	4695	1,357,863
5/2/60		1,511,174

Final mileage 1,593,367

Tenders
First	2392
11/12/29	2389
16/7/30	2401
6/11/31	2394
3/34	2440
4/7/34	2434
24/4/39	2550
7/12/40	2742
8/1/45	2776
19/12/46	2763
29/10/48	2726
13/8/51	2612
15/10/54	2648
5/4/55	2710
27/6/56	2875
5/2/60	2842

Apart from a brief period of time spent at Laira in its very early days, 6006 KING GEORGE I was a Wolverhampton Stafford Road engine throughout virtually all its working life, even being withdrawn from there at the end of its days in February 1962. It was the first King which didn't have the garter crest on the tender, this being replaced by the GWR twin shields. 6006 has one of the early Jaeger type speedometers, fitted to several of the class in around 1933. In the background of this mid-1930s view is Paddington's large goods depot which was in the shadow of the station on the site of the original broad gauge terminus. The original 1850s depot was rebuilt in the 1920s with longer covered roads; it closed at the end of 1975 and was demolished in 1986. www.rail-online.co.uk

6006 KING GEORGE I waits to leave Paddington with the 7.10pm express for Birmingham Snow Hill on July 15, 1937. Its original straight top feed pipes have been changed to ones which curve back behind the nameplates and the Jaeger speedometer has been replaced by the type fitted to the whole class by 1937. John P. Wilson/Rail Archive Stephenson.

A few days before the outbreak of the Second World War, and with a rather strange two-digit reporting number, 6006 KING GEORGE I at Leamington Spa on 10 September 1939. It is in the short-lived 1930s livery with a roundel instead of the Great Western lettering on the tender. Although still retaining its original design of rounded inside valve chest casing, the upper lamp bracket has already been lowered and the footstep removed. After brief spells at Laira and Old Oak, KING GEORGE I moved to Wolverhampton Stafford Road in August 1930 and would stay there until withdrawn in 1962. www.rail-online.co.uk

6006 KING GEORGE I may have failed, resting as it does at Leamington Spa on 27 March 1948, with stopping train lamp. It is in the final version of GWR lined green with the simplified 'GW' tender lettering. www.rail-online.co.uk

6006 KING GEORGE I backs out of Platform 1 at Paddington after bringing in an express from Wolverhampton in 1953, and is now about to cross the approach tracks and points to go onto Ranelagh yard. This was a stabling point for engines which were not required to go out to Old Oak Common following arrival at Paddington, but which could be turned, oiled, watered and examined by their respective footplate crews prior to their return working. This arrangement was used for locomotives arriving from Bristol and Wolverhampton and they would therefore need to have arrived with sufficient coal for the return duty, as illustrated by the generous load remaining on 6006. It did not apply to locomotives working up from the west country, in view of the longer distances involved. P. Kerslake, www.rail-online.co.uk

The embankments are neatly trimmed back at Hatton Bank as 6006 KING GEORGE I heads a Paddington bound express in the early 1960s. It was one of 16 Kings which did not receive replacement frames and inside cylinder block incorporating the later pattern of cover for the inside valves. KING GEORGE I was the first of the class to be withdrawn, in February 1962, and was cut up at Swindon some two months later. www.rail-online.co.uk

6007 KING WILLIAM III

To stock March 1928

Officially withdrawn after Shrivenham accident, but actually repaired

Modifications

WB boiler	27/6/55
New front frames, inside cylinders	21/9/56
Double chimney	21/9/56

Livery changes

BR standard blue	12/1/50
BR green	1/10/52

Allocations

7/3/28	Old Oak Common
18/3/59	Laira
22/9/59	Stafford Road

Withdrawn 21/9/62

Sold to Cox & Danks
Langley Green 27/2/63

Repairs

26/3/28-31/3/28**L**	Swindon Factory
15/6/28-22/6/28**L**	Swindon Factory
24/9/28-18/10/28**L**	Swindon Factory
20/2/29-9/4/29**L**	Swindon Factory
13/8/29-23/8/29**L**	Swindon Factory
8/1/30-2/4/30**H**	Swindon Factory
22/9/30-2/10/30**L**	Swindon Factory
1/1/31-22/1/31**R**	Old Oak Common Shops
10/3/31-13/5/31**G**	Swindon Factory
25/11/31-15/12/31**R**	Old Oak Common Shops
11/1/32-4/2/32**L**	Swindon Factory
1/7/32-19/7/32**R**	Old Oak Common Shops
12/8/32-27/9/32**G**	Swindon Factory
10/7/33-12/7/33**L**	Swindon Factory
13/10/33-13/12/33**I**	Swindon Factory
24/2/34-27/2/34**Expt**	Swindon Factory
2/7/34-4/7/34**L**	Swindon Factory
27/8/34-29/8/34**L**	Swindon Factory
23/11/34-12/12/34**R**	Old Oak Common Shops
14/1/35-5/4/35**G**	Swindon Factory
15/1/36-24/3/36**Renewal**	Swindon Factory
15/6/36-30/6/36**R**	Laira Shops
1/2/37-3/2/37**L**	Stafford Road Factory
19/4/37-5/6/37**G**	Swindon Factory
4/10/37-27/10/37**R**	Old Oak Common Shops
20/6/38-17/8/38**I**	Swindon Factory
9/11/38-23/11/38**L**	Swindon Factory
11/1/39-3/2/39**L**	Old Oak Common Shops
30/5/39-26/6/39**L**	Swindon Factory
18/11/39-5/1/40**G**	Swindon Factory
28/11/40-25/1/41**I**	Swindon Factory
2/2/42-23/2/42**R**	Old Oak Common Shops
6/7/42-26/8/42**I**	Swindon Factory
22/10/42-4/11/42**R**	Old Oak Common Shops
28/4/43-13/5/43**R**	Old Oak Common Shops
9/6/43-29/6/43**R**	Old Oak Common Shops
2/11/43-16/11/43**L**	Old Oak Common Shops
12/1/44-26/2/44**G**	Swindon Factory
14/3/45-18/4/45**L**	Old Oak Common Shops
20/7/45-12/9/45**I**	Swindon Factory
15/5/46-14/6/46**L**	Swindon Factory
11/9/46-1/11/46**G**	Swindon Factory
7/3/47-25/3/47**L**	Swindon Factory
24/4/47-27/5/47**L**	Laira Shops
22/10/47-28/11/47**I**	Swindon Factory
30/3/48-17/4/48**R**	Laira Shops
4/5/48-27/5/48**R**	Swindon Factory
24/6/48-30/7/48**L**	Swindon Factory
29/9/48-25/10/48**L**	Swindon Factory
23/2/49-25/3/49**LC**	Swindon Factory
10/6/49-4/7/49**LC**	Swindon Factory
15/7/49-12/8/49**U**	Taunton Shops
6/12/49-12/1/50**HG**	Swindon Factory
1/6/50-14/6/50**U**	Swindon Factory
21/9/50-19/10/50**U**	Old Oak Common Shops
4/12/50-29/1/51**HI**	Swindon Factory
24/4/51-8/5/51**U**	Old Oak Common Shops
19/6/51-2/7/51**LC**	Swindon Factory
27/8/51-3/10/51**LC**	Old Oak Common Shops
12/2/52-1/4/52**U**	Taunton Shops
6/8/52-1/10/52**HG**	Swindon Factory
13/10/53-16/11/53**U**	Old Oak Common Shops
14/1/54-27/1/54**U**	Old Oak Common
8/2/54-1/4/54**HI**	Swindon Factory
8/4/54-1/5/54**U**	Taunton Shops
30/9/54-29/10/54**LC**	Old Oak Common Shops
13/12/54-12/1/55**U**	Old Oak Common Shops
2/2/55-25/2/55**U**	Old Oak Common
12/5/55-27/6/55**HG**	Swindon Factory
12/8/55-1/9/55**U**	Swindon Factory
14/10/55-17/11/55**HC**	Swindon Factory
26/11/55-24/12/55**U**	Westbury Shops
27/1/56-24/2/56**LC**	Bath Road Shops
28/4/56-21/9/56**HG**	Swindon Factory
22/7/57-21/8/57**U**	Old Oak Common Shops
26/8/57-28/10/57**HI**	Swindon Factory
25/1/58-31/1/58**U**	Old Oak Common Shops
7/5/58-29/5/58**U**	Bath Road Shops
31/7/58-15/8/58**U**	Old Oak Common Shops
22/8/58-8/9/58**U**	Old Oak Common
29/9/58-17/10/58**U**	Old Oak Common Shops
13/1/59-25/2/59**HG**	Swindon Factory
3/3/59-18/3/59**U**	Swindon Factory
21/4/59-8/5/59**U**	Laira Shops
27/7/59-20/8/59**U**	Laira Shops
1/3/60-9/4/60**U**	Stafford Road
1/5/60-27/5/60**U**	Old Oak Common Shops
9/9/60-26/9/60**U**	Banbury Shops
20/10/60-18/11/60**U**	Tyseley Shops
25/11/60-9/12/60**U**	Stafford Road Factory
19/1/61-4/2/61**U**	Stafford Road
20/3/61-20/4/61**U**	Stafford Road
12/6/61-18/8/61**LI**	Swindon Factory
7/2/62-3/3/62**U**	Stafford Road
12/3/62-28/3/62**U**	Tyseley Shops
3/5/62-12/6/62**U**	Stafford Road

Boilers and mileages

First	4668*	
2/4/30		107,132
13/5/31	4676	164,385
27/9/32	4662	243,614
13/12/33		320,030
5/4/35	4661	393,119

'renewed' after accident – mileage on 15/1/36 at accident 453,512

24/3/36	4661	
5/6/37	4667	81,209
17/8/38		175,211
5/1/40	4669	266,617
25/1/41		339,685
26/8/42		449,303
26/2/44	4667	530,387
12/9/45		616,835
1/11/46	4691	687,065
28/11/47	4687	742,228
12/1/50	4662	836,241
29/1/51		897,557
1/10/52	4683	978,241
1/4/54		1,067,779
27/6/55	8606	1,124,419
21/9/56	8607	1,157,768
28/10/57		1,225,759
25/2/59	8600	1,295,741
18/8/61		1,389,004

Final mileage 1,437,609 (since renewal in 1936)

Below. 6007 KING WILLIAM III has just passed Iver with the up 'Cornish Riviera Express' in 1935. The train is made up of the luxurious 1935 'Centenary' stock with their characteristic recessed doors. 6007 was one of the class fitted with a Jaeger speedometer, readily identifiable by the long drive in front of the cab. It would be badly damaged in the accident at Shrivenham in January 1936, and was condemned. Despite the seemingly damning report on the state of the original locomotive, the replacement - also numbered 6007 – incorporated a not insignificant proportion of the old one; indeed, it was not even necessary to lift the boiler of the damaged engine from the frames. The 'new' 6007 entered traffic on 24 March 1936. F.R. Hebron, Rail Archive Stephenson.

Bottom. 6007 KING WILLIAM III has just come off a busy Laira shed on to the former Southern Railway line in 1956, its fireman having telephoned the signalman at Lipson Junction for clearance, and it will now run tender first to North Road station to take the 'Cornish Riviera' at 12.30pm to Paddington. In addition to the rather grubby 6007, this photograph which was taken from the banking round the Laira Sports Arena, provides an interesting view of Laira Depot, packed full of locomotives with the coal store and its coal trucks visible as well as the rear of the coaling plant complete with a Pannier tank on the ramp. The origin of what was known as the "Mullet Pond" immediately behind the engine, is shrouded in mystery. P. Kerslake, www.rail-online.co.uk

Tenders			
First	2387		
2/10/30	2395	12/9/45	2710
13/5/31	2392	27/5/48	2612
19/7/32	2465	2/7/51	2726
27/9/32	2392	1/10/52	2815
13/12/33	2388	1/4/54	2428
5/4/35	2572	1/6/54	2630
'renewed' after accident		29/1/55	2723
24/3/36	2572	27/6/55	2531
23/11/38	2715	21/9/56	2923
25/1/41	2790	28/10/57	2838
25/4/42	2665	25/2/59	2854
26/8/42	2704	18/8/61	2597
26/2/44	2695		

147

An interesting place to park a motor cycle as KING WILLIAM III runs light engine through Bath Spa on 25 February 1956. 6007 still has a single chimney although a double chimney would be fitted during a five month long Heavy General repair which was completed in September 1956. The original style of inside valve casing (in front of the smokebox saddle) had a curved top but this has been replaced by the square top type with tread plates, but the front frames have not yet been replaced nor inside cylinders changed. www.rail-online.co.uk

The class were given improved draughting, mechanical lubricators and self-cleaning smokeboxes enhancing the performance of the class on their heavily loaded workings, especially between Paddington and Plymouth. These had taken their toll on the main frames in the early 1950s, and severe cracking had been discovered in a number of engines. The strengthened lifting holes in the front sideframes and modified inside cylinder block show that 6007 KING WILLIAM III had received new front frames and inside cylinder block during an overhaul at Swindon Works between April and September 1956. 6007 is rounding the severe curve through Teignmouth station, running non-stop to Paddington, complete with the stylish 'Cornish Riviera Limited' headboard which was introduced from 11th June 1956. www.rail-online.co.uk

6007 KING WILLIAM III, an Old Oak Common engine for over 30 years before transfer to Stafford Road in September 1959, passes through Gerrards Cross on the 8.55am Birkenhead-Paddington. www.rail-online.co.uk

Arriving at Banbury with a Down Birkenhead train on 26 April 1962, KING WILLIAM III had less than six months left in traffic. After withdrawal in September 1962 it was scrapped by Cox and Danks at Langley Green in February 1963. www.rail-online.co.uk

6008 KING JAMES II

To stock March 1928

Modifications
WB boiler	13/12/55
New front frames, inside cylinders	11/7/57
Double chimney	11/7/57

Livery changes
BR standard blue	16/11/49
BR green	9/1/53

Allocations
27/4/28	Laira
15/7/30	Old Oak Common
30/8/30	Stafford Road
11/6/52	Laira
2/2/59	Stafford Road

Withdrawn
	19/6/62
Cut up at Swindon	26/1/63

Repairs
12/4/28-27/4/28**L**	Swindon Factory
11/6/28-18/6/28**L**	Swindon Factory
15/10/28-6/11/28**L**	Swindon Factory
9/4/29-8/6/29**L**	Swindon Factory
4/12/29-16/12/02**L**	Laira Shops
20/2/30-22/2/30**L**	Swindon Factory
30/4/30-30/6/30**H**	Swindon Factory
12/8/31-15/10/03**G**	Swindon Factory
21/1/32-22/1/32**L**	Swindon Factory
19/2/32-7/3/32**L**	Swindon Factory
27/7/32-30/8/32**L**	Swindon Factory
21/12/03-10/2/33**I**	Swindon Factory
24/10/33-16/11/33**L**	Swindon Factory
6/1/34-27/3/34**G**	Swindon Factory
27/10/34-16/11/34**L**	Stafford Road Shops
27/3/35-27/5/35**G**	Swindon Factory
9/8/35-13/8/35**L**	Stafford Road Factory
11/9/35-1/10/35**L**	Swindon Factory
26/2/36-15/4/36**L**	Swindon Factory
2/9/36-4/9/36**L**	Stafford Road Factory
26/10/36-5/12/36**I**	Swindon Factory
31/12/37-21/2/38**G**	Swindon Factory
29/3/39-22/5/39**I**	Swindon Factory
14/6/40-7/8/40**G**	Swindon Factory
6/9/41-31/10/41**L**	Swindon Factory
24/2/42-14/4/42**L**	Swindon Factory
5/5/42-23/5/42**L**	Swindon Factory
13/10/42-23/11/42**I**	Swindon Factory
6/1/43-18/1/43**L**	Swindon Factory
3/3/43-26/3/43**L**	Stafford Road Factory
25/6/43-27/8/43**L**	Swindon Factory
25/10/43-13/12/43**L**	Swindon Factory
24/5/44-30/6/44**L**	Swindon Factory
17/11/44-19/12/44**R**	Stafford Road
13/1/45-28/2/45**I**	Swindon Factory
10/4/45-27/4/45**R**	Stafford Road
3/7/45-1/9/45**L**	Stafford Road Factory
21/11/45-28/12/45**L**	Swindon Factory
3/1/46-21/1/46**R**	Stafford Road
14/8/46-9/9/46**L**	Swindon Factory
21/9/46-16/10/46**R**	Stafford Road
31/10/46-10/11/46**L**	Stafford Road
11/11/46-14/12/46**L**	Stafford Road Factory
9/1/47-22/2/47**L**	Swindon Factory
1/3/47-22/3/47**R**	Old Oak Common
31/5/47-3/6/47**R**	Stafford Road Factory
6/8/47-20/8/47**R**	Old Oak Common
31/10/47-17/12/47**I**	Swindon Factory
11/8/48-21/9/48**L**	Swindon Factory
10/10/49-16/11/49**HG**	Swindon Factory
12/6/50-17/7/50**LC**	Swindon Factory
19/11/50-8/1/51**U**	Old Oak Common Shops
14/2/51-22/3/51**HG**	Swindon Factory
5/12/51-23/1/52**LC**	Swindon Factory

29/4/52-11/6/52**LC**	Swindon Factory
16/9/52-9/10/52**U**	Laira Shops
18/11/52-9/1/53**HI**	Swindon Factory
19/6/53-11/7/53**U**	Laira Shops
9/11/53-16/12/53**LC**	Swindon Factory
4/5/54-18/6/54**HI**	Swindon Factory
1/10/54-31/10/54**U**	Laira Shops
8/2/55-30/3/55**LC**	Swindon Factory
31/10/55-13/12/55**HG**	Swindon Factory
31/1/56-17/2/56**LC**	Old Oak Common Shops
27/8/56-18/9/56**U**	Bath Road Shops
2/10/56-9/10/56**U**	Laira Shops
24/11/56-6/12/56**U**	Laira Shops
18/1/57-4/2/57**U**	Laira Shops
8/4/57-11/7/57**HG**	Swindon Factory
23/10/57-6/11/57**U**	Laira Shops
13/2/58-25/2/58**U**	Laira Shops
9/6/58-27/6/58**U**	Laira Shops
13/11/58-30/12/58**HG**	Swindon Factory
16/10/59-10/11/59**U**	Stafford Road
18/1/60-5/2/60**U**	Stafford Road
25/6/60-22/9/60**LI**	Swindon Factory
23/2/61-22/3/61**U**	Stafford Road
28/12/61-19/1/62**U**	Stafford Road
23/1/62-23/2/62**U**	Stafford Road

Boilers and mileages
First	4669*	
30/6/30		109,671
15/10/31	4674	178,973
10/2/33		239,016
27/3/34	4673	295,875
27/5/35	4663	359,794
5/12/36		441,862
21/2/38	4673	510,795
22/5/39		581,236
7/8/40	4661	640,453
23/11/42		733,679
13/12/43	4684	761,992
28/12/45	4686	835,021
22/2/47	4672	867,490
17/12/47		895,774
21/9/48	4669	932,207
16/11/49	4693	988,363
22/3/51	4679	1,057,531
9/1/53	4673	1,143,490
18/6/54	4687	1,230,307
13/12/55	8600	1,328,750
11/7/57	8611	1,405,184
30/12/58	4699	1,509,100
22/9/60		1,598,699

Final mileage		1,695,925

Tenders
First	2396
4/28	2401
8/6/29	2399
16/12/29	2392
22/3/30	2398
30/6/30	2394
15/10/31	2401
15/4/36	2394
22/5/39	2629
14/4/42	2642
23/11/42	2606
18/1/43	2762
28/2/45	2775
22/2/47	2629
21/7/48	2728
22/3/51	2772
11/6/52	2743
1/1/55	2762
30/3/55	2715
13/12/55	2931
1/12/56	2398
11/7/57	2569
30/12/58	2775
23/2/62	2436

An almost brand new 6008 KING JAMES II with the Down 'Cornish Riviera Express' in 1928, not long after it entered traffic in March. F.R. Hebron, Rail Archive Stephenson.

An immaculate 6008 KING JAMES II, still with unmarked buffers, at Leamington Spa on 25 June 1939. It had recently completed an Intermediate overhaul and is in the late 1930s livery with the GWR roundel on the tender. www.rail-online.co.uk

This is one of those hybrid liveries which were a feature of the engines repainted in 1948. Although BRITISH RAILWAYS now adorns the tender, 6008 KING JAMES II at Leamington Spa in 1948 working an Up express, is still in GWR lined green and the tender lettering is in pre-war GWR style. It has yet to be fitted with a smokebox number plate and the front bufferbeam still has its stock number. 6008 was repainted in BR express passenger light blue in late 1949. The SRD code on the front footplate angle shows it was allocated to Stafford Road; it was there from 1930 until 1952. 6008 retains the original design of smooth casing over the inside valve chest, and the front cover over one of the inside valves is missing for some reason. www.rail-online.co.uk

Laira's 6008 KING JAMES II was in Swindon Works for a Light Casual Overhaul which lasted from early February until the end of March 1955, and was on a two-coach local stopping duty at Didcot, before resuming express duties based at Laira. The engine had not been repainted while in the Works, although this shot shows that the outside steam pipes and outside cylinder casings appear to be freshly painted. 6008 still has the original inside valve spindle covers fitted to the first twenty members of the class when built. It returned to Swindon again in the October 1955, this time for a Heavy General Overhaul which lasted until mid-December. www.rail-online.co.uk

It is eleven in the morning at Laira shed on Sunday 15 April 1956 and on its home shed 6008 KING JAMES II has been re-coaled and prepared for its next duty, probably the following morning. It is likely that 6008 had worked home from Paddington overnight, probably on one of the three workings running via Bristol Temple Meads during the hours of darkness. It had been transferred to Laira from Stafford Road in June 1952 but returned to the Wolverhampton shed in February 1959 for its final three years in traffic when diesels displaced the Kings from Laira. P. Kerslake, www.rail-online.co.uk

A lady holidaymaker admires one of Laira's finest in the shape of 6008 KING JAMES II, a regular choice by Laira's Running Foremen for the Up 'Cornish Riviera Limited', which it will work from Plymouth through to Paddington, returning the following day with the Down 'Riviera'. 6008 was about to pass under Black Bridge (some know it as Rockstone Bridge) at Dawlish, probably in the summer of 1958. 6008 had received new front frames and replacement inside cylinder block during an overhaul at Swindon Works in mid-1957. www.rail-online.co.uk

6009 KING CHARLES II

To stock March 1928

Modifications

WB boiler	28/7/54
New front frames and inside cylinders	25/5/56
Double chimney	25/5/56

Livery changes

BR dark blue	28/5/48
BR standard blue	4/11/49
BR green	19/3/53

Allocations

3/4/28	Old Oak Common

Withdrawn 21/9/62

Sold as scrap to J.Cashmore;
probably cut up at Great Bridge 14/11/62

Repairs

18/6/28-26/6/28**L**	Swindon Factory
15/10/28-20/11/28**L**	Swindon Factory
20/11/28-28/11/28**L**	Swindon Factory
9/4/29-23/5/29**L**	Swindon Factory
23/11/29-2/12/29**L**	Laira Shops
24/12/29-6/3/30**H**	Swindon Factory
17/3/30-8/4/30**L**	Swindon Factory
21/1/31-9/2/31**R**	Old Oak Common Shops
6/3/31-18/3/31**R**	Old Oak Common Shops
22/4/31-19/6/31**G**	Swindon Factory
14/1/32-23/3/32**L**	Swindon Factory
26/7/32-19/8/32**L**	Swindon Factory
1/2/33-11/4/33**I**	Swindon Factory
19/9/33-13/10/33**L**	Swindon Factory
3/4/34-30/5/34**G**	Swindon Factory
28/7/34-1/8/34**L**	Swindon Factory
13/2/35-7/3/35**R**	Old Oak Common Shops
30/4/35-20/6/35**I**	Swindon Factory
29/6/36-17/8/36**G**	Swindon Factory
12/10/37-27/11/37**I**	Swindon Factory
18/4/38-7/5/38**R**	Old Oak Common Shops
24/1/39-7/3/39**I**	Swindon Factory
30/3/40-27/5/40**G**	Swindon Factory
10/1/41-7/2/41**L**	Swindon Factory
12/7/41-2/8/41**R**	Swindon Factory
18/2/42-1/4/42**I**	Swindon Factory
26/11/42-30/12/42**R**	Old Oak Common Shops
9/2/43-25/3/43**I**	Swindon Factory
16/12/43-25/1/44**L**	Swindon Factory
29/1/44-3/2/44**L**	Swindon Factory
24/6/44-28/7/44**L**	Old Oak Common Shops
27/9/44-23/11/44**L**	Swindon Factory
15/2/45-17/3/45**L**	Old Oak Common Shops
12/4/45-4/5/45**R**	Old Oak Common Shops
3/10/45-15/11/45**G**	Swindon Factory
12/7/46-27/7/46**R**	Old Oak Common
26/9/46-17/10/46**R**	Old Oak Common
19/11/46-31/12/46**I**	Swindon Factory
11/2/47-1/3/47**R**	Old Oak Common Shops
27/5/47-13/6/47**R**	Old Oak Common
26/9/47-13/10/47**R**	Old Oak Common Shops
2/11/47-25/11/47**R**	Old Oak Common Shops
15/12/47-31/12/47**R**	Old Oak Common Shops
22/1/48-17/2/48**R**	Old Oak Common Shops
23/4/48-28/5/58**G**	Swindon Factory
22/10/48-12/11/48**L**	Swindon Factory
17/3/49-1/4/49**U**	Old Oak Common Shops
22/5/49-27/6/49**LC**	Old Oak Common Shops
22/9/49-4/11/49**HG**	Swindon Factory
27/6/50-22/7/50**U**	Old Oak Common
21/10/50-20/12/50**U**	Taunton Shops
30/12/50-11/1/51**U**	Old Oak Common
25/2/51-21/3/51**LC**	Old Oak Common Shops
2/5/51-5/6/51**HG**	Swindon Factory
25/1/52-27/2/52**LC**	Swindon Factory
4/6/52-17/6/52**U**	Taunton Shops
29/7/52-3/9/52**LC**	Swindon Factory
2/10/52-6/11/52**U**	Old Oak Common Shops
23/1/53-19/3/53**HI**	Swindon Factory
21/9/53-13/10/53**U**	Old Oak Common Shops
19/11/53-3/12/53**U**	Old Oak Common Shops
15/2/54-14/3/54**U**	Laira Shops
22/4/54-6/5/54**U**	Old Oak Common Shops
1/6/54-28/7/54**HG**	Swindon Factory
1/10/54-27/10/54**U**	Laira Shops
27/1/55-18/2/55**U**	Old Oak Common Shops
22/9/55-14/10/55**U**	Laira Shops
28/10/55-20/11/55**U**	Bath Road Shops
2/1/56-25/5/56**HG**	Swindon Factory
4/3/57-19/3/57**U**	Old Oak Common Shops
26/4/57-20/5/57**U**	Taunton Shops
8/8/57-27/9/57**HI**	Swindon Factory
29/5/58-12/6/58**U**	Old Oak Common Shops
12/9/58-21/11/58**LC**	Swindon Factory
20/2/59-16/4/59**HI**	Swindon Factory
25/12/59-14/1/60**U**	Stafford Road Factory
5/2/60-29/2/60**U**	Old Oak Common Shops
6/7/60-15/9/60**U**	Old Oak Common Shops
7/3/61-12/5/61**HG**	Swindon Factory
16/3/62-18/6/62**LC**	Swindon Factory

Boilers and mileages

First	4670*	
6/3/30		99,071
19/6/31	4664	167,259
11/4/33		267,305
30/5/34	4678	339,193
20/6/35		409,733
17/8/36	4670	493,861
27/11/37		590,274
7/3/39		681,599
27/5/40	4692	761,225
1/4/42		879,304
25/3/43		947,120
15/11/45	4665	1,091,500
31/12/46	4674	1,162,488
28/5/48	4673	1,230,724
4/11/49	4676	1,301,199
5/6/51	4669	1,373,490
19/3/53	4677	1,467,149
28/7/54	8615*	1,541,390
25/5/56	4697	1,617,561
27/9/57		1,711,198
16/4/59	8623	1,790,290
12/5/61	8615	1,887,913

Final mileage	1,935,102

Tenders

First	2384
23/5/29	2390
9/2/31	2389
18/3/31	2390
19/6/31	2402
13/10/33	2548
26/7/34	2428
17/11/34	2642
7/2/41	2759
23/11/44	2763
31/12/46	2788
28/5/48	2800
19/3/53	2695
27/2/54	2648
28/7/54	2564
25/5/56	2805
26/1/57	2913
10/8/57	2870
21/11/58	2727
12/5/61	2929
18/6/62	2818
11/8/62	2841

6009 KING CHARLES II passes Kensal Green with a Down express from Paddington in October 1932. The flyover and skew girder bridge in the background was built in 1911/2 to remove the conflicting lines into Paddington. It carried a double track from Old Oak to Ladbroke Bridge box, allowing empty carriage and light engine movements to be kept separate from the main running lines; it was singled in 1967. Kensal Green gasworks was opened in 1845 by the Western Gas Company; it was rebuilt in the 1930s and after closure in 1970 most of the site was cleared and a Sainsbury's supermarket built on the eastern portion in 1989. Colling Turner, Rail Archive Stephenson.

British Railways experimented with ultramarine with cream, red and grey lining for its principal express locomotives, and this was applied to four Kings, including 6009 KING CHARLES II in May 1948. The tenders of those four locomotives were lettered BRITISH RAILWAYS in full in unshaded cream characters. On 6009 it was replaced by the standard lighter blue in November 1949 as shown in this picture taken at Leamington. www.rail-online.co.uk

Old Oak Common's 6009 KING CHARLES II is at the very end of Laira shed's coaling line in this photograph from 1953 and is waiting to be moved forward to have its fire dropped and to be re-coaled further down the coaling line. The chalked '100' Reporting Number indicates that it had worked down to Plymouth on the early 5.30am from Paddington, running via Bristol Temple Meads to arrive at Plymouth around mid-day. 6009 clearly displays the first style of inside valve spindle covers, borne by the early members of the class. P. Kerslake, www.rail-online.co.uk

6009 KING CHARLES II rushes through Brent with an Up express in early 1959, shortly after completion of a Heavy overhaul in February. Brent was the junction on the main line for the Kingsbridge branch which lies out of shot on the far left of this view. The southern fringes of Dartmoor visible in the background, and the line closely skirting that edge of the moor at this location. www.rail-online.co.uk

6009 KING CHARLES II with a two-coach local train near South Brent in 1959. Why 6009 was working an 'All Stations' stopping train here is a mystery, unless it was on a 'Running-in' turn, but the records show that 6009 had not been in Swindon since February 1959, and such turns were carried out on the main line between Swindon and Bristol and certainly not this far west. Possibly it had undergone some kind of minor repair whilst at Laira depot following a run down from Paddington. 6009 was one of the fourteen Kings to have replacement front main frames and a new inside cylinder block fitted, receiving these during a five-month Heavy General Overhaul between early January and late May 1956 when it was also fitted with a double chimney. 6009 is in the final form for a King, with a mechanical lubricator now situated ahead of the main steam pipe, a double chimney, high superheat boiler and modified cover over the inside valve chest. www.rail-online.co.uk

6009 KING CHARLES II at Didcot on 25 June 1961. It was allocated to Old Oak from new in March 1928 until withdrawn in 1962, the only King to stay at one shed throughout. www.rail-online.co.uk

6010 KING CHARLES I

To stock April 1928

Modifications
WB boiler	1/10/51
Double chimney	1/3/56

Livery changes
BR standard blue	1/6/50
BR green	1/2/53

Allocations
21/4/28	Laira
21/12/29	Newton Abbot
15/2/30	Laira
2/4/59	Old Oak Common
11/9/61	Canton

Withdrawn
22/6/62
Cut up at Swindon

Repairs
22/6/28-26/6/28**L**	Swindon Factory
1/1/29-22/1/29**L**	Swindon Factory
15/6/29-22/6/29**R**	Swindon Factory
24/7/29-9/8/29**L**	Laira Shops
25/10/29-14/12/29**H**	Swindon Factory
3/5/30-7/6/30**L**	Swindon Factory
25/8/30-1/9/30**L**	Laira Shops
11/11/30-3/12/30**L**	Newton Abbot Factory
6/5/31-29/6/31**I**	Swindon Factory
20/2/32-14/3/32**I**	Swindon Factory
22/6/32-15/7/32**R**	Laira Shops
10/10/32-7/12/32**G**	Swindon Factory
11/1/33-10/2/33**L**	Swindon Factory
24/5/33-2/6/33**L**	Swindon Factory
2/9/33-6/9/33**Speedo**	Swindon Factory
14/9/33-29/9/33**R**	Laira Shops
2/1/34-15/2/34**I**	Swindon Factory
5/6/34-8/6/34**L**	Swindon Factory
10/11/34-24/11/34**R**	Laira Shops
8/2/35-23/2/35**R**	Laira Shops
4/4/35-1/6/35**G**	Swindon Factory
28/8/35-27/9/35**L**	Swindon Factory
12/10/35-25/10/35**L**	Swindon Factory
15/7/36-25/7/36**L**	Swindon Factory
17/11/36-30/12/36**I**	Swindon Factory
16/6/37-8/7/37**L**	Swindon Factory
29/10/37-18/11/37**R**	Laira Shops
29/12/37-16/2/38**G**	Swindon Factory
19/7/38-13/8/38**L**	Swindon Factory
30/3/39-18/5/39**I**	Swindon Factory
9/6/39-17/6/39**L**	Swindon Factory
6/10/39-26/10/39**R**	Laira Shops
16/11/39-13/12/39**L**	Swindon Factory
8/2/40-1/3/40**L**	Swindon Factory
30/10/40-30/12/40**I**	Swindon Factory
10/9/41-3/10/41**R**	Laira Shops
14/4/42-1/6/42**I**	Swindon Factory
25/9/42-18/10/42**R**	Laira Shops
16/3/43-8/4/43**R**	Laira Shops
26/5/43-6/7/43**G**	Swindon Factory
11/11/43-31/12/43**L**	Laira Shops
16/5/44-6/6/44**R**	Laira Shops
31/7/44-8/9/44**I**	Swindon Factory
1/2/45-16/2/45**R**	Laira Shops
23/4/45-7/5/45**R**	Laira Shops
26/7/45-10/8/45**R**	Laira Shops
22/9/45-17/10/45**R**	Laira Shops
7/1/46-14/2/46**G**	Swindon Factory
19/6/46-11/7/46**R**	Laira Shops
23/9/46-24/10/46**R**	Laira Shops
27/12/46-22/1/47**R**	Laira Shops
8/2/47-17/3/47**I**	Swindon Factory
7/7/47-16/7/47**R**	Laira Shops
12/9/47-3/10/47**R**	Taunton Shops
1/3/48-23/4/48**R**	Laira Shops
3/8/48-13/8/48**L**	Swindon Factory
28/9/48-16/10/48**L**	Laira Shops
17/12/48-31/1/49**HG**	Swindon Factory
17/5/49-31/5/49**HC**	Swindon Factory
8/8/49-26/8/49**U**	Laira Shops
22/11/49-15/12/49**U**	Laira Shops
17/3/50-30/3/50**U**	Laira Shops
2/5/50-5/6/50**HG**	Swindon Factory
5/9/50-15/9/50**U**	Laira Shops
20/10/50-13/11/50**LC**	Swindon Factory
27/2/51-21/3/51**LC**	Swindon Factory
17/8/51-9/10/51**HG**	Swindon Factory
15/10/51-17/10/51**U**	Swindon Factory
7/11/51-5/12/51**LC**	Swindon Factory
25/2/52-12/3/52**U**	Laira Shops
22/4/52-14/5/52**LC**	Swindon Factory
16/9/52-15/10/52**LC**	Swindon Factory
9/1/53-23/2/53**HI**	Swindon Factory
9/4/53-25/5/53**HI**	Swindon Factory
5/8/53-15/10/53**LC**	Swindon Factory
17/12/53-7/1/54**LC**	Swindon Factory
5/4/54-25/5/54**LC**	Swindon Factory
6/7/54-23/7/54**U**	Laira Shops
11/9/54-3/10/54**U**	Laira Shops
23/10/54-19/11/54**U**	Laira Shops
26/1/55-2/3/55**HG**	Swindon Factory
1/9/55-21/9/55**U**	Taunton Shops
21/10/55-5/11/55**U**	Laira Shops
28/1/56-27/3/56**HI**	Swindon Factory
3/1/57-31/1/57**U**	Bath Road Shops
17/6/57-12/9/57**HI**	Swindon Factory
26/9/57-10/10/57**LC**	Swindon Factory
22/11/57-3/12/57**U**	Laira Shops
1/5/58-21/5/58**U**	Taunton Shops
6/8/58-23/8/58**U**	Laira Shops
22/11/58-10/12/58**U**	Laira Shops
15/1/59-2/4/59**HI**	Swindon Factory
27/4/60-12/5/60**U**	Old Oak Common Shops
19/7/60-5/8/60**U**	Old Oak Common Shops
7/9/60-31/10/60**HG**	Swindon Factory
6/5/61-1/6/61**U**	Banbury Shops
7/7/61-26/7/61**U**	Reading Shops
12/3/62-2/4/62**U**	Canton Shops
1/5/62-21/5/62**U**	Ebbw Junction Shops

Boilers and mileages
First	4671*	
14/12/29		92,950
29/6/31		170,284
7/12/32	4676	244,377
15/2/34		307,157
1/6/35	4668	383,765
30/12/36		477,919
16/2/38	4662	553,302
18/5/39		640,246
30/12/40		736,802
1/6/42		829,503
6/7/43	4685	894,287
8/9/44		969,800
14/2/46	4692	1,061,543
17/3/47		1,125,239
31/1/49	4680	1,216,808
31/5/49	4683	1,239,222
5/6/50	4672	1,303,891
9/10/51	4696*	1,381,345
23/2/53		1,439,893
2/3/55	8622*	1,522,407
27/3/56		1,594,275
12/9/57	8625	1,682,902
2/4/59	8611	1,779,147
31/10/60	8628	1,859,765
Final mileage		1,928,258

Below. 6010 KING CHARLES I near Iver with the 3.30pm Paddington to Plymouth express in June 1930. It had been transferred back to its original shed, Laira, from Newton Abbot in February. George R. Grigs, Rail Archive Stephenson.

Bottom. Laira have turned out their own 6010 KING CHARLES I in superb condition and it is in Platform 8 at North Road with three strengthening coaches, awaiting the arrival into Platform 7 of the 9.30am from Falmouth. Upon its arrival the engine from Cornwall will come off and go to Laira, allowing 6010 to add its strengthening coaches to the train before leaving for Paddington. It has a neatly chalked '623' Reporting Number in place of the customary metal numbers in a metal frame. Peter Kerslake believes that Laira shed had a set of stencils used for this purpose.6010 had been fortunate to escape destruction from enemy bombs whilst at Newton Abbot during the war, although its cabsides took a substantial amount of machine gun fire from an accompanying fighter plane during a bombing raid on the station and its surrounds. P. Kerslake, www.rail-online.co.uk

6010 KING CHARLES I sets off from Plymouth for Paddington on 16 January 1954. Its driver is looking back to check that all is well and with no grubby pilot engine attached the King can be seen in all its splendour, its load being within the ten coach maximum for an unassisted King over the banks to Newton Abbot. The large red brick building in the background is the Royal Eye Infirmary which was operational in this capacity until 2013. P. Kerslake, www.rail-online.co.uk

On Sunday 24 April 1955, 6010 KING CHARLES is caught by a shaft of sunlight as it waits to leave Paddington with the 1.30 pm to Plymouth, due there at 6.25 pm. 6010 had been in Swindon Works from January to March 1955 for a Heavy General Overhaul. P. Kerslake, www.rail-online.co.uk

6010 KING CHARLES I has been checked by a distant signal as it runs along the estuary of the River Plym on 25 April 1956, working home on the 1.30pm from Paddington due into Plymouth at 6.25pm. The line on the extreme left is the 4ft 6in gauge Lee Moor tramway, running down from Lee Moor to Cattewater and worked by horses hauling china clay from the quarry. It crossed the main line at Laira Junction and by ancient agreement had priority of the Great Western main line; commercial operations on the tramway ceased in 1945 but the owning company did not wish to relinquish the right of way and token movements continued until 26 August 1960, the last time the Lee Moor Tramway horses pulled wagons across the main line. P. Kerslake, www.rail-online.co.uk

6010 KING CHARLES I at Westbury on a wet day in 1957 hauling the 8.30am 'Mayflower' from Plymouth North Road to Paddington. www.rail-online.co.uk

6011 KING JAMES I

To stock April 1928

Modifications
WB boiler	3/12/52
Double chimney	26/3/56

Livery changes
BR standard blue	1/7/49
BR green	3/12/52

Allocations
1/5/28	Old Oak Common
12/11/39	Bath Road
6/43	Old Oak Common
17/1/46	Stafford Road
7/9/62	Old Oak Common

Withdrawn
Withdrawn	18/12/62
Cut up at Swindon	25/1/64

Repairs
30/5/28-5/6/28**L**	Swindon Factory
6/7/28-20/7/28**L**	Swindon Factory
14/1/29-6/3/29**L**	Swindon Factory
15/6/29-21/6/29**R**	Swindon Factory
27/6/29-12/7/29**L**	Swindon Factory
19/11/29-5/12/29**L**	Swindon Factory
16/1/30-15/4/30**H**	Swindon Factory
13/1/31-20/2/31**L**	Swindon Factory
5/5/31-24/6/31**G**	Swindon Factory
13/10/31-6/11/31**L**	Swindon Factory
6/4/32-22/4/32**R**	Old Oak Common Shops
6/10/32-22/11/32**I**	Swindon Factory
12/8/33-25/8/33**L**	Swindon Factory
18/11/33-11/1/34**I**	Swindon Factory
11/6/34-12/7/34**L**	Swindon Factory
10/10/34-5/11/34**L**	Swindon Factory
18/2/35-26/4/35**G**	Swindon Factory
2/10/35-18/10/35**R**	Old Oak Common Shops
28/2/36-24/3/36**R**	Old Oak Common Shops
24/3/36-15/5/36**I**	Swindon Factory
19/9/36-30/9/36**L**	Swindon Factory
4/11/36-28/11/36**L**	Swindon Factory
25/9/37-10/11/37**G**	Swindon Factory
11/4/38-4/5/38**L**	Swindon Factory
12/11/38-30/12/38**I**	Swindon Factory
11/12/39-24/1/40**I**	Swindon Factory
3/4/40-20/4/40**R**	Bath Road
29/7/40-3/9/40**L**	Swindon Factory
21/10/40-23/11/40**R**	Old Oak Common Shops
26/1/41-11/3/41**R**	Bath Road
28/4/41-23/5/41**R**	Taunton Shops
24/7/41-8/8/41**R**	Bath Road
25/8/41-13/9/41**R**	Old Oak Common Shops
4/12/41-24/1/42**G**	Swindon Factory
14/2/42-30/3/42**L**	Swindon Factory
12/4/42-6/5/42**R**	Taunton Shops
14/5/42-30/5/42**R**	Swindon Factory
16/10/42-10/11/42**R**	Bath Road
11/12/42-16/1/43**L**	Swindon Factory
20/4/43-5/5/43**R**	Old Oak Common Shops
9/1/44-17/2/44**I**	Swindon Factory
9/3/44-10/3/44**L**	Old Oak Common Shops
26/7/44-8/8/44**L**	Swindon Factory
2/12/44-29/12/44**L**	Swindon Factory
20/4/45-10/5/45**R**	Old Oak Common Shops
10/6/45-11/7/45**R**	Old Oak Common Shops
26/9/45-12/10/45**R**	Old Oak Common Shops
8/12/45-17/1/46**G**	Swindon Factory
8/1/47-6/2/47**I**	Swindon Factory
27/2/47-13/3/47**Hot box**	Swindon Factory
21/3/47-2/4/47**Hot box**	Swindon Factory
26/5/47-11/6/47**R**	Stafford Road Factory
10/1/48-26/1/48**R**	Stafford Road
28/1/48-30/1/48**Tender**	Banbury
10/3/48-12/4/48**L**	Swindon Factory
5/5/48-11/6/48**L**	Swindon Factory
19/9/48-5/10/48**R**	Stafford Road
9/11/48-10/12/48**L**	Stafford Road Factory
10/5/49-26/5/49**U**	Old Oak Common Shops
27/5/49-1/7/49**HI**	Swindon Factory
28/2/50-29/3/50**U**	Old Oak Common Shops
16/6/50-10/8/50**HC**	Swindon Factory
10/11/50-30/11/50**U**	Old Oak Common Shops
22/3/51-17/4/51**LC**	Swindon Factory
7/9/51-16/10/51**HI**	Swindon Factory
23/10/52-3/12/52**HG**	Swindon Factory
28/4/53-5/6/53**U**	Swindon Factory
10/11/53-6/1/54**U**	Stafford Road Factory
30/1/54-24/3/54**LC**	Swindon Factory
25/9/54-9/10/54**U**	Stafford Road Factory
2/11/54-21/12/54**HI**	Swindon Factory
26/2/55-11/3/55**U**	Swindon Factory
16/5/55-23/5/55**U**	Tyseley Shops
29/9/55-26/10/55**U**	Old Oak Common Shops
26/1/56-26/3/56**HG**	Swindon Factory
16/3/57-7/6/57**LI**	Swindon Factory
8/7/57-19/7/57**U**	Stafford Road Factory
7/4/58-21/4/58**U**	Old Oak Common Shops
20/5/58-8/6/58**U**	Stafford Road Factory
20/9/58-14/11/58**LI**	Swindon Factory
17/3/59-10/4/59**U**	Stafford Road Factory
5/12/59-2/1/60**U**	Stafford Road
1/3/60-20/5/60**LI**	Swindon Factory
18/11/60-16/12/60**U**	Stafford Road
14/8/61-6/9/61**U**	Stafford Road
28/10/61-23/2/62**HI**	Swindon Factory

Boilers and mileages
First	4673*	
15/4/30		100,838
24/6/31	4668	165,733
22/11/32		243,155
11/1/34		307,902
26/4/35	4662	372,819
15/5/36		440,189
10/11/37	4664	537,466
30/12/38		623,268
24/1/40		698,095
24/1/42	4678	786,161
17/2/44		892,033
17/1/46	4688	985,710
6/2/47	4666	1,037,901
11/6/48	4689	1,083,252
1/7/49		1,124,055
10/8/50	4688	1,176,312
16/10/51	4672	1,232,482
3/12/52	8605*	1,292,833
21/12/54	4695	1,359,584
26/3/56	8608	1,413,714
20/5/60		1,595,247
23/2/62		1,679,040

Final mileage	1,718,295

Tenders
First	2395
15/4/30	2547
24/6/31	2442
25/8/33	2425
24/1/40	2710
3/9/40	2775
24/1/42	2643
16/1/43	2728
8/8/44	2409
29/12/44	2800
17/1/46	2629
6/2/47	2775
16/10/51	2808
21/12/54	2715
11/3/55	2815
7/6/57	2922
8/57	2815
14/9/57	2829
14/6/58	2742
23/2/62	2386

Still with its workshop burnished metalwork, brand new 6011 KING JAMES I in 1928. It was allocated to Old Oak Common until the end of 1939.

6011 KING JAMES I passes the old Kensal Green gasworks with a Down express from Paddington in August 1931. George R. Grigs, Rail Archive Stephenson.

6011 KING JAMES I at Paddington in 1955. It had been repainted green at the end of 1952 after spending over three years in light blue. The first coach in its train is a GWR design buffet car.

A gleaming 6011 KING JAMES I is admired by two trainspotters at Bath in 1957. It is probably on a running-in turn after a lengthy Light Intermediate overhaul completed in June. 6011 had been fitted with a double chimney in March 1956 during a Heavy General repair. Allocated from new in 1928 to Old Oak Common KING JAMES I was to spend the wartime years at Bristol Bath Road and again at Old Oak before being reallocated to Stafford Road in 1946, remaining there until moving back to Old Oak Common in late 1962. www.rail-online.co.uk

The chalked 'A05' reporting number on the smokebox of 6011 KING JAMES I in April 1961 was for the 6.45am from Wolverhampton; 6011 would have been turned at Ranelagh yard and the crew has not attempted to remove the number before returning to the Midlands. It had been fitted with a double chimney in March 1956 and had been allocated to Stafford Road since January 1946. 6011 is underneath Bishop's Road bridge and on the extreme left is 'Paddington Arrival Signal Box' which dated from 1933. www.rail-online.co.uk

6011 KING JAMES I on the 1.10pm Paddington-Birkenhead passes through the lunar-like industrial landscape at Wednesbury, in the Black Country between Birmingham and Wolverhampton, in 1962. The last normal revenue-earning trip by a King is believed to have been by 6011 with reliefs to the Down and Up 'Cambrian Coast Express' on 21 December 1962, the 10.50am Paddington to Shrewsbury and return. It was withdrawn immediately after but was not cut up at Swindon Works until more than twelve months later, in January 1964. It is said that the staff at Swindon didn't take kindly to cutting up the Kings in the infamous 'C' Shop, and several of them languished within the Works for some time following withdrawal until eventual disposal. www.rail-online.co.uk

6012 KING EDWARD VI

To stock April 1928

Modifications
WB boiler	1/10/54
New front frames, inside cylinders	12/2/58
Double chimney	12/2/58

Livery changes
BR standard blue	23/5/50
BR green	21/4/53

Allocations
21/4/28	Newton Abbot
5/7/28	Laira
19/6/54	Old Oak Common
3/4/62	Stafford Road

Withdrawn
Withdrawn	21/9/62
Sold to Cox & Danks, Langley Green	9/10/63

Repairs
16/6/28-5/7/28**L**	Swindon Factory
1/9/28-30/10/28**L**	Swindon Factory
3/1/29-14/1/29**L**	Laira Shops
19/2/29-28/3/29**L**	Swindon Factory
20/6/29-24/6/29**R**	Swindon Factory
26/8/29-6/9/29**L**	Laira Shops
11/11/29-22/11/29**L**	Laira Shops
1/1/30-19/3/30**H**	Swindon Factory
25/3/30-4/4/30**R**	Swindon Factory
27/8/30-28/8/30**R**	Swindon Factory
10/10/30-29/10/30**R**	Newton Abbot Factory
19/1/31-5/2/31**R**	Newton Abbot Factory
27/4/31-28/4/31**R**	Swindon Factory
10/6/31-31/7/31**L**	Swindon Factory
3/11/31-26/11/31**L**	Swindon Factory
3/3/32-23/3/32**R**	Laira Shops
25/4/32-6/7/32**G**	Swindon Factory
7/6/33-27/6/33**R**	Laira Shops
3/10/33-24/11/33**I**	Swindon Factory
8/6/34-27/6/34**R**	Laira Shops
13/11/34-8/1/35**G**	Swindon Factory
19/11/35-7/1/36**I**	Swindon Factory
14/5/36-25/5/36**L**	Swindon Factory
3/2/37-23/3/37**I**	Swindon Factory
2/9/37-14/9/37**L**	Stafford Road Factory
21/10/37-3/12/37**R**	Taunton Shops
8/2/38-23/2/38**R**	Laira Shops
21/4/38-5/5/38**R**	Laira Shops
19/7/38-13/9/38**G**	Swindon Factory
28/4/39-26/5/39**L**	Swindon Factory
22/8/39-7/9/39**R**	Laira Shops
7/11/39-13/12/39**I**	Swindon Factory
11/12/40-30/1/41**I**	Swindon Factory
11/8/41-25/9/41**R**	Old Oak Common Shops
3/10/41-13/10/41**R**	Laira Shops
6/12/41-13/1/42**R**	Swindon Factory
8/2/42-19/3/42**R**	Laira Shops
5/9/42-21/10/42**I**	Swindon Factory
16/12/42-21/1/43**R**	Laira Shops
29/6/43-13/7/43**R**	Laira Shops
23/9/43-14/10/43**R**	Laira Shops
13/11/43-3/12/43**R**	Stafford Road
31/12/43-1/2/44**G**	Swindon Factory
21/6/44-6/7/44**R**	Laira Shops
20/11/44-30/11/44**R**	Laira Shops
12/2/45-6/3/45**R**	Laira Shops
24/5/45-6/6/45**L**	Newton Abbot Shops
19/6/45-23/8/45**I**	Swindon Factory
10/1/46-8/2/46**L**	Newton Abbot Factory
1/4/46-19/4/46**R**	Laira Shops
23/4/46-8/5/46**R**	Laira Shops
5/7/46-26/7/46**R**	Laira Shops
28/10/46-12/12/46**G**	Swindon Factory
18/12/46-12/2/47**R**	Laira Shops
4/6/47-27/6/47**R**	Laira Shops
18/11/47-24/12/47**L**	Swindon Factory
2/1/48-8/1/48**L**	Swindon Factory
16/3/48-2/4/48**R**	Laira Shops
9/7/48-23/7/48**R**	Laira Shops
21/9/48-2/11/48**I**	Swindon Factory
22/12/48-5/1/49**U**	Swindon Factory
16/1/49-31/1/49**U**	Old Oak Common Shops
13/7/49-11/8/49**U**	Laira Shops
2/11/49-23/11/49**U**	Old Oak Common Shops
6/12/49-5/1/50**U**	Laira Shops
14/4/50-23/5/50**HG**	Swindon Factory
2/10/50-12/10/50**U**	Laira Shops
3/12/50-11/1/51**U**	Laira Shops
13/2/51-2/3/51**U**	Laira Shops
2/5/51-8/6/51**U**	Laira Shops
18/9/51-27/11/51**HG**	Swindon Factory
28/4/52-11/5/52**U**	Laira Shops
18/8/52-9/9/52**U**	Laira Shops
25/11/52-15/12/52**U**	Laira Shops
28/1/53-13/2/53**U**	Laira Shops
10/3/53-21/4/53**HI**	Swindon Factory
29/7/53-23/9/53**LC**	Swindon Factory
26/12/53-29/12/53**U**	Laira Shops
18/5/54-4/6/54**U**	Laira Shops
20/9/54-28/10/54**HG**	Swindon Factory
26/2/55-19/4/55**LC**	Swindon Factory
4/9/55-30/9/55**U**	Taunton Shops
5/11/55-30/12/55**LC**	Swindon Factory
9/1/56-7/2/56**LC**	Swindon Factory
14/3/56-6/4/56**U**	Old Oak Common Shops
19/4/56-4/5/56**U**	Old Oak Common Shops
27/7/56-10/9/56**HI**	Swindon Factory
20/9/56-5/10/56**U**	Swindon Factory
16/8/57-7/9/57**U**	Bath Road Shops
1/10/57-15/10/57**U**	Old Oak Common Shops
29/11/57-12/2/58**HG**	Swindon Factory
21/7/58-8/8/58**LC**	Old Oak Common Shops
2/1/59-6/1/59**U**	Old Oak Common Shops
8/5/59-2/6/59**U**	Old Oak Common Shops
15/8/59-16/10/59**HG**	Swindon Factory
25/1/60-12/2/60**LC**	Swindon Factory
26/2/60-11/4/60**LC**	Swindon Factory
24/10/60-10/11/60**U**	Old Oak Common Shops
18/3/61-12/5/61**LI**	Swindon Factory
1/8/61-31/8/61**U**	Stafford Road
12/1/62-14/3/62**LC**	Swindon Factory
20/3/62-3/4/62**U**	Old Oak Common Shops

Boilers and mileages
	First	4672*	
19/3/30			103,618
6/7/32		4679	215,099
24/11/33			303,075
8/1/35		4681	372,480
7/1/36			443,494
23/3/37			520,729
13/9/38		4663	618,950
13/12/39			704,639
30/1/41			779,648
21/10/42			879,232
1/2/44		4694	953,754
23/8/45			1,041,250
12/12/46		4680	1,117,311
2/11/48		4666	1,201,139
23/5/50		4661	1,277,968
25/10/51		4687	1,356,948
21/4/53		4669	1,448,053
28/10/54		8619	1,539,048
10/9/56			1,614,691
12/2/58		8617	1,691,805
16/10/59		8603	1,786,212
12/5/61			1,858,321
Final mileage			1,910,525

Tenders				
First	2396		12/12/46	2743
28/4/31	2548		2/11/48	2763
31/7/31	2554		5/1/49	2716
26/11/31	2550		28/10/54	2395
23/3/37	2547		19/4/55	2775
30/1/41	2695		13/8/55	2931
21/10/42	2707		30/12/55	2544
23/8/45	2695		10/9/56	2717
3/11/45	2759		30/11/57	2620
			12/2/58	2846
			16/10/59	2646
			12/5/61	2564
			14/3/62	2413

Below. Built with straight feed pipes, 6012 KING EDWARD VI now has the modified pipes which curved back behind the nameplates, dating this picture at Old Oak Common to the early 1930s. It was originally allocated to Newton Abbot in April 1928 but moved to Laira within three months, remaining there until 1954.

Bottom. 6012 KING EDWARD VI at Old Oak on 6 February 1955 where it had been allocated since a transfer in June 1954 from Laira. Although it had only completed a Heavy Overhaul the previous October when it was fitted with a WB higher superheat boiler, it returned to Swindon three weeks after this picture for a Light Casual repair. www.rail-online.co.uk

It's Whit Saturday 19 May 1956 and Old Oak Common's 6012 KING EDWARD VI has worked down to Plymouth on the 11.0am relief from Paddington, running behind the 'Cornish Riviera' by 30 minutes. On Laira's coaling line 6012 is having its smokebox and tubes cleared, is being re-coaled and has already had its fire 'dropped' as evidenced by the ash on the cabside. P. Kerslake, www.rail-online.co.uk

Old Oak's 6012 KING EDWARD VI with second emblem at Paddington with the 'Express' – compare with the view of the same engine on the 'Limited' on page 59. The 10.30am departure had reverted to 'Express' from the 'Limited' which had been briefly used from mid-1956. www.rail-online.co.uk

6012 KING EDWARD VI at Shrewsbury in mid-1958 after it had been fitted with a double chimney in February. The Kings began regular working on the Wolverhampton-Shrewsbury line, following satisfactory clearance trials with 6011 on 13 April 1958. As from 20 April, Kings formally took over the Paddington-Shrewsbury 'Cambrian Coast' diagram formerly worked by Castles, but this came to an end in late August when the Castles returned. www.rail-online.co.uk

The chalked 'A07' code had been left on when 6012 KING EDWARD VI was turned at Ranelagh Bridge after bringing in the 7.25am Wolverhampton-Paddington on 24 May 1962. Here it is at Banbury with the return working. 6012 had been transferred from Old Oak Common to Stafford Road the previous month. www.rail-online.co.uk

6013 KING HENRY VIII

To stock April 1928

Modifications
WB boiler	10/10/51
New front frames, inside cylinders	22/9/54
Double chimney	27/6/56

Livery changes
BR standard blue	9/6/50
BR green	13/3/53

Allocations
15/5/28	Old Oak Common
2/4/59	Laira
4/3/60	Old Oak Common
16/6/61	Stafford Road

Withdrawn 12/6/62
Cut up at Swindon 29/12/62

Repairs
20/6/28-29/6/28**L**	Swindon Factory
15/9/28-28/9/28**L**	Swindon Factory
6/3/29-24/4/29**L**	Swindon Factory
24/6/29-27/6/29**R**	Swindon Factory
31/10/29-25/11/29**L**	Swindon Factory
8/1/30-7/4/30**H**	Swindon Factory
8/5/30-27/5/30**R**	Taunton Shops
15/9/30-1/10/30**R**	Old Oak Common Shops
18/11/30-16/1/31**L**	Swindon Factory
20/6/31-24/6/31**R**	Swindon Factory
11/1/32-17/2/32**L**	Old Oak Common Shops
21/4/32-17/6/32**I**	Swindon Factory
10/3/33-18/5/33**G**	Swindon Factory
5/10/33-27/10/33**R**	Old Oak Common Shops
17/4/34-31/5/34**I**	Swindon Factory
11/8/34-4/9/34**L**	Swindon Factory
14/9/34-10/10/34**R**	Taunton Shops
4/3/35-23/3/35**R**	Old Oak Common Shops
18/5/35-11/7/35**G**	Swindon Factory
14/9/35-18/9/35**L**	Swindon Factory
28/9/35-2/10/35**L**	Swindon Factory
28/1/36-15/2/36**R**	Old Oak Common Shops
14/4/36-15/5/36**R**	Old Oak Common Shops
23/9/36-5/11/36**I**	Swindon Factory
5/7/37-20/7/37**L**	Old Oak Common Shops
23/7/37-6/8/37**L**	Swindon Factory
30/8/37-25/9/37**R**	Taunton Shops
11/1/38-18/3/38**G**	Swindon Factory
22/8/38-6/9/38**L**	Swindon Factory
31/1/39-14/3/39**I**	Swindon Factory
12/10/39-24/10/39**R**	Old Oak Common Shops
13/3/40-2/4/40**R**	Old Oak Common Shops
8/4/40-16/5/40**I**	Swindon Factory
23/4/41-16/6/41**I**	Swindon Factory
19/5/42-24/6/42**R**	Old Oak Common Shops
4/8/42-25/9/42**G**	Swindon Factory
1/6/43-21/6/43**R**	Old Oak Common
1/10/43-24/11/43**I**	Swindon Factory
23/12/43-1/1/44**R**	Swindon Factory
23/1/44-2/2/44**R**	Swindon Factory
25/5/44-15/6/44**R**	Old Oak Common Shops
15/9/44-24/10/44**R**	Old Oak Common Shops
9/2/45-23/2/45**R**	Old Oak Common Shops
24/4/45-14/6/45**I**	Swindon Factory
23/11/45-12/12/45**L**	Swindon Factory
16/12/45-16/1/46**R**	Old Oak Common Shops
22/5/46-29/6/46**L**	Swindon Factory
2/11/46-15/12/46**L**	Old Oak Common Shops
29/1/47-4/3/47**G**	Swindon Factory
11/3/47-22/3/47**G**	Swindon Factory
17/4/47-14/5/47**R**	Laira Shops
12/9/47-15/10/47**L**	Old Oak Common Shops
13/11/47-4/12/47**R**	Old Oak Common
6/1/48-5/2/48**L**	Old Oak Common Shops
15/3/48-14/4/48**L**	Swindon Factory
11/6/48-8/7/48**R**	Old Oak Common Shops
28/10/48-26/11/48**R**	Old Oak Common Shops
7/1/49-10/2/49**HG**	Swindon Factory
10/6/49-24/6/49**U**	Old Oak Common Shops
26/8/49-9/9/49**LC**	Old Oak Common Shops
28/10/49-25/11/49**LC**	Swindon Factory
3/3/50-30/3/50**U**	Laira Shops
12/5/50-19/6/50**HG**	Swindon Factory
15/3/51-2/4/51**U**	Old Oak Common
26/4/51-11/5/51**LC**	Swindon Factory
22/8/51-10/10/51**HG**	Swindon Factory
10/3/52-18/4/52**LC**	Swindon Factory
10/9/52-30/9/52**U**	Old Oak Common
24/11/52-11/12/52**U**	Old Oak Common
26/1/53-13/3/53**HI**	Swindon Factory
12/8/53-21/9/53**LC**	Swindon Factory
13/5/54-29/5/54**U**	Old Oak Common Shops
30/6/54-22/9/54**HG**	Swindon Factory
18/11/54-1/12/54**U**	Swindon Factory
26/5/55-27/6/55**U**	Laira Shops
19/7/55-19/8/55**U**	Old Oak Common Shops
29/8/55-11/10/55**U**	Bath Road Shops
26/1/56-17/2/56**LC**	Old Oak Comn Shops
1/5/56-27/6/56**HI**	Swindon Factory
15/6/57-16/6/57**U**	Taunton Shops
27/7/57-15/8/57**U**	Old Oak Common Shops
4/9/57-17/10/57**HI**	Swindon Factory
23/10/58-12/11/58**U**	Old Oak Common Shops
2/12/58-18/12/58**U**	Old Oak Common Shops
22/12/58-21/1/59**U**	Taunton Shops
3/2/59-18/3/59**HG**	Swindon Factory
6/5/60-25/5/60**U**	Old Oak Common Shops
3/6/60-8/8/60**LI**	Swindon Factory
8/5/61-16/6/61**LC**	Stafford Road Factory
8/8/61-24/8/61**U**	Stafford Road
1/3/62-21/3/62**U**	Stafford Road

Boilers and mileages
First	4675*	
7/4/30		104,476
16/1/31	4665	146,440
17/6/32		232,808
18/5/33	4682	291,138
31/5/34		361,742
11/7/35	4676	427,691
5/11/36		513,129
18/3/38	4680	596,455
14/3/39		664,920
16/5/40		752,850
16/6/41		825,770
25/9/42	4679	908,197
24/11/43		983,833
14/6/45		1,060,125
22/3/47	4667	1,149,519
10/2/49	4682	1,239,835
19/6/50	4686	1,318,911
10/10/51	4697*	1,398,986
13/3/53		1,486,161
22/9/54	8616*	1,536,060
27/6/56		1,618,928
17/10/57	8622	1,705,808
18/3/59	8621	1,785,249
8/8/60		1,862,985
Final mileage		1,950,462

Below. 6013 KING HENRY VIII poses at Old Oak soon after it entered service in April 1928. It has the original straight top feed pipes.

Bottom. A work-stained 6013 KING HENRY VIII at Leamington Spa on 4 August 1947 was in the final GWR version of lined green with the abbreviated G and W on the tender under the grime. It has a standard speedometer and curved top feed pipes. Original features visible are the step on the smokebox door, although the top lamp bracket has already been repositioned, the original smooth casing over the inside cylinder block, cover from front of boiler to smokebox for oil feeds and the original style of steam pipes. 6013 was allocated to Old Oak at this date, having gone there from new in 1928. www.rail-online.co.uk

171

6013 KING HENRY VIII at Old Oak in late 1950. It was repainted in BR blue during a Heavy General overhaul completed in June but still has the PDN shed allocation code on the footplate angle. The curved top cover for the inside valves has been covered by a square top with tread plates.

Old Oak's 6013 KING HENRY VIII has been taken off the road for some attention by Laira's fitters after having worked down earlier from Paddington in 1953. In fact not all was rosy in the world of King availability; in the 1930s it had not been unknown for only a single Laira King to be 'present and correct' and the 1950s saw some regular 'lows' too. P. Kerslake, www.rail-online.co.uk

6013 KING HENRY VIII at Birmingham Snow Hill with the 9.10am Paddington-Birkenhead, probably in 1959 or early 1960. The all numeric train reporting codes such as the '908' carried by 6013 were replaced by alpha-numeric codes from 1961. 6013 had been fitted with a double chimney in June 1956 and replacement front frames and inside cylinders, possibly at the same time. 6013 moved briefly away from Old Oak, having gone there from new in 1928, transferring to Laira in April 1959 before returning to the London shed in March 1960. www.rail-online.co.uk

Led by a Castle and 6022 KING EDWARD III, 6013 KING HENRY VIII moves off Wolverhampton Stafford Road shed in the early 1960s. It had been transferred from Laira to Old Oak in March 1960, moving to Stafford Road in June 1961 for its final year in service. www.rail-online.co.uk

6014 KING HENRY VII

To stock May 1928

Modifications
Streamlined	11/3/35
WB boiler	11/10/56
Double chimney	20/9/57

Livery changes
BR standard blue	18/8/50
BR green	6/2/54

Allocations
18/6/28	Newton Abbot
3/6/29	Laira
30/7/30	Old Oak Common
30/8/30	Stafford Road
26/3/35	Old Oak Common
4/10/52	Laira
27/3/54	Stafford Road

Withdrawn   21/9/62
Sold to Cox & Danks,	
Langley Green	7/3/63

Repairs
2/6/28-18/6/28**L**	Swindon Factory
28/11/28-12/12/28**L**	Newton Abbot Factory
3/4/29-27/5/29**L**	Swindon Factory
7/10/29-7/11/29**L**	Swindon Factory
7/3/30-19/3/30**L**	Laira Shops
16/6/30-17/7/30**H**	Swindon Factory
6/10/30-3/11/30**L**	Swindon Factory
18/11/30-26/11/30**L**	Swindon Factory
11/6/31-13/8/31**L**	Swindon Factory
20/2/32-10/3/32**L**	Swindon Factory
30/5/32-6/7/32**L**	Swindon Factory
25/10/32-16/12/32**I**	Swindon Factory
19/6/33-23/6/33**L**	Stafford Road Factory
15/7/33-26/9/33**G**	Swindon Factory
29/6/34-26/7/34**L**	Stafford Road Factory
15/10/34-19/10/34**L**	Stafford Road Factory
19/1/35-11/3/35**G**	Swindon Factory
20/8/35-22/8/35**L**	Swindon Factory
10/12/35-20/12/35**L**	Swindon Factory
13/3/36-29/4/36**I**	Swindon Factory
31/8/36-11/9/36**L**	Swindon Factory
13/10/36-9/11/36**L**	Swindon Factory
14/1/37-2/2/37**L**	Swindon Factory
28/4/37-15/5/37**R**	Old Oak Common Shops
6/7/37-12/7/37**L**	Swindon Factory
8/11/37-24/12/37**G**	Swindon Factory
17/1/38-12/2/38**R**	Old Oak Common Shops
17/10/38-8/11/38**R**	Old Oak Common Shops
14/3/39-4/5/39**I**	Swindon Factory
10/9/39-30/9/39**R**	Old Oak Common Shops
25/12/39-8/1/40**R**	Old Oak Common Shops
13/4/40-31/5/40**I**	Swindon Factory
3/10/41-29/11/41**G**	Swindon Factory
11/12/42-21/1/43**I**	Swindon Factory
7/4/43-11/5/43**R**	Old Oak Common Shops
10/2/44-29/2/44**R**	Old Oak Common Shops
11/4/44-26/4/44**R**	Old Oak Common
1/5/44-16/6/44**R**	Old Oak Common Shops
23/8/44-19/10/44**G**	Swindon Factory
11/7/45-27/7/45**R**	Old Oak Common
23/1/46-28/2/46**I**	Swindon Factory
18/9/46-3/10/46**R**	Old Oak Common
10/10/46-27/10/46**R**	Old Oak Common
19/11/46-16/12/46**R**	Stafford Road
21/1/47-28/2/47**L**	Swindon Factory
28/3/47-2/5/47**R**	Old Oak Common
16/7/47-14/8/47**R**	Westbury Shops
26/8/47-9/10/47**G**	Swindon Factory
18/10/47-21/10/47**L**	Newton Abbot Factory
6/1/48-9/2/48**R**	Old Oak Common Shops
12/3/48-10/4/48**R**	Old Oak Common
22/8/48-16/9/48**R**	Laira Shops
31/12/48-8/2/49**U**	Bath Road Shops
11/2/49-15/3/49**HG**	Swindon Factory
19/5/49-2/6/49**U**	Swindon Factory
10/7/49-28/7/49**U**	Old Oak Common Shops
7/11/49-28/11/49**U**	Old Oak Common Shops
20/6/50-18/8/50**HG**	Swindon Factory
30/11/50-2/1/51**U**	Old Oak Common Shops
9/4/51-24/4/51**U**	Laira Shops
2/10/51-16/10/51**U**	Old Oak Common
19/11/51-11/1/52**HG**	Swindon Factory
17/3/52-2/4/52**HG**	Swindon Factory
23/7/52-14/8/52**U**	Old Oak Common Shops
27/10/52-2/11/52**U**	Laira Shops
29/12/52-16/1/53**U**	Laira Shops
25/2/53-27/3/53**LC**	Taunton Shops
12/7/53-13/8/53**U**	Reading Shops
17/9/53-6/10/53**U**	Laira Shops
11/1/54-16/2/54**HG**	Swindon Factory
22/2/54-3/3/54**U**	Stafford Road Factory
29/9/54-5/11/54**U**	Old Oak Common Shops
19/7/55-25/8/55**LI**	Swindon Factory
6/9/55-1/11/55**HC**	Swindon Factory
24/1/56-14/2/56**LC**	Stafford Road
8/6/56-11/10/56**HG**	Swindon Factory
14/6/57-17/6/57**U**	Stafford Road Factory
25/7/57-20/9/57**HG**	Swindon Factory
9/10/57-15/10/57**LC**	Stafford Road Factory
28/6/58-19/7/59**U**	Stafford Road
25/8/58-17/9/58**U**	Old Oak Common Shops
8/10/58-22/10/58**U**	Stafford Road
17/6/59-2/10/59**LI**	Swindon Factory
14/10/59-30/10/59**U**	Stafford Road
24/5/60-7/7/60**LC**	Stafford Road Factory
3/8/60-19/8/60**U**	Stafford Road Factory
11/10/60-3/11/60**U**	Banbury Shops
5/12/60-29/12/60**U**	Stafford Road
15/9/61-6/12/61**HG**	Swindon Factory
28/2/62-16/3/62**U**	Old Oak Common Shops
23/5/62-18/6/62**U**	Old Oak Common Shops

Boilers and mileages
First	4674*	
17/7/30		112,531
13/8/31		155,755
16/12/32		216,546
26/9/33	4661	255,639
11/3/35	4679	337,637
29/4/36		417,908
24/12/37	4666	512,685
4/5/39		608,165
31/5/40		683,749
29/11/41	4682	787,300
21/1/43		870,143
19/10/44	4669	958,324
28/2/46	4685	1,048,781
9/10/47	4690	1,104,751
15/3/49	4667	1,175,302
18/8/50	4682	1,257,504
11/1/52	4686	1,335,152
16/2/54	4679	1,452,577
11/10/56	8604	1,564,734
20/9/57	8614	1,607,661
2/10/59	-	1,705,088
6/12/61	8612	1,794,324
Final mileage		1,830,386

Tenders
First	2398
27/5/29	2401
17/7/30	2557
13/8/31	2388
26/9/33	2572
11/3/35	2612
22/8/36	2442
4/5/39	2728
21/1/43	2648
2/6/49	2715
1/8/52	2742
20/9/57	2564
2/10/59	2867
6/12/61	2685

6014 KING HENRY VII inside the Old Oak Common Factory prior to being streamlined in 1935. Rail Archive Stephenson.

6014 KING HENRY VII arrives at Paddington with an express from Plymouth in 1937. Its full set of streamlining lasted for only five months. The coverings over and around the cylinders were regarded as a major hindrance to routine lubrication and were soon removed - along with the tender cowling - in August 1935. 6014 has the special bracket on the inside valve chest to hold the Reporting Number frame. C.R.L. Coles, Rail Archive Stephenson.

6014 KING HENRY VII at Leamington Spa on 9 October 1937 had been modified at Swindon during a Works visit from January to March of 1935, but only five months later some of the additional panels covering the outside cylinders and hiding the inside valve gear were removed, as was the cowling on the tender, and it is in this later condition that the engine appears in this photograph. The 'bull nose' was not the smokebox door, which remained in its proper place on its own hinges underneath; instead it was no more than a hinged cover. It was a confounded nuisance, you'd think, and along with the chimney and safety valve fairings was removed by early 1943, and the original splashers and nameplates which had been kept in safe-keeping at Swindon were refitted during the engine's overhaul there in late 1944. All that was left for the engine's remaining years in service were the wedge fronted cab, the special bracket on the inside valve chest for the Reporting Number frame and concealed snifting valves. www.rail-online.co.uk

6014 KING HENRY VII, the last of the blue liveried Kings to revert to green (during a Heavy General completed in February 1954) at Birmingham Snow Hill. The period will be the mid-1950s as it still has a single chimney (the double chimney was not fitted until 1957) and there is no sign of Lloyd House (HQ of West Midlands police) being built in the left-hand background. While in the Works in 1954 it had been fitted with a new type of blow-down apparatus. It was also fitted with a device in the cab which enabled samples of boiler water to be taken, to check the formation of deposit in the boiler. The equipment was developed in conjunction with ICI and after re-entering traffic 6014 was transferred to Stafford Road so that it could be nearer to the ICI technicians. www.rail-online.co.uk

Two former Laira engines, side by side after arrival at Paddington in around 1955; 6014 KING HENRY VII had worked up to London with the 7.30am from Shrewsbury. The Castle is 5057 EARL WALDEGRAVE, which had been at Bristol Bath Road since June 1954. The wedge-fronted cab fitted to 6014 in 1935 survived until withdrawal, although the rest of the adornments were removed during the war. The small bracket which was welded to the front face of the inside valve chest was designed and intended to do just what it's doing here, namely to carry the Reporting Number frame. When 6014 had been fitted with a rounded smokebox front in its streamlined days it was impossible to locate on 6014 the frames on their customary fitting over the smokebox door handles. www.rail-online.co.uk

Working the 8.55am Birkenhead-Paddington, 6014 KING HENRY VII at Wednesbury in around 1960. Oddly the reporting number has taken up the traditional position – compare with the view on page 114 for instance.www.rail-online.co.uk

6015 KING RICHARD III

To stock June 1928

Modifications
WB boiler	10/10/52
New front frames, inside cylinders	8/9/55
Double chimney	8/9/55

Livery changes
BR standard blue	14/10/49
BR green	10/10/52

Allocations
15/6/28	Old Oak Common
4/6/62	Stafford Road

Withdrawn 21/9/62
Sold to Cox & Danks, Langley Green 5/4/63

Repairs

21/6/28-7/7/28**L**	Swindon Factory
13/8/28-16/8/28**L**	Swindon Factory
17/9/28-18/9/28**L**	Swindon Factory
21/1/29-25/3/29**R**	Swindon Factory
22/6/29-26/6/29**R**	Swindon Factory
19/7/29-27/7/29**L**	Swindon Factory
19/8/29-27/8/29**L**	Swindon Factory
23/9/29-4/10/29**R**	Old Oak Common Shops
14/1/30-28/3/30**H**	Swindon Factory
11/4/30-16/4/30**R**	Swindon Factory
30/7/30-4/8/30**L**	Old Oak Common Shops
15/9/30-11/10/30**L**	Swindon Factory
1/12/30-16/12/30**R**	Old Oak Common Shops
28/2/31-10/4/31**G**	Swindon Factory
20/12/31-14/1/32**L**	Swindon Stock
14/9/32-2/11/32**G**	Swindon Factory
27/9/33-9/11/33**I**	Swindon Factory
28/8/34-15/10/34**G**	Swindon Factory
29/10/34-13/11/34**R**	Stafford Road
11/3/35-29/3/35**R**	Old Oak Common Shops
30/7/35-31/7/35**L**	Swindon Factory
2/10/35-23/10/35**L**	Swindon Factory
1/1/36-19/2/36**I**	Swindon Factory
11/3/36-25/3/36**L**	Swindon Factory
7/10/36-6/11/36**L**	Swindon Factory
28/11/36-6/1/37**L**	Swindon Factory
30/1/37-19/2/37**L**	Swindon Factory
13/5/37-3/7/37**G**	Swindon Factory
31/8/38-14/10/38**I**	Swindon Factory
21/3/39-5/4/39**L**	Swindon Factory
12/6/39-4/7/39**L**	Swindon Factory
31/10/39-22/12/39**I**	Swindon Factory
10/4/40-29/4/40**L**	Swindon Factory
1/2/41-29/3/41**I**	Swindon Factory
3/2/42-16/2/42**L**	Old Oak Common Shops
28/4/42-12/6/42**I**	Swindon Factory
11/7/42-1/8/42**L**	Old Oak Common Shops
9/5/43-27/5/43**R**	Old Oak Common
28/6/43-12/7/43**L**	Old Oak Common Shops
30/8/43-4/10/43**G**	Swindon Factory
21/8/44-5/9/44**R**	Old Oak Common
29/3/45-17/5/45**I**	Swindon Factory
30/10/45-8/11/45**R**	Laira Shops
27/5/46-29/6/46**G**	Swindon Factory
24/11/46-13/12/46**R**	Old Oak Common Shops
11/6/47-26/6/47**R**	Old Oak Common
30/6/47-7/8/47**R**	Old Oak Common
2/10/47-22/10/47**R**	Old Oak Common
9/11/47-9/12/47**R**	Taunton Shops
18/2/48-24/3/48**I**	Swindon Factory
21/9/48-1/11/48**R**	Bath Road Shop
2/12/48-31/12/48**R**	Old Oak Common Shops
1/5/49-26/5/49**U**	Old Oak Common Shops
10/6/49-18/7/49**U**	Taunton Shops
25/7/49-18/8/49**U**	Laira Shops
6/9/49-14/10/49**HG**	Swindon Factory
3/11/49-23/11/49**U**	Taunton Shops
4/12/49-22/12/49**U**	Old Oak Common Shops
16/6/50-30/6/50**U**	Swindon Factory
19/9/50-19/10/50**U**	Old Oak Common Shops
8/11/50-12/12/50**U**	Laira Shops
10/1/51-30/1/51**U**	Old Oak Common Shops
10/5/51-14/6/51**HG**	Swindon Factory
20/2/52-19/3/52**LC**	Swindon Factory
1/9/52-10/10/52**HG**	Swindon Factory
16/1/53-26/2/53**LC**	Swindon Factory
31/7/53-12/8/53**U**	Laira Shops
5/10/53-29/10/53**U**	Bath Road
16/12/53-19/2/54**HI**	Swindon Factory
9/4/54-28/4/54**U**	Bath Road Shops
13/10/54-23/12/54**LC**	Swindon Factory
23/2/55-31/3/55**U**	Bath Road Shops
20/4/55-12/5/55**U**	Swindon Factory
28/6/55-8/9/55**HG**	Swindon Factory
24/1/56-18/2/56**LC**	Stafford Road
9/8/56-25/8/56**U**	Old Oak Common
6/12/57-23/12/57**U**	Old Oak Common Shops
22/3/58-2/5/58**HG**	Swindon Factory
22/5/58-12/6/58**LC**	Swindon Factory
26/1/59-9/2/59**U**	Old Oak Common Shops
29/5/59-18/6/59**U**	Old Oak Common Shops
2/1/60-24/2/60**HG**	Swindon Factory
27/7/60-10/8/60**U**	Old Oak Common Shops
23/2/61-21/3/61**U**	Old Oak Common
18/10/61-11/12/61**LI**	Swindon Factory
22/3/62-30/3/62**U**	Stafford Road Factory

Boilers and mileages

First	4676*	
28/3/30		93,308
10/4/31	4675	149,135
2/11/32	4672	252,249
9/11/33		326,991
15/10/34	4666	393,627
19/2/36		475,568
3/7/37	4694	546,469
14/10/38		655,486
22/12/39		727,312
29/3/41		807,681
12/6/42		891,483
4/10/43	4691	961,252
17/5/45		1,049,255
29/6/46	4662	1,124,746
24/3/48	4676	1,204,007
14/10/49	4692	1,273,601
14/6/51	4673	1,339,886
10/10/52	8603	1,412,058
19/2/54		1,471,133
8/9/55	8609	1,519,261
6/12/56		1,585,782
2/5/58	8613	1,673,305
24/2/60	8606	1,767,531
11/12/61		1,861,296
Final mileage		1,901,585

Tenders			
First	2399	17/5/45	2815
25/3/29	2425	10/10/52	2726
28/3/30	2395	19/2/54	2788
11/10/30	2390	23/12/54	2759
10/4/31	2395	8/9/55	2922
14/1/32	2557	3/11/56	2565
13/11/33	2402	6/12/56	2878
6/2/37	2547	2/5/58	2629
19/2/37	2550	21/2/59	2583
21/10/38	2548	24/2/60	2846
22/12/39	2401	22/4/61	2875
29/3/41	2665	11/12/61	2850
25/4/42	2790		
12/6/42	2612		

Below. The driver is oiling round 6015 KING RICHARD III outside Swindon Works after a General repair completed in July 1937. The inside valve covers, buffer heads and motion are all polished and it has the 1930s roundel on the tender. The top feed pipes are now curved behind the nameplate and the top lamp bracket moved down onto the smokebox door but the footstep on the door has not been taken off. Rail Archive Stephenson.

Bottom. During a lengthy works visit in 1955, 6015 KING RICHARD III was experimentally fitted with a double chimney which had been fabricated from sheet steel as shown by this picture taken at Bath on a 'Running-in' local stopper after it returned to traffic on 8 September, following which its performances were closely monitored. Within the space of a week on two runs with the 'Cornish Riviera', 6015 reached a speed of 103mph on a section where 85mph had been the norm for single chimney Kings and three days later, it was timed at over 107mph - the highest authenticated speed achieved by any Great Western locomotive. 6015 had also been fitted with new front frames and has a mechanical lubricator in front of the outside steam pipe, high degree superheating and a self-cleaning smokebox. www.rail-online.co.uk

6015 KING RICHARD III passes Westbury North Box with 'The Mayflower', the 8.30am from Plymouth North Road, in 1957. The train which ran between Paddington and Plymouth was given the name in June of that year.www.rail-online.co.uk

In absolutely sparkling condition fresh from Swindon Works 6015 KING RICHARD III displays a single local passenger lamp on the smokebox, ready for a running-in duty with a tender piled high with coal in this view taken from Swindon station. It had just completed a Heavy General Overhaul which lasted from March until May 1958, and its narrow fabricated double chimney has been replaced by a far more pleasing cast iron chimney of elliptical cross-section. The tender has the final BR crest.www.rail-online.co.uk

6015 KING RICHARD III in the early 1960s at Royal Oak. It was allocated to Old Oak Common throughout apart from the last three months in service when it was transferred to Wolverhampton Stafford Road; the double chimney was fitted in September 1955. Behind 6015 is the former GWR Muniment Store, later the home of the British Transport Commission Historical Records. Although facing Paddington, it has the M16 reporting code for the 1.10pm Paddington-Birkenhead. It appears that this had been fixed for the return working, and that 6015 has backed out with the stock of its incoming train before turning on the Ranelagh Bridge table. www.rail-online.co.uk

The cameramen are out in force at Saunderton on the Paddington to Birmingham main line, where the Up and Down lines are on different levels and running some way apart from each other. 6015 KING RICHARD III, photographed here in its final year of service, had been the first of the class to receive a double chimney. It was withdrawn from Stafford Road in September 1962 and was one of those scrapped by Cox and Danks at Langley Green. www.rail-online.co.uk

6016 KING EDWARD V

To stock June 1928

Modifications

WB boiler	19/2/53
New front frame, inside cylinders	9/12/54
Double chimney	14/1/58

Livery changes

BR standard blue	16/12/49
BR green	19/2/53

Allocations

2/7/28	Laira
10/5/30	Newton Abbot
30/8/30	Laira
5/6/52	Stafford Road
9/12/54	Old Oak Common
2/12/58	Stafford Road
2/2/59	Laira
16/9/60	Old Oak Common
15/6/62	Stafford Road

Withdrawn 13/9/62

Sold to Cox & Danks, Langley Green	14/11/63

Repairs

28/8/28-6/9/28**L**	Laira Shops
13/11/28-18/12/28**L**	Swindon Factory
18/3/29-19/3/29**R**	Swindon Factory
7/5/29-25/5/29**L**	Swindon Factory
6/6/29-13/6/29**R**	Swindon Factory
9/8/29-16/8/29**L**	Taunton Shops
1/10/29-26/11/29**H**	Swindon Factory
6/5/30-10/5/30**L**	Laira Shops
14/10/30-13/11/30**L**	Swindon Factory
9/2/31-7/3/31**L**	Swindon Factory
30/4/31-24/6/31**I**	Swindon Factory
4/1/32-12/2/32**L**	Swindon Factory
23/5/32-22/6/32**R**	Laira Shops
29/6/32-7/7/32**L**	Swindon Factory
6/10/32-22/10/32**R**	Laira Shops
1/11/32-24/1/33**G**	Swindon Factory
19/9/33-17/10/33**L**	Swindon Factory
25/1/34-12/3/34**I**	Swindon Factory
12/1/35-2/2/35**R**	Laira Shops
1/5/35-21/6/35**I**	Swindon Factory
12/8/36-1/10/36**G**	Swindon Factory
8/9/37-20/10/37**I**	Swindon Factory
2/3/38-24/3/38**R**	Laira Shops
20/6/38-7/7/38**L**	Swindon Factory
22/8/38-3/10/38**L**	Swindon Factory
2/1/39-16/2/39**I**	Swindon Factory
14/6/39-4/7/39**L**	Swindon Factory
30/8/39-27/9/39**R**	Newton Abbot Factory
9/10/39-20/10/39**L**	Swindon Factory
29/12/39-12/1/40**R**	Laira Shops
29/3/40-9/5/40**L**	Swindon Factory
12/7/40-31/8/40**G**	Swindon Factory
13/3/41-4/4/41**R**	Laira Shops
7/7/41-21/7/41**R**	Laira Shops
16/1/42-6/3/42**I**	Swindon Factory
17/9/42-7/10/42**R**	Old Oak Common Shops
8/11/42-25/11/42**R**	Laira Shops
17/3/43-22/6/43**G**	Swindon Factory
27/10/43-24/11/43**R**	Laira Shops
16/2/44-6/3/44**R**	Laira Shops
18/3/44-17/4/44**R**	Taunton Shops
22/7/44-23/8/44**L**	Swindon Factory
27/10/44-13/11/44**R**	Laira Shops
15/12/44-25/12/44**R**	Laira Shops
19/1/45-11/2/45**R**	Laira Shops
22/2/45-7/4/45**I**	Swindon Factory
19/4/45-28/4/45**R**	Swindon Factory
31/8/45-2/10/45**L**	Swindon Factory
5/2/46-25/2/46**R**	Laira Shops
8/5/46-11/6/46**G**	Swindon Factory
23/10/46-7/11/46**R**	Laira Shops
6/12/46-22/1/47**R**	Bath Road
17/2/47-22/3/47**R**	Laira Shops
30/4/47-17/6/47**R**	Laira Shops
1/7/47-22/7/47**R**	Old Oak Common Shops
6/8/47-11/9/47**L**	Laira Shops
26/9/47-17/10/47**R**	Old Oak Common Shops
8/12/47-6/1/48**R**	Laira Shops
19/1/48-3/3/48**R**	Laira Shops
5/3/48-22/3/48**R**	Laira Shops
1/6/48-28/7/48**I**	Swindon Factory
30/8/48-10/9/48**R**	Laira Shops
28/9/48-9/10/48**R**	Laira Shops
1/5/49-18/5/49**U**	Old Oak Common Shops
5/9/49-11/10/49**U**	Laira Shops
11/11/49-16/12/49**HG**	Swindon Factory
24/5/50-9/6/50**U**	Laira Shops
8/8/50-30/8/50**U**	Old Oak Common Shops
22/9/50-11/10/50**U**	Swindon Factory
24/10/50-8/11/50**U**	Laira Shops
14/1/51-2/2/51**U**	Laira Shops
2/3/51-10/4/51**HG**	Swindon Factory
12/6/51-23/6/51**U**	Laira Shops
8/8/51-28/9/51**U**	Taunton
15/10/51-31/10/51**U**	Laira Shops
7/5/52-5/6/52**LC**	Swindon Factory
24/8/52-11/9/52**U**	Old Oak Common
12/12/52-19/2/53**HG**	Swindon Factory
19/5/53-16/6/53**LC**	Swindon Factory
14/7/53-31/7/53**U**	Old Oak Common Shops
2/11/53-22/12/53**LC**	Swindon Factory
3/5/54-11/6/54**LC**	Swindon Factory
27/7/54-9/12/54**HG**	Swindon Factory
30/5/55-29/6/55**LC**	Swindon Factory
26/7/55-19/8/55**U**	Old Oak Common Shops
29/12/55-27/1/56**U**	Old Oak Common Shops
30/1/56-20/2/56**LC**	Stafford Road
24/2/56-22/3/56**U**	Old Oak Common Shops
20/7/56-7/9/56**HI**	Swindon Factory
2/5/57-17/5/57**U**	Old Oak Common
10/9/57-25/9/57**U**	Old Oak Common Shops
27/11/57-14/1/58**HG**	Swindon Factory
18/1/58-3/2/58**LC**	Swindon Factory
21/2/58-13/3/58**LC**	Swindon Factory
2/1/59-16/1/59**U**	Stafford Road
27/2/59-14/3/59**U**	Old Oak Common
5/8/59-3/11/59**HG**	Swindon Factory
14/3/60-29/3/60**U**	Laira Shops
24/8/60-16/9/60**U**	Laira Shops
20/9/60-25/10/60**U**	Taunton Shops
31/10/60-23/11/60**U**	Taunton Shops
8/12/60-22/12/60**U**	Old Oak Common Shops
4/1/61-27/1/61**U**	Old Oak Common Shops
19/5/61-14/6/61**U**	Old Oak Common Shops
12/9/61-9/11/61**LI**	Swindon Factory

Boilers and mileages

	First	4677*	
	26/11/29		71,419
	24/6/31		150,328
	24/1/33	4675	219,787
	12/3/34		283,855
	21/6/35		360,390
	1/10/36	4688	444,450
	20/10/37		530,543
	16/2/39		607,044
	31/8/40	4670	697,722
	6/3/42		794,881
	22/6/43	4693	864,712
	7/4/45		965,820
	11/6/46	4681	1,038,013
	28/7/48	4662	1,111,874
	16/12/49	4673	1,190,541
	10/4/51	4677	1,264,430
	19/2/53	8607*	1,355,861
	9/12/54	8618*	1,410,645
	7/9/56		1,500,596
	14/1/58	8616	1,585,269
	3/11/59	8622	1,673,986
	9/11/61		1,762,327
Final mileage			1,811,207

Tenders

First	2400
25/5/29	2384
13/6/29	2402
26/11/29	2399
12/2/32	2551
1/10/36	2549
3/10/38	2552
6/3/42	2776
22/6/43	2665
23/8/44	2728
28/7/48	2710
16/12/49	2772
10/4/51	2710
11/6/54	2694
9/12/54	2931
9/12/54	2808
7/9/56	2846
15/6/57	2544
14/1/58	2745
29/11/58	2771
3/11/59	2793
9/11/61	2815

6016 KING EDWARD V at Swindon Works on 5 February 1939, fresh from an Intermediate overhaul; it was not formally returned to traffic until 17th. It exhibits a few changes from when it was built there over a decade earlier, including curved top feed pipes, the upper lamp bracket moved down onto the smokebox and the mid-1930s GWR roundel on the tender. Apart from a few months in 1930, 6015 had been allocated to Laira since July 1928. Note borrowed tender for initial steaming. www.rail-online.co.uk

6016 KING EDWARD V at Taunton in early 1948 has BRITISH RAILWAYS in GWR-style letters on the tender, but has not yet received a smokebox number plate. The step which had been left on the smokebox to allow staff to reach the upper lamp bracket when in its original position on top of the smokebox, has been removed. 6016 was repainted into BR light blue in December 1949. Colour-rail

This is the 8.50.a.m. from Paddington to Paignton, worked here by Old Oak's 6016 KING EDWARD V which is running over Red Cow Crossing and into Exeter St. David's station, probably during 1955. 6016 was one of the first of Kings to receive replacement front frames and new inside cylinders, during a five month long Heavy General overhaul lasting from late July until early December 1954.www.rail-online.co.uk

Heading west out of Swindon with just four coaches in the mid-1950s, 6016 KING EDWARD V despite its express passenger headcode, appears to be on a running-in turn with a rather strange chalked '375' reporting number on the smokebox door. It was allocated to Old Common from December 1954 until December 1958 when it moved to Stafford Road. www.rail-online.co.uk

Proof that the lighting at Paddington made it a difficult place for photographers, 6016 KING EDWARD V prepares to depart with 'The Inter-City' to Wolverhampton in March 1961. It had been transferred to Old Oak for the second time in September 1960. www.rail-online.co.uk

6016 KING EDWARD V rushes through Beaconsfield with the 3.10pm Paddington-Wolverhampton on 13 May 1961. One of the Kings to receive new front frames together with a new inside cylinder block at Swindon in the 1950s, 6016 moved around between Laira, Old Oak and Stafford Road sheds several times over the years before its withdrawal from service at Stafford Road shed in September 1962. www.rail-online.co.uk

6017 KING EDWARD IV

To stock June 1928

Modifications
Speedometer	20/9/33
WB boiler	7/8/52
New front frames, inside cylinders	5/12/55
Double chimney	5/12/55

Livery changes
BR standard blue	26/5/50
BR green	7/8/52

Allocations
2/7/28	Old Oak Common
16/7/28	Stafford Road
5/11/39	Bath Road
8/43	Laira
10/7/48	Old Oak Common
26/1/52	Laira
2/2/59	Stafford Road

Withdrawn 24/7/62
Sold to Cox & Danks, Langley Green	24/4/63

Repairs
1/9/28-20/9/28**R**	Swindon Factory
1/5/29-25/6/29**L**	Swindon Factory
12/4/30-28/6/30**L**	Swindon Shed
4/7/30-10/7/30**R**	Swindon Shed
3/1/31-14/2/31**G**	Swindon Factory
11/4/32-22/6/32**G**	Swindon Factory
8/2/33-9/3/33**L**	Swindon Factory
5/6/33-15/6/33**L**	Stafford Road
30/10/33-22/12/33**I**	Swindon Factory
3/3/34-5/3/34**L**	Swindon Factory
14/8/34-26/9/34**L**	Swindon Factory
7/1/35-14/1/35**L**	Stafford Road Factory
21/2/35-13/4/35**I**	Swindon Factory
19/3/36-6/5/36**I**	Swindon Factory
19/11/36-12/12/36**L**	Stafford Road
12/4/37-22/4/37**L**	Stafford Road Factory
4/5/37-22/6/37**G**	Swindon Factory
11/10/38-23/11/38**I**	Swindon Factory
18/2/39-6/3/39**L**	Swindon Factory
11/7/39-31/7/39**L**	Swindon Factory
12/10/39-5/11/39**R**	Bath Road
22/1/40-9/2/40**R**	Bath Road
22/2/40-6/6/40**G**	Swindon Factory
6/1/41-28/1/41**R**	Bath Road
28/3/41-15/4/41**R**	Swindon Factory
12/5/41-12/7/41**L**	Swindon Factory
26/8/41-3/9/41**L**	Swindon Factory
20/1/42-3/2/42**R**	Bath Road
10/4/42-25/4/42**R**	Bath Road
5/5/42-26/6/42**I**	Swindon Factory
7/8/42-1/9/42**L**	Swindon Factory
24/9/42-10/10/42**R**	Bath Road Shops
5/6/43-21/7/43**R**	Laira Shops
28/10/43-8/12/43**G**	Swindon Factory
6/8/44-2/9/44**R**	Reading Shops
4/9/44-26/9/44**R**	Laira Shops
18/1/45-16/3/45**I**	Swindon Factory
7/8/45-17/9/45**R**	Laira Shops
16/2/46-2/3/46**R**	Laira Shops
30/3/46-7/5/46**G**	Swindon Factory
11/9/46-8/10/46**R**	Laira Shops
10/2/47-5/3/47**R**	Laira Shops
9/6/47-9/6/47**L**	Laira Shops
30/6/47-19/7/47**R**	Laira Shops
4/8/47-27/8/47**R**	Laira Shops
26/9/47-12/11/47**R**	Laira Shops
14/11/47-21/11/47**L**	Newton Abbot Factory
2/12/47-22/12/47**R**	Laira Shops
16/1/48-18/2/48**I**	Swindon Factory

15/11/48-10/12/48**L**	Old Oak Common Shops
23/3/49-3/5/49**HG**	Swindon Factory
6/8/49-27/8/49**U**	Banbury Shops
18/4/50-26/5/50**LC**	Swindon Factory
23/7/50-18/9/50**U**	Taunton Shops
21/9/50-21/10/50**U**	Bath Road
7/12/50-23/1/51**HG**	Swindon Factory
12/8/51-13/9/51**U**	Old Oak Common Shops
1/10/51-16/10/51**U**	Old Oak Common
20/11/51-3/1/52**LC**	Swindon Factory
9/6/52-7/8/52**HG**	Swindon Factory
2/10/52-20/10/52**U**	Swindon Factory
18/1/53-1/2/53**U**	Laira Shops
6/3/53-13/3/53**U**	Laira Shops
8/6/53-16/6/53**U**	Laira Shops
27/1/54-30/3/54**HI**	Swindon Factory
26/10/54-17/11/54**LC**	Taunton Shops
29/12/54-10/1/55**U**	Laira Shops
1/3/55-15/4/55**LC**	Swindon Factory
17/5/55-23/5/55**U**	Newton Abbot Factory
29/8/55-14/9/55**U**	Laira Shops
26/9/55-5/12/55**HG**	Swindon Factory
27/1/56-19/2/56**LC**	Laira Shops
13/6/56-6/7/56**U**	Laira Shops
6/7/56--23/7/56**U**	Bath Road Shops
5/10/56-10/10/56**U**	Laira Shops
29/10/56-6/11/56**U**	Laira Shops
9/2/57-27/2/57**U**	Laira Shops
29/4/57-18/6/57**HI**	Swindon Factory
3/10/57-8/10/57**U**	Laira Shops
3/12/57-20/12/57**LC**	Newton Abbot Factory
16/4/58-26/4/58**U**	Laira Shops
8/7/58-25/7/58**U**	Bath Road Shops
1/9/58-8/9/58**U**	Laira Shops
10/9/58-30/10/58**HG**	Swindon Factory
2/9/59-24/9/59**U**	Stafford Road
30/1/60-26/2/60**U**	Stafford Road
14/4/60-15/6/60**LI**	Swindon Factory
5/11/60-3/12/60**U**	Stafford Road Shops
12/3/61-22/3/61**U**	Stafford Road
10/4/61-30/4/61**U**	Stafford Road
21/6/61-10/7/61**U**	Stafford Road
2/10/61-24/11/61**U**	Stafford Road
9/1/62-24/1/62**U**	Stafford Road
5/3/62-2/4/62**U**	Old Oak Common Shops

Boilers and mileages
Date	Boiler	Mileage
First	4678*	
14/2/31	4662	139,495
22/6/32	4681	211,053
22/12/33		291,843
26/9/34	4664	331,785
13/4/35		358,209
6/5/36		423,673
22/6/37	4674	485,271
23/11/38		567,137
6/6/40	4667	640,798
26/6/42		736,644
8/12/43	4668	814,474
16/3/45		896,435
7/5/46	4664	966,225
18/2/48	4691	1,058,314
3/5/49	4679	1,129,349
23/1/51	4678	1,210,999
7/8/52	8602	1,287,821
30/3/54		1,379,697
5/12/55	8625	1,477,610
18/6/57	8621	1,574,576
30/10/58	8609	1,667,558
15/6/60		1,751,360

Final mileage 1,853,262

Tenders
First	2402
25/6/29	2413
10/7/30	2391
22/6/32	2389
23/11/38	2544
6/6/40	2612
26/6/42	2710
8/12/43	2733
16/3/45	2762
7/5/46	2642
14/5/47	2630
18/2/48	2707
23/1/51	2630
3/1/52	2707
15/4/55	2395
5/12/55	2715
18/6/57	2771
20/10/58	2436
24/1/62	2795

6017 KING EDWARD IV arrives at Paddington with an express from Birkenhead Woodside in 1935. It had been fitted with a Jaeger speedometer in September 1933; other changes since it was built include top feed pipes curved back behind the nameplates instead of straight pipes and the upper lamp bracket moved down from the smokebox top to the smokebox door, although the access footstep has been left on the door. C.R.L. Coles, Rail Archive Stephenson.

6017 KING EDWARD IV at Taunton on the 8.30am Plymouth to Paddington, a regular King duty, in the early 1950s. 6017's mechanical lubricator is in the original position to the rear of the steam pipe, but was later moved forward of the pipe to ease access to the valve gear which remained hand lubricated. Original items which are not yet modified include the front frames, inside cylinders and single chimney. www.rail-online.co.uk

6017 KING EDWARD IV arriving at Westbury with the 8.30am Plymouth-Paddington on 19 May 1956. It was the first of Laira's Kings to receive a double chimney, in December 1955; at the same time it was given new front frames and inside cylinder block. The mechanical lubricator has been moved forward of the outside steam pipe. 6017 was one of three Kings allocated to Bristol Bath Road during the War, although it only stayed there for less than four years. www.rail-online.co.uk

On a rather dull day at Dawlish only a couple of youngsters on Marine Parade show any interest as 6017 KING EDWARD IV emerges from Kennaway tunnel at Dawlish with the Up 'Royal Duchy' in 1957. Everyone on the sea front seems distinctly unimpressed. www.rail-online.co.uk

6017 KING EDWARD IV at Swindon on 16 June 1957, two days before it went back into traffic after completion of a Heavy Intermediate overhaul which started at the end of April. 6017 has the later design of copper capped double chimney, which enjoyed a much better appearance than the earlier fabricated steel version. www.rail-online.co.uk

6017 KING EDWARD IV at Wolverhampton Stafford Road on 18 February 1962. During the 1950s there were six Kings allocated there, until 1959 when this increased to ten in preparation for electrification work on the former LMS line, after the main Birmingham expresses were transferred to Paddington from the Euston line. 6017 had previously spent over a decade at Stafford Road, from 1928 until 1939, and returned in February 1959 for its final years in service. www.rail-online.co.uk

6018 KING HENRY VI

To stock June 1928

Modifications

WB boiler	1/12/53
Double chimney	1/3/58

Livery changes

BR standard blue	1/12/50
BR green	1/4/52

Allocations

1/9/28	Laira
21/2/29	Newton Abbot
10/12/48	Bath Road
15/7/50	Old Oak Common
13/9/60	Cardiff Canton
4/6/62	Old Oak Common

Withdrawn	18/12/62
Cut up Swindon	5/10/63

Repairs

4/8/28-1/9/28**L**	Swindon Factory
14/1/29-16/2/29**L**	Swindon Factory
8/4/29-18/5/29**L**	Swindon Factory
22/5/29-10/6/29**L**	Swindon Factory
29/8/29-13/9/29**L**	Swindon Factory
6/1/30-15/1/30**L**	Newton Abbot Shops
29/4/30-5/7/30**H**	Swindon Factory
23/5/31-24/7/31**I**	Swindon Factory
17/2/32-11/3/32**R**	Newton Abbot Shops
12/4/32-5/7/32**G**	Swindon Factory
11/10/32-21/11/32**L**	Swindon Factory
20/2/33-23/3/33**L**	Swindon Factory
20/7/33-2/8/33**L**	Swindon Factory
2/11/33-4/1/34**I**	Swindon Factory
27/11/34-14/12/34**R**	Newton Abbot Shops
4/2/35-12/4/35**G**	Swindon Factory
4/10/35-21/10/35**R**	Newton Abbot Shops
20/1/36-4/2/36**R**	Newton Abbot Shops
6/2/36-8/2/36**L**	Swindon Factory
11/8/36-26/9/36**I**	Swindon Factory
28/7/37-18/8/37**L**	Swindon Factory
19/10/37-4/11/37**L**	Swindon Factory
25/1/38-22/3/38**G**	Swindon Factory
19/4/38-17/5/38**R**	Taunton Shops
13/8/38-17/9/38**L**	Swindon Factory
6/2/39-25/2/39**R**	Newton Abbot Shops
17/6/39-7/7/39**L**	Swindon Factory
15/2/40-2/4/40**I**	Swindon Factory
27/4/41-14/5/41**R**	Newton Abbot
11/8/41-8/10/41**G**	Swindon Factory
28/8/42-11/9/42**R**	Newton Abbot
20/12/42-27/1/43**I**	Swindon Factory
4/3/44-22/3/44**R**	Newton Abbot
24/5/44-28/6/44**R**	Newton Abbot
14/9/44-2/11/44**G**	Swindon Factory
6/4/45-2/5/45**L**	Swindon Factory
27/8/45-10/9/45**R**	Newton Abbot
27/2/46-1/4/46**I**	Swindon Factory
19/5/46-4/6/46**R**	Newton Abbot
19/8/46-9/9/46**R**	Newton Abbot
5/1/47-11/1/47**R**	Newton Abbot
11/1/47-14/2/47**L**	Newton Abbot Factory
8/3/47-27/3/47**R**	Newton Abbot
20/5/47-1/7/47**R**	Reading Shops
22/9/47-29/10/47**G**	Swindon Factory
8/12/47-8/1/48**L**	Swindon Factory
21/7/48-21/8/48**R**	Swindon Factory
7/9/48-13/9/48**R**	Swindon Factory
28/4/49-27/5/49**HG**	Swindon Factory
12/2/50-8/3/50**LC**	Old Oak Common Shops
17/10/50-4/12/50**HG**	Swindon Factory
25/7/51-24/8/51**U**	Old Oak Common Shops
4/12/51-18/12/51**U**	Old Oak Common
20/12/51-4/2/52**U**	Taunton Shops
14/3/52-25/4/52**HI**	Swindon Factory
7/5/53-1/6/53**U**	Old Oak Common Shops
19/10/53-8/12/53**HG**	Swindon Factory
11/3/55-26/4/55**HI**	Swindon Factory
9/1/56-17/2/56**LC**	Swindon Factory
6/3/56-22/3/56**LC**	Old Oak Common Shops
3/7/56-14/9/56**HI**	Swindon Factory
25/10/57-15/11/57**U**	Old Oak Common Shops
22/1/58-21/3/58**HI**	Swindon Factory
7/7/58-23/7/58**U**	Old Oak Common Shops
13/8/58-10/9/58**U**	Taunton Shops
30/3/59-22/4/59**U**	Old Oak Common Shops
1/9/59-11/11/59**HG**	Swindon Factory
30/4/60-16/5/60**U**	Banbury Shops
19/9/60-11/10/60**U**	Old Oak Common Shops
27/3/61-19/4/61**U**	Canton Shops
19/10/61-9/11/6**U**	Canton Shops
5/12/61-22/2/62**HG**	Swindon Factory

Boilers and mileages

First	4679*	
5/7/30		89,548
24/7/31		141,170
5/7/32	4663	181,618
4/1/34		255,023
12/4/35	4685	325,593
26/9/36		404,001
22/3/38	4679	467,630
2/4/40		559,970
8/10/41	4665	646,946
27/1/43		729,632
2/11/44	4690	818,919
1/4/46	4670	882,849
29/10/47	4677	939,029
27/5/49	4691	1,018,549
4/12/50	4689	1,100,116
25/4/52		1,172,378
8/12/53	8614	1,263,193
26/4/55	8605	1,354,236
14/9/56	8610	1,420,986
21/3/58	8606	1,518,348
11/11/59	8626	1,612,955
22/2/62	8618	1,705,202

Final mileage	1,738,387

Tenders

First	2403
16/2/29	2390
18/5/29	2394
5/7/30	2403
24/7/31	2555
21/11/32	2553
21/11/32	2396
21/10/33	2441
29/6/35	2549
26/9/36	2551
23/7/38	2648
17/9/38	2549
2/4/40	2694
2/11/44	2788
2/5/45	2715
27/5/49	2649
25/4/52	2775
26/4/55	2800
14/9/56	2544
15/6/57	2846
22/3/58	2841
11/11/59	2816
22/2/62	2619
19/3/63	2883

6018 KING HENRY VI still has brightly polished metalwork in this undated picture, probably in the early 1930s since the straight top feed pipes have been modified to the curved type. It was allocated to Laira for just six months after it was built in June 1928, moving to Newton Abbot for the next two decades. 6018 was the Western Region representative in the express passenger category during British Railways 1948 Interchange Trials but, because of loading gauge restrictions, could only work on the Eastern Region runs.

Old Oak Common's 6018 KING HENRY VI arrives at Bath in 1955 with the 7.30am from Paddington to Torquay and Paignton, running via Bristol, and will probably work through to Newton Abbot on this service. Its single chimney was not replaced until 1958, one of the last two to be dealt with. www.rail-online.co.uk

Old Oak's 6018 KING HENRY VI runs non-stop through Teignmouth station in summer 1956 with the 10.0am Newquay to Paddington and heads towards Exeter, its next stop. The impressive lattice Eastcliff Bridge is prominent in this view, as is St. Michael's Church, and there is even one of the war time observation 'pillboxes' still in place. The section from the end of the wall on the left to the station beyond was originally a tunnel in broad gauge days. This was, and still is, a favourite location from which to watch the trains go by, especially when there is a steam special running. www.rail-online.co.uk

6018 KING HENRY VI at Didcot in early 1960 is working the 4.15pm Bristol to Paddington. Although it now has a double chimney, fitted in March 1958, and a mechanical lubricator in front of the outside steam pipe, it retains the original inside valve casings and front frames which it kept until withdrawal. www.rail-online.co.uk

In a delightful rural setting at Holmes Park Farm, between Banbury and Leamington Spa about three miles north of Fenny Compton, 6018 KING HENRY VI on the 'Cambrian Coast Express'. The name was re-introduced in June 1951 for the through service from Paddington to Aberystwyth and Pwllheli, and the revived 'chocolate and cream' livery for the coaching stock on the Western Region's named trains in 1956. www.rail-online.co.uk

Displaying the 'Bristolian' train reporting number but not the headboard, 6018 KING HENRY VI arriving at Temple Meads in 1962. The two leading maroon ex-LMS coaches are strengthening vehicles added in front of the uniform rake of chocolate and cream liveried Mark 1 coaches which were the regular consist for the train at that date. www.rail-online.co.uk

6019 KING HENRY V

To stock July 1928

Modifications
WB boiler	20/9/55
Double chimney	24/4/57

Livery changes
BR standard blue	19/9/49
BR green	17/11/52

Allocations
1/8/28	Stafford Road
29/6/35	Laira
14/6/39	Newton Abbot (?)
22/7/39	Laira
1/1/49	Bath Road
16/7/49	Newton Abbot (loan?)
19/9/49	Bath Road
15/7/50	Old Oak Common
19/9/60	Canton
14/3/62	Old Oak Common

Withdrawn
	21/9/62
Sold to J.Cashmore, Newport	14/11/62

Repairs
26/9/28-29/9/28**L**	Swindon Factory
5/10/28-24/10/28**L**	Swindon Factory
1/3/29-24/4/29**L**	Swindon Factory
22/6/29-27/6/29**L**	Swindon Factory
3/12/29-2/4/30**H**	Swindon Factory
12/4/30-24/4/30**L**	Swindon Factory
16/5/30-5/6/30**L**	Swindon Factory
21/4/31-16/6/31**I**	Swindon Factory
31/3/32-25/5/32**G**	Swindon Factory
3/5/33-22/6/33**I**	Swindon Factory
16/3/34-3/5/34**G**	Swindon Factory
30/4/35-18/6/35**I**	Swindon Factory
25/11/35-11/12/35**R**	Laira Shops
7/5/36-30/5/36**L**	Swindon Factory
8/10/36-18/11/36**G**	Swindon Factory
3/1/38-22/2/38**I**	Swindon Factory
20/4/38-4/5/38**L**	Swindon Factory
28/7/38-20/8/38**L**	Swindon Factory
16/1/39-1/2/39**L**	Swindon Factory
26/4/39-12/6/39**I**	Swindon Factory
13/11/39-30/11/39**R**	Laira Shops
9/5/40-27/6/40**G**	Swindon Factory
19/4/41-14/5/41**R**	Laira Shops
19/8/41-15/10/41**I**	Swindon Factory
7/4/42-29/4/42**R**	Laira Shops
6/8/42-20/8/42**R**	Laira Shops
10/12/42-14/1/43**I**	Swindon Factory
5/7/43-29/7/43**R**	Laira Shops
30/9/43-29/10/43**L**	Swindon Factory
3/11/43-6/11/43**L**	Swindon Factory
24/2/44-14/3/44**R**	Laira Shops
24/5/44-12/6/44**R**	Laira Shops
30/8/44-26/10/44**G**	Swindon Factory
20/3/45-9/4/45**R**	Laira Shops
19/6/45-5/7/45**R**	Laira Shops
30/7/45-5/9/45**L**	Swindon Factory
23/10/45-13/11/45**R**	Laira Shops
2/2/46-12/3/46**I**	Swindon Factory
13/5/46-30/5/46**R**	Laira Shops
6/8/46-26/9/46**R**	Laira Shops
27/11/46-22/12/46**R**	Laira Shops
24/1/47-26/2/47**L**	Swindon Factory
15/8/47-6/9/47**R**	Laira Shops
17/10/47-3/11/47**R**	Laira Shops
8/12/47-13/1/48**R**	Laira Shops
5/3/48-15/4/48**G**	Swindon Factory
12/7/48-4/8/48**R**	Taunton Shops
8/9/48-22/9/48**R**	Swindon Factory
7/12/48-1/1/49**U**	Reading Shops
17/8/49-19/9/49**HG**	Swindon Factory
9/2/50-3/3/50**LC**	Swindon Factory
9/3/50-28/3/50**U**	Swindon Factory
8/9/50-18/10/50**U**	Taunton Shops
29/12/50-2/2/51**HG**	Swindon Factory
26/6/51-19/7/51**LC**	Swindon Factory
3/1/52-21/2/52**LC**	Swindon Factory
22/5/52-10/6/52**U**	Old Oak Common Shops
21/10/52-17/11/52**HI**	Swindon Factory
22/9/53-27/10/53**U**	Old Oak Common Shops
8/2/54-18/3/54**HG**	Swindon Factory
22/11/54-31/12/54**U**	Bath Road Shops
3/8/55-20/9/55**HI**	Swindon Factory
5/12/55-16/12/55**U**	Old Oak Common Shops
31/1/56-2/3/56**LC**	Swindon Factory
26/4/56-5/6/56**LC**	Swindon Factory
22/2/57-24/4/57**HG**	Swindon Factory
1/8/58-15/8/58**U**	Taunton Shops
27/8/58-8/9/58**U**	Exeter Shops
9/10/58-12/12/58**HI**	Swindon Factory
7/1/59-10/2/59**U**	Stafford Road
30/6/60-19/9/60**HG**	Swindon Factory
30/8/61-9/1/62**HC**	Swindon Factory

Boilers and mileages
First	4680*	
2/4/30	4681	77,003
16/6/31		135,150
25/5/32	4680	184,440
22/6/33		246,295
3/5/34	4674	293,354
18/6/35		361,651
18/11/36	4675	453,402
22/2/38		549,836
12/6/39		628,883
27/6/40	4689	698,385
15/10/41		782,989
14/1/43		864,969
26/10/44	4670	971,345
12/3/46	4669	1,058,579
15/4/48	4675	1,155,049
19/9/49	4680	1,215,159
2/2/51	4690	1,289,907
17/11/52	4678	1,384,512
18/3/54	4694	1,468,274
20/9/55	4698	1,557,963
24/4/57	8612	1,643,648
12/12/58		1,736,179
19/9/60	8605	1,817,502

Final mileage	1,912,309

Tenders
First	2428
2/4/30	2425
16/6/31	2389
25/5/32	2391
15/11/37	2398
22/2/38	2694
1/2/39	2612
27/6/40	2762
14/1/43	2606
26/10/44	2694
5/9/45	2707
12/3/46	2695
19/7/51	2922
20/9/55	2398
5/6/56	2776
1/8/56	2398
3/11/56	2776
24/4/57	2815
8/57	2922
11/57	2775
12/12/58	2613
18/4/59	2786
19/6/60	2399
9/1/62	2558

The driver poses proudly in front of the last of the 1928 engines, 6019 KING HENRY V at Old Oak Common in 1934. The straight top feed pipes have been replaced by the curved type, but the upper lamp bracket is still to be moved down from the smokebox top. George R. Grigs, Rail Archive Stephenson.

Pictured at Reading on a stopper, shortly after a General overhaul completed in April 1948, 6019 KING HENRY V had been repainted in lined green with BRITISH RAILWAYS in GWR small pattern lettering on the tender but had yet to receive its smokebox number plate. It still had the original style of casing, in front of the smokebox saddle. The green livery only lasted until September 1949 when it was replaced by light blue. Colour-rail

Old Oak's 6019 KING HENRY V on a running-in turn at Bath Spa on 9 June 1956 after a Light Casual repair. It had returned to lined green livery in November 1952 and has the typical early 1950s modifications, a mechanical lubricator and curved top casing in front of the smokebox saddle, but was a year away from the fitting of a double chimney. www.rail-online.co.uk

6019 KING HENRY V departs from Reading in the early 1950s on the Down Main with the westward facing bay platforms on the right. Unlike a number of the class which spent virtually their whole working lives at one of the three principal Motive Power Depots, 6019 did the rounds, being allocated initially from new in 1928 to Stafford Road followed by spells at Laira, Newton Abbot, Bristol Bath Road, Old Oak Common and Cardiff Canton before returning to Old Oak for its last six months in service. www.rail-online.co.uk

6019 KING HENRY V emerges from the Snow Hill tunnel past Birmingham Moor Street with the Up 'Inter-City' on 23 April 1959. Its single chimney had been replaced by a double chimney in April 1957 and it had also been fitted with the later type of covers for the inside valves. M. Mensing.

There is rather a large amount of steam leakage from 6019 KING HENRY V as it sets off from Banbury with the 11.40am Birkenhead-Paddington on 24 May 1962. Following a spell allocated to Cardiff Canton from September 1960 until March 1962, 6019 returned to Old Oak Common for its last six months in traffic. www.rail-online.co.uk

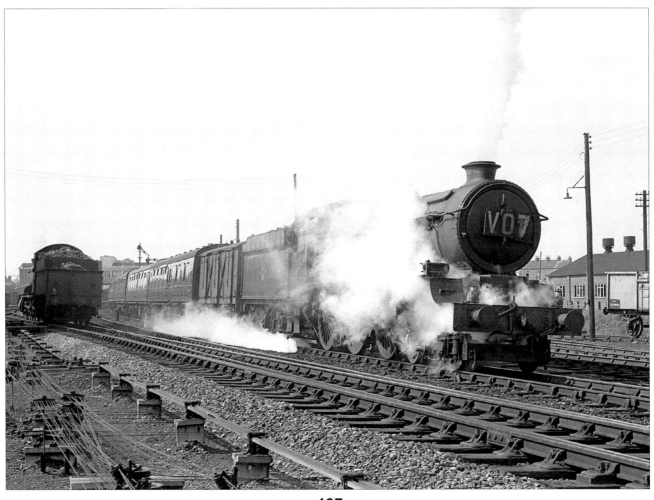

197

6020 KING HENRY IV

To stock May 1930

Modifications
WB boiler	11/3/52
Double chimney	15/8/56

Livery changes
BR standard blue	28/7/49
BR green	11/3/52

Allocations
4/6/30	Newton Abbot
4/7/30	Laira
22/8/30	Old Oak Common
4/10/30	Laira
5/1/49	Stafford Road

Withdrawn — 24/7/62
Sold to Cox & Danks,	
Langley Green	9/5/63

Repairs
7/6/30-30/6/30**L**	Swindon Factory
14/7/30-9/8/30**L**	Swindon Factory
25/9/30-30/9/30**R**	Swindon Factory
20/12/30-21/1/31**L**	Swindon Factory
27/4/31-10/6/31**L**	Swindon Factory
31/8/31-13/9/31**R**	Laira Shops
9/11/31-15/12/31**I**	Swindon Factory
3/1/32-20/1/32**R**	Laira Shops
24/7/32-13/8/32**R**	Swindon Factory
26/9/32-9/11/32**L**	Swindon Factory
6/4/33-25/4/33**R**	Laira Shops
26/4/33-7/7/33**I**	Swindon Factory
12/1/34-26/1/34**R**	Laira Shops
27/3/34-7/5/34**L**	Swindon Factory
26/5/34-21/6/34**L**	Swindon Factory
3/7/34-10/7/34**L**	Swindon Factory
31/12/34-28/2/35**G**	Swindon Factory
4/10/35-23/10/35**R**	Laira Shops
5/2/36-23/3/36**I**	Swindon Factory
28/1/37-12/2/37**R**	Laira Shops
7/4/37-24/5/37**I**	Swindon Factory
5/10/37-22/10/37**R**	Laira Shops
29/11/37-5/1/38**L**	Swindon Factory
4/5/38-7/6/38**L**	Swindon Factory
8/9/38-21/10/38**G**	Swindon Factory
19/4/39-5/5/39**L**	Swindon Factory
27/12/39-16/2/40**I**	Swindon Factory
8/7/40-26/7/40**R**	Newton Abbot Factory
21/12/40-31/1/41**L**	Swindon Factory
10/5/41-8/7/41**I**	Swindon Factory
8/10/41-19/10/41**R**	Old Oak Common Shops
23/12/41-7/1/42**R**	Laira Shops
9/4/42-9/5/42**R**	Laira Shops
7/7/42-29/7/42**R**	Laira Shops
7/8/42-10/8/42**R**	Newton Abbot Factory
14/10/42-28/11/42**G**	Swindon Factory
12/2/43-28/2/43**R**	Laira Shops
4/6/43-25/6/43**R**	Laira Shops
28/8/43-16/9/43**R**	Taunton Shops
18/10/43-2/11/43**R**	Laira Shops
20/2/44-3/4/44**I**	Swindon Factory
7/6/44-26/6/44**R**	Laira Shops
10/11/44-28/11/44**R**	Laira Shops
4/5/45-6/6/45**R**	Laira Shops
10/7/45-28/8/45**I**	Swindon Factory
5/1/46-19/1/46**R**	Laira Shops
29/3/46-13/4/46**R**	Laira Shops
23/7/46-9/8/46**R**	Laira Shops
22/10/46-10/12/46**G**	Swindon Factory
15/2/47-26/2/47**R**	Laira Shops
27/8/47-19/9/47**R**	Laira Shops
9/2/48-12/3/48**I**	Swindon Factory
19/9/48-8/10/48**R**	Laira Shops
18/12/48-5/1/49**U**	Stafford Road
8/6/49-28/7/49**HG**	Swindon Factory
21/9/50-25/10/50**HG**	Swindon Factory
13/6/51-9/7/51**LC**	Swindon Factory
13/9/51-1/10/51**U**	Swindon Factory
1/1/52-29/1/52**U**	Old Oak Common Shops
4/3/52-18/4/52**HG**	Swindon Factory
18/6/52-3/7/52**U**	Swindon Factory
23/9/52-28/10/52**U**	Stafford Road
19/11/52-19/12/52**U**	Stafford Road Factory
6/5/53-22/6/53**HC**	Swindon Factory
5/1/54-15/3/54**HI**	Swindon Factory
27/10/54-10/12/54**HC**	Swindon Factory
2/2/55-28/3/55**LC**	Swindon Factory
16/6/55-5/8/55**LC**	Swindon Factory
22/12/55-28/2/56**HG**	Swindon Factory
7/6/56-15/8/56**HC**	Swindon Factory
13/8/57-4/10/57**HG**	Swindon Factory
21/2/58-19/3/58**U**	Stafford Road
24/9/58-7/10/58**U**	Stafford Road
9/6/59-19/8/59**LI**	Swindon Factory
31/12/59-25/1/60**U**	Stafford Road
4/4/60-19/4/60**U**	Banbury Shops
9/6/60-15/7/60**LC**	Stafford Road Factory
19/8/60-12/9/60**U**	Stafford Road
2/11/60-18/11/60**U**	Stafford Road
15/2/61-6/3/61**U**	Stafford Road
18/4/61-20/6/61**LI**	Swindon Factory
27/11/61-14/12/61**U**	Tyseley Shops
2/5/62-29/5/62**U**	Stafford Road

Boilers and mileages
First	4683*	
15/12/31		63,297
7/7/33		134,424
28/2/35	4687	215,628
23/3/36		286,056
24/5/37		364,634
21/10/38	4683	456,906
16/2/40		541,849
8/7/41		631,572
28/11/42	4672	716,541
3/4/44		796,277
28/8/45		885,018
10/12/46	4675	969,531
12/3/48	4684	1,045,276
28/7/49	4678	1,114,800
25/10/50	4667	1,179,411
18/4/52	8601	1,244,400
10/12/54	4697	1,350,064
28/2/56	8628	1,390,550
15/8/56	8603	1,407,954
4/10/57	4698	1,460,824
19/8/59		1,544,375
20/6/61		1,621,858

Final mileage	1,686,568

Tenders
First	2548
10/6/31	2396
15/12/31	2553
9/11/32	2403
23/7/35	2543
31/1/41	2715
28/11/42	2726
3/4/44	2710
28/8/45	2907
10/12/46	2776
12/3/48	2606
28/7/49	2922
9/7/51	2695
18/4/52	2649
15/3/54	2815
28/3/55	2707
28/2/56	2564
4/10/57	2815
19/8/59	2564
20/6/61	2749

6020 KING HENRY IV climbs Rattery bank with the 3.30pm Paddington to Truro on 21 June 1939. It was the first of the 1930 engines, all of which had modified covers for the inside valves. After moving between Newton Abbot, Laira and Old Oak in its first three months, it settled down at the Plymouth shed and remained there until 1949. H. Harman, Rail Archive Stephenson.

Apart from the addition of a BR smokebox number plate, the outward appearance of 6020 KING HENRY IV had changed little since pre-war days as it waits at Leamington Spa in the early 1950s. It had been transferred to Stafford Road from Laira in January 1949. www.rail-online.co.uk

A King on shed at Leamington was an unusual event. 6020 KING HENRY IV had failed and been taken off its train for attention; the vigorous discharge of steam confirms it had been taken off in mid-flight.

Climbing Hatton Bank with the 2.10pm from Paddington to Birkenhead on 22 April 1957, 6020 KING HENRY IV had been fitted with a double chimney during a HC overhaul completed in June 1956. R.C. Riley, transporttreasury

6020 KING HENRY IV roars through West Bromwich on Saturday 20 September 1958 with the 7.30am Shrewsbury-Paddington. It has the final type of cover over the inside valves which came about when the exhaust passages were altered, the centre portion of the tread plate (above the valve covers) being raised to provide the necessary clearance. M. Mensing.

Two Kings flanked by two Castles inside Wolverhampton Stafford Road on 18 March 1961, with from left to right, 5042 WINCHESTER CASTLE, 6008 KING JAMES II, 6020 KING HENRY IV and 5031 TOTNES CASTLE. 6020 was allocated there from January 1949 until its withdrawal in July 1962. www.rail-online.co.uk

6021 KING RICHARD II

To stock June 1930

Modifications
WB boiler	2/3/56
Double chimney	4/3/57

Livery changes
BR standard blue	26/11/51
BR green	28/5/53

Allocations
12/6/30	Old Oak Common
8/9/56	Laira
11/12/59	Old Oak Common

Withdrawn 21/9/62
Sold to J.Cashmore,
Newport 14/11/62

Repairs

20/6/30-3/7/30**L**	Swindon Factory
19/7/30-11/8/30**R**	Old Oak Common Shops
16/8/30-1/9/30**L**	Swindon Factory
17/9/31-2/10/31**R**	Old Oak Common Shops
14/1/32-24/3/32**I**	Swindon Factory
31/8/32-7/9/32**R**	Old Oak Common Shops
12/10/32-11/11/32**L**	Swindon Factory
7/3/33-7/4/33**L**	Swindon Factory
10/10/33-29/11/33**G**	Swindon Factory
6/1/34-11/1/34**L**	Swindon Factory
15/1/34-18/1/34**L**	Swindon Factory
23/5/34-14/6/34**R**	Old Oak Common Shops
20/11/34-17/1/35**I**	Swindon Factory
2/4/35-18/4/35**R**	Laira Shops
14/9/35-16/10/35**L**	Swindon Factory
19/3/36-9/4/36**R**	Old Oak Common Shops
14/4/36-1/5/36**R**	Old Oak Common Shops
16/5/36-3/7/36**G**	Swindon Factory
7/12/36-21/12/36**R**	Old Oak Common Shops
5/5/37-1/6/37**R**	Old Oak Common Shops
14/6/37-5/7/37**L**	Swindon Factory
28/7/37-10/8/37**L**	Swindon Factory
6/9/37-22/10/37**I**	Swindon Factory
8/11/37-23/11/37**L**	Swindon Factory
16/3/38-30/3/38**R**	Old Oak Common Shops
10/8/38-14/9/38**L**	Swindon Factory
2/1/39-9/2/39**G**	Swindon Factory
22/1/40-8/3/40**I**	Swindon Factory
25/9/40-31/10/40**L**	Swindon Factory
13/2/41-11/3/41**L**	Swindon Factory
30/7/41-23/9/41**I**	Swindon Factory
8/1/42-25/2/42**L**	Swindon Factory
19/8/42-2/9/42**R**	Old Oak Common Shops
30/12/42-12/2/43**G**	Swindon Factory
19/5/43-6/6/43**R**	Old Oak Common Shops
8/9/43-29/9/43**R**	Old Oak Common
14/3/44-27/4/44**L**	Swindon Factory
5/6/44-24/7/44**L**	Old Oak Common Shops
12/8/44-1/9/44**R**	Old Oak Common Shops
22/11/44-10/1/45**I**	Swindon Factory
2/5/45-14/6/45**L**	Laira Shops
27/7/45-14/8/45**R**	Old Oak Common
8/11/45-26/1/46**L**	Old Oak Common Shops
29/4/46-24/5/46**I**	Swindon Factory
26/9/46-16/10/46**L**	Old Oak Common Shops
2/1/47-5/1/47**R**	Reading Shops
16/2/47-13/3/47**R**	Old Oak Common Shops
6/5/47-16/6/47**G**	Swindon Factory
28/6/47-8/7/47**L**	Swindon Factory
30/7/47-12/8/47**L**	Swindon Factory
16/4/48-19/5/48**L**	Swindon Factory
9/11/48-20/12/48**I**	Swindon Factory
15/4/49-5/5/49**U**	Exeter Shops
30/9/49-20/10/49**U**	Old Oak Common Shops
23/1/50-24/2/50**U**	Bath Road Shops
4/4/50-10/5/50**HG**	Old Oak Common
16/5/50-23/5/50**U**	Swindon Factory
12/9/50-9/10/50**LC**	Old Oak Common Shops
23/1/51-7/2/51**U**	Taunton Shops
17/4/51-25/5/51**HC**	Swindon Factory
1/9/51-1/10/51**U**	Swindon Factory
19/10/51-26/11/51**HI**	Swindon Factory
18/9/52-3/10/52**U**	Old Oak Common
29/10/52-10/12/52**U**	Shops
9/2/53-26/2/53**U**	Taunton Shops
26/2/53-17/3/53**U**	Swindon Factory
17/4/53-28/5/53**HG**	Swindon Factory
21/9/53-14/10/53**U**	Bath Road Shops
29/12/53-19/1/54**U**	Old Oak Common Shops
25/5/54-14/6/54**U**	Old Oak Common Shops
20/9/54-26/10/54**HI**	Swindon Factory
28/2/55-24/3/55**U**	Old Oak Common Shops
9/8/55-7/9/55**U**	Old Oak Common Shops
12/10/55-8/11/55**U**	Old Oak Common Shops
9/1/56-2/3/56**HG**	Swindon Factory
20/11/56-4/3/57**HC**	Swindon Factory
26/4/57-5/6/57**U**	Taunton Shops
31/10/57-15/11/57**U**	Laira Shops
6/1/58-28/2/58**HI**	Swindon Factory
12/6/58-26/6/58**U**	Taunton Shops
11/8/58-27/8/58**U**	Taunton Shops
15/1/59-30/1/59**U**	Newton Abbot Factory
6/10/59-11/12/59**HI**	Swindon Factory
19/12/60-9/1/61**U**	Leamington Shops
16/2/61-13/3/61**U**	Old Oak Common Shops
5/5/61-25/5/61**U**	Old Oak Common
22/7/61-7/9/62**HG**	Swindon Factory

Boilers and mileages

First	4684*	
24/3/32		87,140
29/11/33	4670	179,060
17/1/35		244,108
3/7/36	4692	332,473
22/10/37		418,234
9/2/39	4690	502,604
8/3/40		575,622
23/9/41		673,294
12/2/43	4681	755,146
10/1/45		850,583
24/5/46	4677	914,104
16/6/47	4668	976,614
20/12/48	4672	1,058,473
10/5/50	4664	1,131,620
25/5/51	4665	1,186,136
26/11/51		1,211,453
28/5/53	4672	1,295,882
26/10/54		1,385,001
2/3/56	8602	1,446,856
28/2/58		1,549,090
11/12/59	8617	1,657,589
26/9/61	8604	1,741,591
Final mileage		1,793,439

Tenders

First	2549
7/4/33	2552
14/9/38	2648
9/2/39	2441
8/3/40	2759
31/10/40	2556
23/9/41	2800
10/1/45	2808
1/10/51	2694
26/11/51	2742
9/8/52	2715
28/5/53	2630
1/6/54	2428
19/6/54	2759
26/10/54	2694
26/3/55	2648
5/11/55	2583
2/3/56	2762
3/11/56	2666
4/3/57	2695
28/2/58	2899
11/12/59	2740
3/12/60	2865
26/9/61	2696

This low angle picture of 6021 KING RICHARD II at Banbury in 1936 shows a number of original King features that were changed over the years. Firstly, the rounded casing over the inside valve chest which must have provided a less than satisfactory foothold for shed staff and footplatemen, especially in wet or icy conditions, and which was replaced by a squared version from about the late 1940s. The later design of inside valve spindle covers, applied to the final ten of the class from new, shows clearly here, as does the small footstep on the smokebox door, which was later dispensed with, and the brass axlebox cover on the leading wheel bogie was the original design which was later changed. www.rail-online.co.uk

In typical post-war condition, 6021 KING RICHARD II waits at Leamington Spa on 31 August 1946. It is in unlined green with the simplified G W lettering on the tender and had been allocated to Old Oak from new in 1930. www.rail-online.co.uk

With its lining restored after a General overhaul completed three months earlier, 6021 KING RICHARD II climbing out of Hockley No.1 Tunnel with an Up express and into Birmingham Snow Hill on 6 September 1947. On the left is the distinctive North Signal Box which was opened in 1909 and was taken out of use in 1960. It was one of the first all-electric signalling systems on the Great Western Railway. In the centre background is the factory of Taylor & Challen Ltd which made industrial presses. It was built of red brick with superb decorative stone. www.rail-online.co.uk

6021 KING RICHARD II after arrival at Bristol with the Down 'Merchant Venturer' on 31 December 1955. The mid-morning train from Paddington to Bristol and Weston-super-Mare had been given the name in June 1951. 6021 was transferred from Old Oak to Laira in September 1956, and returned there three years later. www.rail-online.co.uk

With Old Oak's 6015 KING RICHARD III on the left, Laira's 6021 KING RICHARD II has just replenished its tender on the Laira coaling line in the late 1950s. Its double chimney was fitted in March 1957 and it returned to Old Oak's allocation in December 1959 as the diesels took over Laira's express work. The impact of the dieselisation already at Laira is shown by the absence of any other engines waiting for attention, a complete contrast with pictures taken just two or three years earlier. transporttreasury

A classic Birmingham Snow Hill scene as 6021 KING RICHARD II arrives at Platform 7 with the 3 o'clock to Paddington, the 11.40am from Birkenhead, on 28 October 1961. The famous clock shows the train was a few minutes late: it had been held outside the station while a parcels van was removed from the rear of a preceding local. R. Darlaston.

6022 KING EDWARD III

To stock June 1930

Modifications
WB boiler	21/6/51
New front frames, inside cylinders	1/11/54
Double chimney	31/5/56

Livery changes
BR standard blue	12/12/49
BR green	16/6/53

Allocations
5/7/30	Laira
27/9/48	Newton Abbot
24/4/49	Laira
24/10/55	Old Oak Common
18/6/59	Stafford Road

Withdrawn
	21/9/62
Sold to Cox & Danks, Langley Green	5/6/63

Repairs
5/1/31-29/1/31**L**	Swindon Factory
15/10/31-16/11/31**L**	Swindon Factory
26/1/32-4/3/32**I**	Swindon Factory
2/6/32-6/6/32**L**	Swindon Factory
11/7/32-27/7/32**R**	Laira Shops
14/11/32-9/12/32**L**	Swindon Factory
20/2/33-17/3/33**L**	Swindon Factory
10/11/33-27/11/33**R**	Laira Shops
10/1/34-23/2/34**I**	Swindon Factory
15/1/35-27/3/35**G**	Swindon Factory
22/11/35-14/1/36**L**	Swindon Factory
7/2/36-22/2/36**L**	Swindon Factory
15/4/36-22/5/36**I**	Swindon Factory
27/4/37-12/6/37**I**	Swindon Factory
25/10/37-10/11/37**R**	Laira Shops
27/12/37-14/1/38**R**	Laira Shops
26/5/38-6/8/38**G**	Swindon Factory
19/9/38-29/9/38**L**	Swindon Factory
11/1/39-7/2/39**L**	Bath Road Shops
30/3/39-5/4/39**L**	Swindon Factory
16/8/39-6/9/39**L**	Swindon Factory
15/12/39-30/1/40**I**	Swindon Factory
16/3/40-9/4/40**L**	Swindon Factory
26/10/40-15/11/40**L**	Swindon Factory
4/2/41-22/2/41**L**	Swindon Factory
2/5/41-24/5/41**R**	Laira Shops
23/6/41-27/8/41**I**	Swindon Factory
24/9/41-29/10/41**L**	Swindon Factory
26/11/41-10/12/41**L**	Swindon Factory
4/5/42-27/5/42**R**	Laira Shops
24/6/42-9/7/42**L**	Newton Abbot Factory
23/9/42-8/10/42**R**	Laira Shops
23/2/43-30/4/43**G**	Swindon Factory
11/2/44-6/3/44**R**	Laira Shops
18/7/44-4/8/44**R**	Laira Shops
7/9/44-24/10/44**I**	Swindon Factory
2/3/45-28/3/45**R**	Taunton Shops
30/4/45-8/5/45**R**	Laira Shops
7/8/45-2/10/45**L**	Laira Shops
29/10/45-9/11/45**R**	Laira Shops
19/11/45-8/12/45**R**	Laira Shops
29/1/46-1/3/46**I**	Swindon Factory
25/4/46-17/5/46**R**	Laira Shops
15/7/46-3/8/46**R**	Laira Shops
9/10/46-9/11/46**R**	Laira Shops
1/1/47-3/2/47**R**	Old Oak Common Shops
4/2/47-8/3/47**L**	Swindon Factory
15/5/47-21/5/47**R**	Laira Shops
8/11/47-5/12/47**R**	Laira Shops
9/1/48-5/3/48**G**	Swindon Factory
9/1/48-5/3/48**G**	Swindon Factory
10/3/48-23/4/48	Swindon Factory Test Plant
4/6/48-1/7/48**L**	Swindon Factory
20/8/48-27/9/48**L**	Swindon Factory
11/4/49-24/4/49**U**	Laira Shops
23/8/49-6/9/49**U**	Laira Shops
31/10/49-12/12/49**HI**	Swindon Factory
30/12/49-26/1/50**LC**	Swindon Factory
27/4/50-11/5/50**U**	Laira Shops
19/5/50-5/6/50**U**	Exeter Shops
27/6/50-14/7/50**U**	Laira Shops
30/8/50-26/9/50**LC**	Swindon Factory
15/11/50-6/12/50**U**	Laira Shops
22/1/51-7/2/51**U**	Old Oak Common Shops
15/5/51-21/6/51**HG**	Swindon Factory
19/9/51-8/11/51**U**	Taunton Shops
28/12/51-16/1/52**U**	Old Oak Common
28/3/52-16/4/52**U**	Laira Shops
22/5/52-17/6/52**LC**	Swindon Factory
25/8/52-21/9/52**U**	Taunton Shops
25/9/52-7/10/52**U**	Laira Shops
19/11/52-16/1/53**LC**	Swindon Factory
12/2/53-6/3/53**U**	Laira Shops
29/4/53-16/6/53**HI**	Swindon Factory
6/1/54-10/2/54**LC**	Swindon Factory
16/4/54-27/4/54**U**	Laira Shops
17/5/54-1/6/54**U**	Old Oak Common Shops
26/7/54-1/11/54**HG**	Swindon Factory
3/11/54-9/11/54**U**	Swindon Factory
13/11/54-10/12/54**U**	Taunton Shops
23/2/55-27/2/55**U**	Laira Shops
18/5/55-6/6/55**U**	Laira Shops
24/9/55-24/10/55**LC**	Swindon Factory
28/1/56-21/2/56**LC**	Laira Shops
12/4/56-31/5/56**HI**	Swindon Factory
6/6/56-21/6/56**U**	Swindon Factory
9/3/57-23/4/57**U**	Swindon Factory
1/10/57-5/11/57**HI**	Swindon Factory
16/4/58-25/4/58**U**	Laira Shops
12/6/58-22/7/58**LC**	Swindon Factory
6/3/59-18/6/59**HG**	Swindon Factory
13/11/59-8/12/59**U**	Stafford Road
10/2/60-3/3/60**U**	Old Oak Common Shops
21/8/60-23/9/60**U**	Stafford Road
29/11/60-9/2/61**LI**	Swindon Factory
30/8/61-11/10/61**U**	Stafford Road
30/3/62-19/4/62**U**	Stafford Road
30/3/62-23/4/62**U**	Stafford Road
28/6/62-20/7/62**U**	Oxley Shops

Boilers and mileages
First	4685*	
4/3/32		91,289
23/2/34		199,363
27/3/35	4683	261,556
22/5/36		329,508
12/6/37		413,097
6/8/38	4685	493,414
30/1/40		587,341
27/8/41		670,792
30/4/43	4683	755,282
24/10/44		855,342
1/3/46	4684	928,866
5/3/48	4670	1,025,375
12/12/49		1,096,713
21/6/51	4695*	1,171,458
16/6/53		1,255,402
1/11/54	8617*	1,320,524
31/5/56		1,406,598
15/11/57	8603	1,490,382
18/6/59	8625	1,572,653
9/2/61		1,650,274
Final mileage		1,733,189

Tenders
First	2550
4/3/32	2554
30/1/40	2556
15/11/40	2642
27/8/41	2743
24/10/44	2759
3/11/45	2695
1/3/46	2707
5/3/48	2776
1/7/48	2716
17/5/49	2763
21/6/51	2743
17/6/52	2788
10/2/54	2849
22/5/54	2759
1/6/54	2648
1/11/54	2788
31/5/56	2775
15/11/57	2598
22/7/58	2565
18/6/59	2438

6022 KING EDWARD III has just passed Tigley signal box as it slogs up Rattery with the 3.30pm Paddington to Truro on 22 June 1939. The 1930 built engine was shedded at Laira until September 1948. Hugh Harman/ Rail Archive Stephenson.

Transferred from Laira to Old Oak the previous October, 6022 KING EDWARD III slows as it arrives at Bath Spa for its only intermediate stop from Paddington to Bristol Temple Meads with the Down 'Merchant Venturer' on 10 July 1956. The engine was diagrammed to work back home from Bristol later that same afternoon, on the 'Bristolian'. The strengthened lifting holes in the front frames show up very well in this view, confirming that 6022 had new front frames and inside cylinder block, probably fitted during its recent Heavy Intermediate Overhaul completed at the end of May. www.rail-online.co.uk

6022 KING EDWARD III at Bristol Temple Meads on 11 November 1956 on a down working from Paddington. It had been fitted with a double chimney during a Heavy Overhaul at Swindon earlier in the year when its mechanical lubricator was re-positioned ahead of the right-hand outside steam pipe. From late 1949, all of the class had been fitted with mechanical lubricators for cylinders, valves and regulators. Initially, most had the lubricators on the running plate immediately to the rear of the right-hand outside steam pipe, but this was found to hinder access to the inside cylinder motion and so the lubricators were re-sited. www.rail-online.co.uk

With an LMR style of Reporting Number with an 'X' indicating a Special working from that Region, 6022 KING EDWARD III arrives at Paddington on 26 July 1959. It had been transferred from Old Oak to Stafford Road a month earlier. A run out to Old Oak will not be necessary for 6022 because its tender is well filled with coal and it will be turned, watered and prepared for its return journey at Ranelagh Yard. www.rail-online.co.uk

On the 7.30am from Shrewsbury, 6022 KING EDWARD III runs through West Ruislip on 6 May 1961. www.rail-online.co.uk

6022 KING EDWARD III arrives at Banbury with the 5.10pm Paddington-Wolverhampton on 26 April 1962. The Stafford Road engine had less than six months left in service, and was condemned in September 1962. www.rail-online.co.uk

6023 KING EDWARD II

To stock June 1930

Modifications
WB boiler	8/2/55
Double chimney	4/6/57

Livery changes
BR standard blue	1/8/50
BR green	7/3/52

Allocations
19/7/30	Newton Abbot
23/11/36	Laira
12/12/36	Newton Abbot
2/2/49	Laira
30/8/56	Old Oak Common
13/9/60	Canton

Withdrawn
	19/6/62
Sold to T.W.Ward,	
Briton Ferry	10/10/62
Re-sold to Woodhams Barry	26/11/62

Repairs
9/7/30-19/7/30**L**	Swindon Factory
13/1/31-19/1/31**R**	Newton Abbot Factory
2/2/31-16/2/31**R**	Newton Abbot Factory
28/10/31-3/11/31**L**	Swindon Factory
16/11/31-17/11/31**L**	Swindon Factory
2/2/32-7/4/32**I**	Swindon Factory
4/7/32-23/7/32**R**	Newton Abbot Factory
19/10/32-7/11/32**L**	Swindon Factory
30/1/33-7/4/33**G**	Swindon Factory
25/8/33-30/8/33**Speedo**	Swindon Factory
24/4/34-19/6/34**I**	Swindon Factory
11/2/35-26/2/35**R**	Newton Abbot Factory
8/4/35-10/4/35**Bogie change**	Swindon Factory
25/5/35-10/7/35**L**	Swindon Factory
11/10/35-18/10/35**L**	Swindon Factory
28/1/36-9/3/36**G**	Swindon Factory
15/4/36-24/4/36**L**	Swindon Factory
11/5/36-13/5/36**Tender**	Swindon Factory
11/1/37-3/2/37**L**	Swindon Factory
15/6/37-9/7/37**L**	Swindon Factory
14/12/37-4/2/38**I**	Swindon Factory
29/12/38-10/2/39**G**	Swindon Factory
29/2/40-13/4/40**I**	Swindon Factory
21/10/40-5/11/40**R**	Newton Abbot Shops
27/8/41-21/10/41**I**	Swindon Factory
8/4/42-9/4/42**L**	Newton Abbot Shops
5/8/42-21/8/42**R**	Newton Abbot Shops
12/10/42-19/11/42**L**	Swindon Factory
18/1/43-27/1/43**R**	Newton Abbot Factory
20/4/43-5/6/43**I**	Swindon Factory
16/8/43-21/9/43**L**	Swindon Factory
23/2/44-8/3/44**R**	Newton Abbot
26/6/44-27/7/44**L**	Swindon Factory
3/3/45-21/4/45**G**	Swindon Factory
19/10/45-4/11/45**R**	Newton Abbot
8/2/46-25/2/46**R**	Swindon Factory
14/3/46-16/4/46**R**	Laira Shops
1/5/46-5/6/46**L**	Swindon Factory
2/10/46-22/10/46**R**	Exeter Shops
6/11/46-12/11/46**R**	Newton Abbot Factory
25/1/47-13/3/47**L**	Newton Abbot
9/4/47-16/5/47**I**	Swindon Factory
20/5/47-30/5/47**L**	Swindon Factory
16/9/47-1/10/47**L**	Newton Abbot
31/1/48-16/2/48**L**	Exeter Shops
25/2/48-22/3/48**R**	Old Oak Common Shops
1/12/48-11/1/49**HG**	Swindon Factory
18/1/49-2/2/49**HG**	Swindon Factory
20/5/49-12/6/49**U**	Laira Shops
3/8/49-17/8/49**U**	Laira Shops
6/9/49-28/9/49**U**	Laira Shops
10/10/49-27/10/49**U**	Laira Shops
30/12/49-19/1/50**LC**	Swindon Factory

8/6/50-1/8/50**HG**	Swindon Factory
23/10/50-8/11/50**U**	Laira Shops
10/1/51-26/1/51**U**	Laira Shops
13/4/51-24/4/51**U**	Laira Shops
28/4/51-12/6/51**U**	Taunton Shops
26/6/51-14/7/51**LC**	Newton Abbot Factory
22/8/51-18/9/51**LC**	Swindon Factory
20/11/51-30/11/51**U**	Swindon Factory
29/1/52-7/3/52**HG**	Swindon Factory
19/6/52-3/7/52**U**	Laira Shops
3/9/52-24/9/52**U**	Laira Shops
14/11/52-14/1/53**LC**	Swindon Factory
10/4/53-14/5/53**U**	Laira Shops
30/5/53-17/8/53**HI**	Swindon Factory
26/12/53-28/12/53**U**	Laira Shops
29/3/54-20/4/54**U**	Laira Shops
20/8/54-4/9/54**U**	Laira Shops
18/9/54-15/10/54**U**	Taunton Shops
3/1/55-8/2/55**HG**	Swindon Factory
28/5/55-5/8/55**U**	Reading Shops
5/9/55-10/10/55**U**	Laira Shops
9/11/55-30/11/55**U**	Taunton Shops
3/1/56-27/2/56**U**	Taunton Shops
23/3/56-27/3/56**U**	Laira Shops
18/4/56-18/5/56**U**	Bath Road Shops
12/6/56-30/8/56**LC**	Swindon Factory
25/12/56-22/1/57**U**	Taunton Shops
13/4/57-4/6/57**HI**	Swindon Factory
25/7/57-13/8/57**LC**	Swindon Factory
27/2/58-14/3/58**U**	Stafford Road Factory
12/8/58-6/10/58**HG**	Swindon Factory
23/6/59-23/8/59**U**	Stafford Road
31/3/60-27/6/60**HG**	Swindon Factory
13/11/60-2/12/60**U**	Canton Shops
23/1/61-9/3/61**LC**	Swindon Factory
23/5/61-8/6/61**U**	Canton Shops
14/9/61-11/10/61**U**	Canton Shops
20/11/61-7/12/61**U**	Canton Shops
19/2/62-12/3/62**U**	Old Oak Common Shops

Boilers and mileages
First	4686*	
7/4/32		87,948
7/4/33	4677	130,971
19/6/34		196,034
9/3/36	4669	289,452
4/2/38		374,751
10/2/39	4687	427,909
13/4/40		496,014
21/10/41		587,165
19/11/42	4666	647,759
5/6/43		675,049
21/4/45	4671	766,707
16/5/47		845,835
11/1/49	4688	916,200
1/8/50	4683	985,969
7/3/52	4670	1,064,561
17/8/53		1,126,074
8/2/55	8621	1,221,295
4/6/57	8600	1,315,191
6/10/58	8624	1,388,709
27/6/60	8619	1,464,528
Final mileage		1,554,201

Tenders
First	2551
3/11/31	2399
17/11/31	2396
7/11/32	2553
10/7/35	2441
10/2/39	2694
13/4/40	2549
21/10/41	2606
19/11/42	2715
5/6/43	2763
21/9/43	2715
21/4/45	2772
16/5/47	2694
18/9/51	2648
7/3/52	2905
17/8/53	2762
1/1/55	2742
3/12/55	2717
30/8/56	2913
26/1/57	2805
4/6/57	2752
6/10/58	2771
29/11/58	2745
10/59	2427
27/6/60	2668

6023 KING EDWARD II takes water from Exminster troughs while working the down 'Cornish Riviera' probably shortly after it entered traffic in June 1930. It spent almost all of its first two decades allocated to Newton Abbot, apart from a few weeks at Laira in late 1936. F.R. Hebron/Rail Archive Stephenson.

6023 KING EDWARD II poses in front of the Old Oak coaling stage in the mid-1930s. The long drive for the Jaeger speedometer, fitted in August 1933, which entered the cab level with the bottom of the side window shows up well as does the later style of inside valve cover which the last ten engines had from new. transporttreasury

Only a few days since leaving Swindon after completion of a Heavy General overhaul and repainting in BR standard light blue livery, 6023 KING EDWARD II is on shed at Didcot on 7 August 1950. It would re-appear in this condition, including the single chimney, almost seventy years later after a protracted restoration following nearly twenty years rotting away at Woodham's Barry scrapyard. It finally returned to the main line in late 2017.

6023 KING EDWARD II with the Up 'Cornish Riviera' leaves Plymouth North Road Platform 7, passing North Road East signal box and heading towards Mutley, probably in or about 1954. It had regained green livery in March 1952 replacing the short-lived light blue livery which it kept for less than eighteen months. P. Kerslake/ www.rail-online.co.uk

A possible 'cop' for the two young lads on the platform at Bath Spa, an immaculate 6023 KING EDWARD II was probably on a running-in turn after completion of a Heavy Intermediate overhaul in June 1957, during which it was fitted with a double chimney. It was an Old Oak Common engine by this date, having moved from Laira in mid-1956. www.rail-online.co.uk

The GWR style of Train Reporting Number, as mentioned earlier, was replaced in 1960 by the British Railways alpha-numeric system with the letter indicating the destination; in the GWR system the first digit indicated the origin of the train. The 'A24' on the smokebox of 6023 KING EDWARD II shows that it was working the 4.55am from Fishguard Harbour, due Paddington at 11.45am, when photographed at Dover Road near Slough in June 1960. It had recently completed a Heavy General Overhaul from 31 March until 27 June. Just two months later 6023, together with 6003, 6004, 6018, 6019 and 6028, was transferred from Old Oak to Cardiff Canton, to be joined the following year by 6024. The move was an attempt to find suitable work for them, but their stay in South Wales lasted only two years; 6023 was condemned at Canton in September 1962. www.rail-online.co.uk

6024 KING EDWARD I

To stock June 1930

Modifications
WB boiler	11/9/53
Double chimney	20/3/57

Livery changes
BR standard blue	7/11/50
BR green	11/9/53

Allocations
10/7/30	Laira
13/1/34	Newton Abbot
29/1/49	Laira
10/8/54	Old Oak Common
11/9/61	Canton

Withdrawn 19/6/62
Sold to T.W.Ward,	
Briton Ferry	10/10/62
Re-sold to Woodhams, Barry	26/11/62

Repairs
12/1/32-26/2/32**I**	Swindon Factory
24/5/32-27/5/32**L**	Swindon Factory
15/8/32-24/8/32**L**	Swindon Factory
30/11/32-15/12/32**L**	Swindon Factory
27/3/33-7/4/33**L**	Swindon Factory
8/5/33-5/7/33**I**	Swindon Factory
10/4/34-25/5/34**L**	Swindon Factory
28/8/34-30/8/34**L**	Swindon Factory
9/11/34-24/1/35**G**	Swindon Factory
8/10/35-6/11/35**L**	Swindon Factory
17/3/36-4/4/36**L**	Swindon Factory
21/4/36-29/5/36**I**	Swindon Factory
11/5/37-22/6/37**L**	Swindon Factory
15/2/38-14/4/38**G**	Swindon Factory
2/5/39-23/6/39**I**	Swindon Factory
6/3/40-20/3/40**R**	Newton Abbot Factory
8/10/40-3/12/40**I**	Swindon Factory
28/4/41-15/5/41**R**	Newton Abbot
14/7/41-30/7/41**R**	Newton Abbot Factory
3/2/42-14/3/42**I**	Swindon Factory
19/8/42-3/9/42**R**	Newton Abbot Factory
28/1/43-4/6/43**L**	Swindon Factory
27/8/43-14/9/43**R**	Laira Shops
9/1/44-23/1/44**R**	Newton Abbot
16/2/44-2/3/44**L**	Newton Abbot Shops
27/3/44-16/4/44**R**	Newton Abbot
25/7/44-4/10/44**G**	Swindon Factory
10/10/45-12/11/45**L**	Swindon Factory
6/4/46-14/5/46**I**	Swindon Factory
16/1/47-1/2/47**R**	Newton Abbot
28/2/47-8/4/47**R**	Newton Abbot Shops
2/8/47-11/9/47**G**	Swindon Factory
4/3/48-8/3/48**L**	Newton Abbot Shops
8/1/49-28/1/49**U**	Laira Shops
9/2/49-24/2/49**U**	Laira Shops
2/3/49-6/4/49**HG**	Swindon Factory
9/7/49-28/7/49**U**	Laira Shops
22/8/49-6/9/49**U**	Laira Shops
21/10/49-17/11/49**LC**	Swindon Factory
9/2/50-9/3/50**LC**	Swindon Factory
15/5/50-20/6/50**LC**	Swindon Factory
2/10/50-7/11/50**HG**	Swindon Factory
22/2/51-7/3/51**U**	Laira Shops
16/5/51-4/7/51**U**	Laira Shops
20/9/51-26/10/51**U**	Laira Shops
3/12/51-23/1/52**HI**	Swindon Factory
6/2/52-22/2/52**LC**	Swindon Factory
29/6/52-20/7/52**U**	Laira Shops
29/8/52-12/9/52**U**	Laira Shops
16/10/52-30/10/52**LC**	Newton Abbot Factory
15/1/53-24/2/53**LC**	Swindon Factory
17/6/53-11/9/53**HG**	Swindon Factory
26/12/53-3/1/54**U**	Laira Shops
8/5/54-30/5/54**U**	Laira Shops
16/6/54-10/8/54**LC**	Swindon Factory
29/9/54-5/11/54**LC**	Old Oak Common Shops
11/4/55-16/6/55**HI**	Swindon Factory
6/9/55-20/10/55**LC**	Swindon Factory
30/12/55-2/1/56**U**	Laira Shops
25/1/56-21/2/56**LC**	Old Oak Common Shops
26/4/56-4/6/56**U**	Bath Road Shops
19/6/56-11/7/56**U**	Southall Shops
12/9/56-12/10/56**U**	Newton Abbot
24/1/57-20/3/57**HG**	Swindon Factory
18/4/57-21/4/57**U**	Laira Shops
28/8/57-11/9/57**U**	Old Oak Common Shops
11/2/58-26/2/58**U**	Taunton Shops
22/7/58-18/9/58**HI**	Swindon Factory
28/10/58-4/12/58**HI**	Swindon Factory
29/1/60-13/4/60**HI**	Swindon Factory
22/2/61-21/3/61**U**	Stafford Road
24/4/61-16/5/61**U**	Old Oak Common Shops
10/10/61-27/10/61**U**	Canton Shops

Boilers and mileages
First	4687*	
26/2/32		96,552
5/7/33		162,665
24/1/35	4672	237,871
29/5/36		312,278
14/4/38	4668	411,054
23/6/39		472,231
3/12/40		554,714
14/3/42		637,629
4/6/43	4690	689,241
4/10/44	4677	735,643
14/5/46	4663	805,304
11/9/47	4679	864,212
6/4/49	4690	941,557
7/11/50	4694	1,015,772
23/1/52	4684	1,074,755
11/9/53	8611*	1,144,028
16/6/55		1,236,039
20/3/57	8605	1,320,206
18/9/58		1,408,510
13/4/60	8610	1,475,631

Final mileage 1,570,015

Tenders
First	2552
7/4/33	2549
29/6/35	2553
3/12/40	2763
4/6/43	2643
18/7/44	2649
4/10/44	2790
14/5/46	2733
22/3/47	2905
11/9/47	2762
11/9/53	2905
9/10/54	2710
26/3/55	2694
16/6/55	2763
20/3/57	2531
19/4/58	2393
18/9/58	2625
16/5/59	2846
13/4/60	2839

6024 KING EDWARD I takes water at Old Oak Common in April 1933. Built in June 1930 it spent the first 3½ years at Laira before moving to Newton Abbot in January 1934, staying there until the year following nationalisation when it returned to the Plymouth shed. Colling Turner, Rail Archive Stephenson.

6024 KING EDWARD I at Torquay on the Down 'Torbay Express' which it will work through to the terminus at Kingswear. It bears the double chimney fitted in March 1957 and has the later 1957 BR emblem. The new headboard and chocolate and cream coaches had been introduced on the 'Torbay Express' on 11 June 1956. Formerly a Laira engine, 6024 was transferred to Old Oak Common in August 1954. www.rail-online.co.uk

Still immaculate following a Heavy Intermediate overhaul which lasted from 29 January until 13 April 1960, 6024 KING EDWARD I rests at Laira on 22 April. It had been fitted with a double chimney in March 1957. B.Penney.

6024 KING EDWARD I at Bristol Bath Road on 28 August 1960. It will have worked down on the 'Bristolian' as the reversed headboard shows and the 'A85' reporting number indicates that it will take over the 2.15pm from Weston-super-Mare back to Paddington. www.rail-online.co.uk

6024 KING EDWARD I at Reading on 28 May 1961, had been the first King to work the 'Capitals United Express' up from Cardiff to Paddington when the class was diagrammed for the service in November 1959. It would move from Old Oak to Canton in September 1961 joining six other Kings transferred there after dieselisation displaced them. www.rail-online.co.uk

6024 KING EDWARD I at Stafford Road shed on 10 June 1961, three months before it was transferred from Old Oak to Cardiff Canton. It is one of the two Kings preserved after spending years at Barry scrapyard. It was restored at Quainton Road by the 6024 Preservation Society Ltd and returned to the main line in 1990. On 9 May 1998 6024 would become the first King authenticated as crossing the Royal Albert Bridge into Cornwall when it worked the 'Par King Pioneer' enthusiast special. It was later the first King to reach Penzance, with the 'Penzance Pirate' special, on 19 September 1998. Colour-rail

6025 KING HENRY III

To stock July 1930

Modifications
WB boiler	14/3/52
Double chimney	22/3/57

Livery changes
BR dark blue	30/6/48
BR standard blue	25/8/50
BR green	15/1/54

Allocations
24/7/30	Old Oak Common
10/7/48	Laira
15/7/59	Old Oak Common

Withdrawn
Withdrawn	18/12/62
Cut up Swindon	16/5/64

Repairs
10/9/30-27/9/30**R**	Exeter Shops
10/10/30-22/11/30**L**	Swindon Factory
24/11/30-2/12/30**R**	Swindon Factory
26/10/31-22/12/31**I**	Swindon Factory
24/10/32-25/11/32**L**	Swindon Factory
12/6/33-1/8/33**G**	Swindon Factory
25/11/33-19/12/33**L**	Swindon Factory
5/2/34-19/2/34**R**	Old Oak Common Shops
17/7/34-17/9/34**I**	Swindon Factory
21/2/35-11/3/35**R**	Old Oak Common Shops
15/10/35-28/11/35**I**	Swindon Factory
14/4/36-1/5/36**R**	Old Oak Common Shops
15/6/36-3/7/36**R**	Old Oak Common Shops
29/9/36-20/11/36**L**	Old Oak Common Shops
22/2/37-19/4/37**G**	Swindon Factory
2/4/38-20/5/38**I**	Swindon Factory
20/12/38-7/2/39**R**	Taunton Shops
27/2/39-14/3/39**L**	Swindon Factory
12/5/39-24/6/39**I**	Swindon Factory
1/3/40-16/3/40**R**	Old Oak Common Shops
21/5/40-21/6/40**I**	Swindon Factory
20/1/41-15/3/41**R**	Old Oak Common Shops
23/5/41-26/6/41**R**	Old Oak Common Shops
8/9/41-11/10/41**R**	Old Oak Common Shops
19/11/41-3/1/42**I**	Swindon Factory
21/7/42-8/8/42**R**	Old Oak Common Shops
3/2/43-26/3/43**G**	Swindon Factory
14/5/43-3/6/43**R**	Laira Shops
20/8/43-7/9/43**L**	Old Oak Common Shops
30/4/44-10/6/44**L**	Old Oak Common Shops
22/6/44-3/8/44**R**	Old Oak Common Shops
30/11/44-30/12/44**R**	Old Oak Common
5/2/45-16/3/45**I**	Swindon Factory
7/11/45-24/11/45**R**	Old Oak Common Shops
25/1/46-15/2/46**R**	Old Oak Common Shops
11/3/46-15/4/46**I**	Swindon Factory
24/10/46-10/12/46**L**	Old Oak Common Shops
17/4/47-22/5/47**G**	Swindon Factory
21/11/47-12/12/47**R**	Old Oak Common Shops
29/12/47-13/1/48**R**	Old Oak Common Shops
11/2/48-16/3/48**L**	Swindon Factory
6/5/48-30/6/48**L**	Swindon Factory
12/10/48-19/11/48**R**	Old Oak Common Shops
10/2/49-24/2/49**U**	Laira Shops
18/3/49-27/4/49**HI**	Swindon Factory
1/9/49-23/9/49**U**	Laira Shops
4/12/49-4/1/50**LC**	Swindon Factory
29/3/50-12/4/50**U**	Laira Shops
13/7/50-25/8/50**HG**	Swindon Factory
15/2/51-27/2/51**U**	Laira Shops
5/3/51-25/3/51**U**	Laira Shops
17/4/51-8/5/51**LC**	Swindon Factory
29/6/51-3/8/51**U**	Laira Shops
31/1/52-14/3/52**HG**	Swindon Factory
24/7/52-20/8/52**U**	Laira Shops
18/2/53-20/3/53**LC**	Swindon Factory
15/7/53-31/7/53**U**	Taunton Shops
23/9/53-25/10/53**U**	Laira Shops
25/11/53-15/1/54**HI**	Swindon Factory
15/4/54-6/5/54**U**	Laira Shops
9/8/54-22/8/54**U**	Laira Shops
22/9/54-6/10/54**U**	Taunton Shops
13/12/54-3/2/55**LC**	Swindon Factory
10/5/55-5/7/55**HG**	Swindon Factory
10/11/55-28/12/55**LC**	Swindon Factory
23/1/56-13/2/56**LC**	Old Oak Common Shops
10/3/56-13/4/56**U**	Laira Shops
15/5/56-30/5/56**U**	Laira Shops
20/6/56-19/7/56**U**	Taunton Shops
4/12/56-22/3/57**HI**	Swindon Factory
24/4/57-14/5/57**U**	Bath Road Shops
9/10/57-12/10/57**LC**	Newton Abbot Factory
7/11/57-27/11/57**U**	Laira Shops
14/2/58-13/3/58**U**	Laira Shops
20/5/58-27/8/58**HI**	Swindon Factory
19/2/60-12/5/60**HI**	Swindon Factory
26/8/60-14/9/60**U**	Swindon Factory
20/1/61-3/2/61**U**	Old Oak Common Shops
24/11/61-9/2/62**HG**	Swindon Factory

Boilers and mileages
First	4688*	
22/12/31		80,851
1/8/33	4665	174,916
17/9/34		242,864
28/11/35		330,623
19/4/37	4693	412,300
20/5/38		499,338
24/6/39		572,162
21/6/40		643,403
3/1/42		734,088
26/3/43	4687	805,600
16/3/45		902,323
15/4/46	4690	968,689
22/5/47	4686	1,029,137
30/6/48	4694	1,078,309
27/4/49		1,115,692
25/8/50	4666	1,192,837
14/3/52	4699	1,280,457
15/1/54		1,383,049
5/7/55	8601	1,465,519
22/3/57		1,549,030
27/8/58		1,631,951
12/5/60	4696	1,727,935
9/2/62	8617	1,810,247

Final Mileage	1,836,713

Tenders
First	2553
22/12/31	2428
22/10/32	2395
14/3/39	2440
24/6/39	2730
21/6/41	2406
3/1/42	2775
16/3/45	2733
15/4/46	2694
22/5/47	2772
30/6/48	2875
3/2/55	2763
5/7/55	2544
28/12/55	2905
3/11/56	2762
22/3/57	2776
19/4/58	2681
27/8/58	2817
14/11/59	2667
28/11/59	2745
12/5/60	2725
9/2/62	2835

6025 KING HENRY III passes Taplow with the 5.30pm Paddington to Plymouth express in 1938. It entered traffic in July 1930 and was at Old Oak Common throughout its GWR career, moving to Laira in July 1948. C.R.L. Coles/Rail Archive Stephenson

The newly formed British Railways experimented with ultramarine with cream, red and grey lining (not dissimilar to the old Great Eastern livery) for its principal express locomotives, and this was applied to 6001, 6009, 6025 and 6026. The livery incorporated blue-backed name and cabside number-plates. The tenders were lettered BRITISH RAILWAYS in full using unshaded cream characters. Repainted in June 1948, 6025 KING HENRY III waits to depart from Paddington in 1949. The dark blue was replaced by the first standard BR express livery of light blue in August 1950. www.rail-online.co.uk

The Reporting Number indicates that this is the Fridays Only from Bradford to Paignton headed by 6025 KING HENRY III at Westbury in 1958. 6025 had been fitted with a double chimney in March 1957 and was the next to last King to retain its blue livery which it kept until January 1954. www.rail-online.co.uk

6025 KING HENRY III at Wolverhampton Stafford Road with a 'Cambrian Coast Express' headboard. It had been ousted from its long-standing home at Laira by the new diesels in 1959 and went to Old Oak Common in July. It was withdrawn from there in December 1962, eventually being broken up at Swindon in May 1964. www.rail-online.co.uk

The industrial wasteland at Wednesbury in the background contrasts with a well turned-out 6025 KING HENRY III with a Down express in 1962. This was the last year that the Kings ruled on the West Midlands expresses, as Western diesel-hydraulics took over from 10 September, and all of the class were withdrawn by the end of the year. www.rail-online.co.uk

One of a handful of stations provided especially for football grounds, The Hawthorns was opened on Christmas Day 1931 for the use of supporters travelling to the nearby West Bromwich Albion FC Hawthorns ground, and was open only on match days. The Halt closed in March 1968, but a new station was built there in 1999 when the Midland Metro line was opened. 6025 KING HENRY III roars through with the Down 'Cambrian Coast Express' in 1961. M. Mensing.

6026 KING JOHN

To stock July 1930

Modifications

WB boiler	17/10/56
Double chimney	6/3/58

Livery changes

BR dark blue	1/6/48
BR standard blue	11/11/49
BR green	6/6/52

Allocations

26/7/30	Old Oak Common
30/3/35	Stafford Road
20/10/39	Bath Road
18/2/43	Laira
18/11/59	Old Oak Common

Withdrawn 12/9/62
Cut up at Swindon 28/12/63

Repairs

29/8/30-12/9/30**R**	Reading Shops
20/9/30-9/10/30**L**	Swindon Factory
25/10/30-19/11/30**L**	Swindon Factory
13/2/31-21/2/31**L**	Swindon Factory
13/7/31-24/7/31**L**	Swindon Factory
7/1/32-15/3/32**I**	Swindon Factory
15/11/32-29/11/32**R**	Old Oak Common Shops
27/12/32-27/1/33**L**	Swindon Factory
26/4/33-23/6/33**L**	Swindon Factory
24/10/33-10/1/34**G**	Swindon Factory
8/1/35-19/3/35**I**	Swindon Factory
13/3/36-4/5/36**G**	Swindon Factory
11/8/37-28/9/37**I**	Swindon Factory
24/12/37-10/1/38**L**	Swindon Factory
12/3/38-25/3/38**L**	Swindon Factory
10/8/38-19/9/38**L**	Swindon Factory
12/12/38-3/2/39**G**	Swindon Factory
27/3/39-5/4/39**L**	Stafford Road Factory
6/10/39-20/10/39**R**	Bath Road Shops
13/11/39-4/12/39**R**	Bath Road Shops
14/12/39-6/1/40**R**	Bath Road Shops
20/4/40-30/5/40**L**	Swindon Factory
3/9/40-29/9/40**R**	Bath Road Shops
12/11/40-16/1/41**I**	Swindon Factory
7/4/41-26/5/41**R**	Swindon Factory
13/6/41-12/7/41**R**	Old Oak Common Shops
31/7/41-23/8/41**R**	Bath Road Shops
18/11/41-6/12/41**R**	Bath Road Shops
8/7/42-25/7/42**R**	Bath Road Shops
29/9/42-16/11/42**I**	Swindon Factory
8/1/43-18/2/43**R**	Laira Shops
20/3/43-13/4/43**R**	Taunton Shops
12/6/43-5/7/43**R**	Laira Shops
26/8/43-17/9/43**R**	Old Oak Common Shops
27/9/43-18/11/43**L**	Swindon Factory
20/1/44-29/1/44**R**	Laira Shops
23/3/44-6/4/44**R**	Laira Shops
26/6/44-11/7/44**R**	Newton Abbot Factory
13/7/44-5/9/44**R**	Taunton Shops
20/9/44-24/10/44**R**	Laira Shops
16/12/44-18/1/45**R**	Laira Shops
10/3/45-30/4/45**I**	Swindon Factory
28/5/45-21/6/45**R**	Swindon Factory
18/10/45-1/11/45**R**	Laira Shops
8/1/46-16/2/46**L**	Swindon Factory
27/3/46-18/5/46**L**	Laira Shops
18/5/46-20/6/46**G**	Swindon Factory
11/10/46-8/11/46**L**	Swindon Factory
17/3/47-2/4/47**R**	Laira Shops
9/4/47-25/4/47**R**	Laira Shops
16/5/47-3/7/47**U**	Reading Shops
16/7/47-31/7/47**R**	Old Oak Common Shops
22/10/47-11/11/47**L**	Old Oak Common Shops
2/12/47-16/12/47**R**	Laira Shops
23/12/47-23/12/47**Tender**	Newton Abbot Factory

29/1/48-5/3/48**L**	Laira Shops
1/4/48-1/6/48**I**	Swindon Factory
24/2/49-27/3/49**U**	Laira Shops
7/6/49-24/6/49**U**	Swindon Factory
8/8/49-19/8/49**U**	Laira Shops
24/8/49-23/9/49**U**	Reading Shops
4/10/49-11/11/49**HG**	Swindon Factory
15/5/50-25/5/50**U**	Laira Shops
11/9/50-3/10/50**U**	Old Oak Common Shops
8/1/51-31/1/51**U**	Laira Shops
1/2/51-9/3/51**HI**	Swindon Factory
26/3/51-1/5/51**U**	Bath Road Shops
12/7/51-3/8/51**U**	Laira Shops
4/9/51-4/10/51**U**	Taunton Shops
17/12/51-17/1/52**U**	Laira Shops
19/2/52-13/3/52**U**	Taunton Shops
20/3/52-25/4/52**U**	Taunton Shops
28/4/52-6/6/52**HG**	Swindon Factory
22/12/52-29/1/53**LC**	Swindon Factory
27/4/53-12/5/53**U**	Exeter Shops
18/6/53-28/9/53**HI**	Swindon Factory
31/3/54-26/4/54**LC**	Laira Shops
17/5/54-26/5/54**U**	Laira Shops
21/6/54-18/7/54**U**	Laira Shops
2/10/54-27/10/54**U**	Laira Shops
23/12/54-31/1/55**U**	Bath Road Shops
2/2/55-21/3/55**HI**	Swindon Factory
13/5/55-20/6/55**LC**	Swindon Factory
8/10/55-24/10/55**U**	Laira Shops
14/1/56-27/2/56**LC**	Taunton Shops
30/8/56-17/10/56**HG**	Swindon Factory
25/10/56-29/10/56**LC**	Swindon Factory
25/4/57-13/5/57**U**	Laira Shops
12/11/57-25/11/57**U**	Taunton Shops
3/1/58-6/3/58**HI**	Swindon Factory
9/4/58-24/4/58**U**	Swindon Factory
29/7/58-22/8/58**U**	Laira Shops
14/11/58-3/12/58**U**	Laira Shops
9/4/59-23/4/59**U**	Newton Abbot Factory
23/9/59-18/11/59**HI**	Swindon Factory
13/7/60-19/8/60**LC**	Swindon Factory
21/9/60-4/11/60**LC**	Old Oak Common Shops
6/1/61-10/2/61**U**	Old Oak Common Shops
26/4/61-19/5/61**U**	Old Oak Common Shops
27/8/61-3/1/62**HG**	Swindon Factory
16/5/62-30/5/62**U**	Old Oak Common Shops
30/6/62-19/7/62**U**	Southall Shops

Boilers and mileages

	First	4689*	
15/3/32		89,560	
10/1/34	4692	192,102	
19/3/35		270,834	
4/5/36	4691	339,384	**Tenders**
28/9/37		423,539	First 2554
3/2/39	4677	487,816	24/7/31 2557
16/1/41		567,265	15/3/32 2395
16/11/42		654,988	22/10/32 2428
18/11/43	4662	694,127	26/7/34 2548
30/4/45		757,558	3/2/39 2648
20/6/46	4673	815,897	16/11/42 2772
1/6/48	4693	894,641	30/4/45 2612
11/11/49	4663	960,569	1/6/48 2788
9/3/51	4680	1,042,398	6/6/52 2772
6/6/52	4666	1,097,364	17/10/56 2881
28/9/53		1,163,975	6/3/58 2730
21/3/55	4684	1,248,665	18/11/59 2820
17/10/56	8620	1,336,473	19/8/60 2779
6/3/58		1,417,752	3/1/63 4013
18/11/59	8618	1,511,455	*Changed after withdrawal,*
3/1/62	8623	1,588,879	*presumably for book purposes*
			or part of the plan to send
Final mileage		1,622,350	*most worn-out tenders for scrap.*

6026 KING JOHN takes water from Ruislip troughs with the 6.10pm Paddington to Birmingham Snow Hill express, about 1935. F.R. Hebron, Rail Archive Stephenson.

6026 KING JOHN on the Laira firepits on the evening of 24 April 1956. The gent in the splendid hat is one of Laira's firedroppers, posing for the cameraman with his long-handled shovel. 6026 will have worked down from Paddington to Plymouth and once the fire has been cleared, will be moved up to have its tender refilled and its smokebox cleared of accumulated ash. Note how the ash levels could build up, particularly by the end of a busy day. P. Kerslake, www.rail-online.co.uk

6026 KING JOHN is working back home to Plymouth with the Down 'Cornish Riviera Limited' in summer 1956, after the train's original title was restored and the introduction of 'chocolate and cream' stock to the service. At the extreme right of this view is Sprey Point on the sea wall, formed by Brunel during construction of the line. After a massive rock fall from the cliffs above, rather than removing all the fallen rocks. he built a wall round them and converted the resultant area into what we can still see today. www.rail-online.co.uk

Laira's 6026 KING JOHN had been fitted with a double chimney during a Heavy Overhaul completed in March 1958. It returned to Swindon Works in April for an Unclassified repair and is on a running in turn at Reading. The 'Cordon' gas cylinder wagon is of interest; these were still being used to replenish restaurant car tanks at that time. www.rail-online.co.uk

6026 KING JOHN heads a Plymouth-Paddington train at Dawlish in late 1959 or early 1960. It might have taken on additional coaches from the Torquay line at Newton Abbot where it would have detached the pilot engine which had assisted it over the banks from Plymouth. Note how low the walkway is at this spot, right down at sea level; the houses on the right were damaged during the storms of 2014. www.rail-online.co.uk

6026 KING JOHN going off shed at Old Oak Common to work the 9.10am Paddington-Birkenhead on 28 April 1962. It had been transferred here from Laira in November 1959. The Kings were concentrated at Old Oak in their twilight years, with no less than seventeen there by early 1960, as the new diesel-hydraulics replaced them on the main express duties to the south west. www.rail-online.co.uk

6027 KING RICHARD I

To stock July 1930

Modifications
WB boiler	9/6/53
Double chimney	31/8/56
New front frames, inside cylinders	13/3/58

Livery changes
BR standard blue	12/5/50
BR green	9/6/53

Allocations
9/8/30	Old Oak Common
2/4/44	Newton Abbot
25/12/48	Laira
4/11/59	Old Oak Common
6/1/60	Stafford Road
9/6/60	Old Oak Common
11/12/61	Stafford Road (loan)
19/12/61	Old Oak Common

Withdrawn 21/9/62
Sold to Cox & Danks, Langley Green	16/7/63

Repairs
17/6/31-14/7/31**L**	Swindon Factory
30/12/31-18/1/32**L**	Swindon Factory
5/4/32-31/5/32**I**	Swindon Factory
1/3/33-24/5/33**G**	Swindon Factory
29/6/33-7/7/33**L**	Swindon Factory
22/5/34-10/7/34**I**	Swindon Factory
23/1/35-8/2/35**L**	Swindon Factory
8/4/35-15/4/35**L**	Swindon Factory
27/5/35-12/7/35**G**	Swindon Factory
6/9/35-10/9/35**L**	Swindon Factory
25/8/36-6/10/36**I**	Swindon Factory
4/10/37-19/11/37**G**	Swindon Factory
2/8/38-15/8/38**L**	Old Oak Common Shops
27/9/38-8/11/38**I**	Swindon Factory
14/12/38-31/12/38**Tender**	Old Oak Common Shops
6/3/39-20/3/39**R**	Taunton Shops
1/5/39-13/5/39**L**	Old Oak Common Shops
19/6/39-7/7/39**R**	Old Oak Common Shops
17/10/39-25/11/39**I**	Swindon Factory
18/10/40-20/12/40**G**	Swindon Factory
21/3/41-25/4/51**L**	Swindon Factory
4/12/41-24/12/41**R**	Old Oak Common Shops
4/7/42-20/8/42**I**	Swindon Factory
9/11/43-17/12/43**I**	Swindon Factory
25/2/44-28/3/44**L**	Swindon Factory
10/5/44-25/5/44**R**	Newton Abbot
23/8/44-28/9/44**L**	Swindon Factory
13/4/45-25/5/45**L**	Swindon Factory
30/7/45-13/8/45**R**	Newton Abbot
5/9/45-27/10/45**L**	Bath Road Shops
18/2/46-27/3/46**G**	Swindon Factory
29/7/46-11/8/46**R**	Newton Abbot
2/12/46-18/12/46**R**	Newton Abbot
12/3/47-21/4/47**I**	Swindon Factory
12/6/47-20/6/47**L**	Swindon Factory
29/9/47-16/10/47**R**	Newton Abbot Shops
5/11/47-1/12/47**L**	Swindon Factory
16/12/47-30/1/48**R**	Reading Shops
10/2/48-25/2/48**R**	Exeter Shops
29/9/48-10/11/48**G**	Swindon Factory
24/3/49-7/4/49**U**	Laira Shops
14/6/49-8/7/49**U**	Laira Shops
16/9/49-7/10/49**LC**	Swindon Factory
3/11/49-10/11/49**U**	Laira Shops
1/12/49-30/12/49**LC**	Taunton Shops
5/4/50-12/5/50**HG**	Swindon Factory
16/10/50-31/10/50**U**	Taunton Shops
12/12/50-16/1/51**LC**	Swindon Factory
18/4/51-2/5/51**U**	Laira Shops
6/6/51-26/6/51**U**	Laira Shops
25/9/51-30/10/51**U**	Old Oak Common Shops
2/11/51-7/12/51**HI**	Swindon Factory
15/4/52-29/4/52**U**	Laira Shops
4/8/52-5/9/52**U**	Laira Shops
12/1/53-30/1/53**U**	Exeter Shops
20/2/53-18/3/53**U**	Laira Shops
26/3/53-9/6/53**HG**	Swindon Factory
22/9/53-27/10/53**LC**	Swindon Factory
19/11/53-16/12/53**U**	Laira Shops
23/2/54-30/3/54**LC**	Swindon Factory
7/10/54-24/10/54**U**	Taunton Shops
24/11/54-17/1/55**HI**	Swindon Factory
21/1/55-8/2/55**U**	Swindon Factory
15/2/55-1/3/55**U**	Laira Shops
1/9/55-6/10/55**U**	Taunton Shops
6/1/56-23/2/56**LC**	Laira Shops
19/5/56-31/8/56**HI**	Swindon Factory
14/3/57-26/3/57**U**	Laira Shops
16/10/57-30/10/57**U**	Laira Shops
28/12/57-13/3/58**HG**	Swindon Factory
17/5/58-19/5/58**U**	Laira Shops
16/7/58-31/7/58**U**	Taunton Shops
24/3/59-10/4/59**U**	Laira Shops
31/7/59-25/9/59**HG**	Swindon Factory
1/10/59-15/10/59**U**	Swindon Factory
12/5/60-3/6/60**U**	Stafford Road
9/11/60-6/12/60**U**	Old Oak Common Shops
27/1/61-21/3/61**HI**	Swindon Factory
27/5/61-22/9/61**LC**	Swindon Factory
20/6/62-4/7/62**U**	Old Oak Common Shops

Boilers and mileages
First	4690*	
31/5/32		117,618
24/5/33	4686	180,609
10/7/34		259,430
12/7/35	4673	321,972
6/10/36		412,200
19/11/37	4665	499,557
8/11/38		567,090
25/11/39		633,082
20/12/40	4673	702,997
20/8/42		813,348
17/12/43		906,385
27/3/46	4683	1,003,776
21/4/47	4682	1,064,354
10/11/48	4686	1,127,797
12/5/50	4684	1,211,576
16/3/51		1,256,044
7/12/51	4661	1,278,987
9/6/53	8610	1,350,740
17/1/55		1,433,809
31/8/56	8613	1,505,800
13/3/58	8618	1,610,775
25/9/59	4697	1,706,396
21/3/61		1,779,233
Final mileage		1,836,535

Tenders
First	2555
14/7/31	2547
31/5/32	2556
24/5/33	2547
15/12/34	2442
22/8/36	2612
7/1/39	2402
25/11/39	2742
20/12/40	2733
17/12/43	2710
28/3/44	2815
25/5/45	2726
10/11/48	2759
16/1/51	2707
7/12/51	2630
9/6/53	2715
8/2/55	2875
31/8/56	2800
13/3/58	2792
25/9/59	2815
21/3/61	2431
22/9/61	2861

In 1934, the GREAT WESTERN lettering and badge on the tenders was replaced by a more fashionable, circular totem formed by the letters 'GWR' - officially described as a roundel but popularly known as the 'shirt button' emblem as illustrated by 6027 KING RICHARD I at Leamington Spa in 1938.

6027 KING RICHARD I restarts the 'Cornish Riviera' at Newton Abbot on Christmas Eve 1953. 6027's pilot engine, which would have assisted over the South Devon banks from Plymouth, has been uncoupled and gone over to Newton Abbot shed leaving the King to run non-stop through the station (it was not booked to call there). 6027 had undergone a Heavy General from March to June of 1953 when it was fitted with a 'WB' 4-row superheater boiler and repainted from light blue to green livery. It was back in the Works again in the autumn for a Light Casual repair, and was still not right because it was then in Laira's Shop from 19 November until 16 December for an Unclassified repair. P. Kerslake/www.rail-online.co.uk

Laira's 6027 KING RICHARD I restarts the 7.15am Plymouth-Paddington from Westbury in 1955. www.rail-online.co.uk

The Down 'Cornish Riviera', diverted because of engineering work at Reading to the Bristol line, away from its normal Berks and Hants line, in 1956. 6027 KING RICHARD I is entering Chippenham from the London direction; Westinghouse Brake and Signal Company factory on the left, the line to Calne in the right background with the branch signal and main line signal both visible behind the coaches. There is a Travelling Post Office exchange apparatus with the net, warning lamp and ladder clearly shown, just ahead of the King. www.rail-online.co.uk

6027 KING RICHARD I is watched by a large group of platform-enders at Paddington as it gets underway with the 'Cornish Riviera Limited' on 13 April 1957. The double chimney had been fitted during a Heavy Intermediate overhaul completed in August 1956. Colour-rail.

6027 KING RICHARD I on a Paddington-Wolverhampton express drifting through the familiar lunarscape at Wednesbury. It had been allocated to Old Oak Common since June 1959, apart from two short spells at Stafford Road in 1960 and 1961. www.rail-online.co.uk

6028 KING HENRY II

(renamed KING GEORGE VI on 12/1/37)
To stock July 1930

Modifications
WB boiler	13/3/52
Double chimney	31/1/57

Livery changes
BR standard blue	23/11/50
BR green	17/11/53

Allocations
31/7/30	Old Oak Common
27/4/44	Newton Abbot
25/12/48	Old Oak Common
13/9/60	Canton
15/6/62	Old Oak Common

Withdrawn
Withdrawn	20/11/62
Sold to Birds of Risca	3/6/64

Repairs
5/8/30-16/9/30**L**	Old Oak Common Shops
29/10/30-17/12/30**L**	Swindon Factory
19/1/32-24/3/32**I**	Swindon Factory
2/2/33-15/3/33**L**	Swindon Factory
28/3/33-7/4/33**L**	Swindon Factory
20/9/33-3/11/33**G**	Swindon Factory
27/2/34-14/3/34**L**	Swindon Factory
14/8/34-14/9/34**L**	Swindon Factory
11/10/34-16/11/34**R**	Old Oak Common Shops
31/1/35-4/4/35**I**	Swindon Factory
2/7/35-9/7/35**L**	Swindon Factory
20/12/35-23/1/36**L**	Swindon Factory
3/6/36-7/8/36**G**	Swindon Factory
24/4/37-4/5/37**R**	Taunton Shops
7/5/37-19/5/37**L**	Swindon Factory
2/6/37-18/6/37**R**	Old Oak Common
15/11/37-3/1/38**I**	Swindon Factory
22/4/38-25/5/38**R**	Old Oak Common Shops
19/9/38-8/10/38**R**	Old Oak Common Shops
13/12/38-23/12/38**L**	Swindon Factory
21/2/39-4/4/39**G**	Swindon Factory
1/4/40-21/5/40**I**	Swindon Factory
3/12/40-13/2/41**I**	Swindon Factory
1/9/41-27/9/41**R**	Old Oak Common Shops
13/10/41-1/12/41**L**	Swindon Factory
3/3/42-4/5/42**L**	Swindon Factory
4/7/42-18/7/42**R**	Old Oak Common Shops
10/8/42-31/8/42**L**	Swindon Factory
2/10/42-22/10/42**L**	Swindon Factory
15/12/42-29/1/43**I**	Swindon Factory
9/3/43-30/3/43**L**	Swindon Factory
1/5/43-26/5/43**L**	Swindon Factory
5/1/44-14/1/44**L**	Old Oak Common Shops
11/4/44-27/4/44**R**	Newton Abbot
18/8/44-10/10/44**G**	Swindon Factory
26/10/45-12/11/45**R**	Newton Abbot
25/3/46-1/5/56**I**	Swindon Factory
24/7/46-22/8/46**L**	Swindon Factory
30/7/47-15/9/47**G**	Swindon Factory
30/9/47-30/9/47**L**	Newton Abbot Factory
9/4/48-21/4/48**R**	Laira Shops
25/2/49-28/3/49**HG**	Swindon Factory
27/4/49-12/5/49**LC**	Swindon Factory
17/11/49-6/12/49**U**	Old Oak Common Shops
19/4/50-10/5/50**U**	Old Oak Common Shops
22/6/50-21/7/50**U**	Bath Road Shops
10/10/50-23/11/50**HI**	Swindon Factory
29/7/51-24/8/51**LC**	Swindon Factory
10/9/51-1/10/51**U**	Taunton Shops
28/11/51-23/12/51**U**	Taunton Shops
18/1/52-13/3/52**HG**	Swindon Factory
26/8/52-18/9/52**LC**	Swindon Factory
13/10/52-17/11/52**U**	Laira Shops
6/1/53-3/2/53**U**	Old Oak Common Shops
9/4/53-20/5/53**LC**	Swindon Factory
4/8/53-1/9/53**U**	Old Oak Common Shops
16/9/53-17/11/53**HI**	Swindon Factory
3/9/54-23/9/54**U**	Old Oak Common Shops
1/11/54-10/12/54**U**	Old Oak Common Shops
5/1/55-7/2/55**U**	Old Oak Common Shops
19/3/55-3/5/55**HI**	Swindon Factory
19/5/55-27/6/55**U**	Swindon Factory
19/7/55-8/8/55**U**	Swindon Factory
12/9/55-14/10/55**U**	Old Oak Common Shops
24/10/55-2/12/55**U**	Old Oak Common Shops
25/1/56-24/2/56**LC**	Old Oak Common Shops
23/7/56-12/9/56**U**	Laira Shops
12/11/56-31/1/57**HG**	Swindon Factory
16/10/57-6/11/57**U**	Old Oak Common Shops
2/1/58-12/2/58**LC**	Swindon Factory
24/6/58-4/9/58**HI**	Swindon Factory
18/9/59-9/10/59**U**	Old Oak Common Shops
12/11/59-27/11/59**U**	Old Oak Common Shops
20/3/60-9/6/60**HI**	Swindon Factory
2/3/61-21/3/61**U**	Canton Shops
5/5/61-20/5/61**U**	Canton Shops
24/8/61-4/10/61**U**	Canton Shops
18/11/61-4/1/62**HG**	Swindon Factory
16/4/62-10/5/62**U**	Swindon Factory

Boilers and mileages
	First	4691*	
24/3/32			89,536
3/11/33	4688		187,149
4/4/35			263,129
7/8/36	4689		349,702
3/1/38			450,783
4/4/39	4671		527,923
21/5/40			608,725
13/2/41			645,334
29/1/43			743,510
10/10/44	4663		819,392
1/5/46	4687		892,916
15/9/47	4683		949,628
28/3/49	4671		1,036,412
23/11/50			1,125,284
13/3/52	4698		1,187,003
17/11/53			1,253,058
3/5/55	8612		1,327,735
31/1/57	8628		1,388,243
4/9/58			1,471,209
9/6/60	8613		1,555,344
4/1/62	8620		1,634,195

Final mileage	1,663,271

Tenders
First	2556
30/6/31	2388
24/3/32	2548
3/11/33	2557
19/5/37	2724
15/11/37	?
23/12/38	2609
4/4/39	2726
21/5/40	2695
13/2/41	2543
1/12/41	2772
22/10/42	2648
29/1/43	2643
30/3/43	2763
26/5/43	2790
10/10/44	2606
1/5/46	2762
15/9/47	2905
13/3/52	2648
27/2/54	2800
27/6/55	2694
31/1/57	2620
30/11/57	2565
4/9/58	2427
10/59	2745
11/59	2667
9/6/60	2695
5/1/62	2544

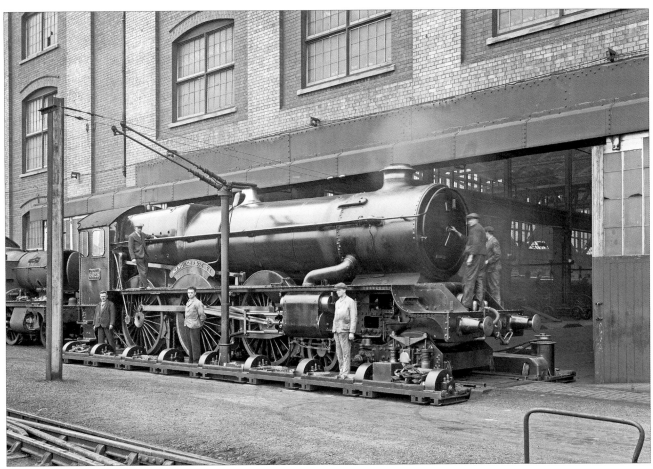

6028, the former KING HENRY II, on the traverser at Swindon Works just after receiving its KING GEORGE VI nameplates on 11 January 1937. Rail Archive Stephenson.

Old Oak Common's 6028 KING GEORGE VI passing Leamington shed in the early 1950s with a Down express made up of Collett and Hawksworth coaches and BR Mark 1s. The remains of a chalked-on Train Reporting number '823' show that it had recently worked the Saturdays Only Birmingham-Paignton. Except for four years allocated to Newton Abbot from April 1944 to December 1948, 6028 had been at Old Oak Common since new in 1930. www.rail-online.co.uk

6028 KING GEORGE VI approaching Pengam Road bridge in the northern suburbs of Cardiff with the 7.20 pm Cardiff to Crewe mail on 13 June 1962. It was transferred back to Old Oak from Canton two days later. R.O. Tuck, Rail Archive Stephenson.

6028 KING GEORGE VI at the head of a packed Laira coaling line, leading a Castle and a second King in May 1956. It had worked down to Plymouth from Paddington and judging by the amounts of ash, it's been a busy day. 6028 has had, or is waiting to have, its smokebox cleared and the white ash on the cabside indicates that its fire has already been cleaned. Note the steam lance by the wall, used for clearing the boiler tubes which would be attached to the small steam valve on the left-hand side of the smokebox door. P. Kerslake, www.rail-online.co.uk

6028 KING GEORGE VI at Bath with the 7.00am Weston-super-Mare to Paddington, probably shortly after completion of a Heavy Intermediate overhaul in June 1955. The mechanical lubricators for cylinders, valves and regulators have been repositioned on the running plate ahead of the right-hand outside steam pipe. In the background is the Grade II listed Royal Hotel which first opened in 1846. www.rail-online.co.uk

There is a considerable loss of steam from both inside and outside cylinders as 6028 KING GEORGE VI comes up through Cornwood, about half-way up the climb to the summit of Hemerdon Bank, on 12 May 1956. The train is the 4.10pm Plymouth-Paddington and the King does not have a pilot engine over the banks to Newton Abbot; this train was invariably headed by a single King at this time, rarely exceeding the ten coach limit for the class over those banks. The 4.10 had started out as the 1.30pm from Penzance; coaches, including a restaurant car, were added at Plymouth and a portion from Kingswear at Newton Abbot from where the formation was typically a prodigious fourteen vehicles. P. Kerslake, www.rail-online.co.uk

The driver of Old Oak's 6028 KING GEORGE VI has shut off steam and is giving the photographer a wave as he runs along the sea wall at Teignmouth with the 9.20am from St Ives to Paddington. The King would have had a pilot engine for the South Devon banks, but this would have been detached at Newton Abbot when the additional coaches were added. The double chimney was fitted in January 1957 and this picture was probably taken during the summer of that year. It was one of six Kings transferred from Old Oak to Cardiff Canton in September 1960; it returned to Old Oak in June 1962 but worked only for a short time before going into store on 3 August, to be withdrawn three months later. www.rail-online.co.uk

6029 KING STEPHEN

(renamed KING EDWARD VIII on 14/5/36)
To stock August 1930

Modifications
WB boiler	6/10/53
Double chimney	18/12/57

Livery changes
BR standard blue	29/6/50
BR green	19/5/52

Allocations
8/9/30	Old Oak Common
10/9/30	On loan for Liverpool & Manchester centenary exhibition
7/10/30	Old Oak Common
14/10/39	Laira
21/5/59	Old Oak Common

Withdrawn
Withdrawn	24/7/62
Sold to J.Cashmore of Newport	14/11/62

Repairs

29/8/30-3/9/30**L**	Swindon Factory
30/10/31-19/11/31**R**	Old Oak Common Shops
8/2/32-14/4/32**I**	Swindon Factory
11/1/33-28/1/33**R**	Old Oak Common Shops
6/2/33-10/3/33**L**	Swindon Factory
14/10/33-1/12/33**G**	Swindon Factory
9/4/34-17/5/34**L**	Swindon Factory
20/11/34-22/1/35**I**	Swindon Factory
28/6/35-11/7/35**L**	Swindon Factory
5/12/35-14/12/35**L**	Swindon Factory
12/2/36-25/4/36**G**	Swindon Factory
24/11/36-9/12/36**L**	Swindon Factory
10/5/37-23/6/37**I**	Swindon Factory
15/11/37-1/12/37**R**	Exeter Shops
2/3/38-23/3/38**R**	Old Oak Common Shops
7/6/38-4/8/38**G**	Swindon Factory
26/4/39-12/5/39**L**	Old Oak Common Shops
15/5/39-30/6/39**I**	Swindon Factory
23/5/40-27/6/40**I**	Swindon Factory
22/5/41-18/6/41**R**	Laira Shops
6/9/41-10/11/41**G**	Swindon Factory
16/1/42-31/1/42**R**	Laira Shops
13/3/42-11/4/42**L**	Swindon Factory
9/9/42-24/9/42**R**	Laira Shops
26/3/43-17/5/43**I**	Swindon Factory
28/9/43-21/10/43**R**	Laira Shops
28/12/43-21/1/44**R**	Laira Shops
23/3/44-6/4/44**R**	Laira Shops
30/6/44-16/8/44**L**	Swindon Factory
5/12/44-21/12/44**R**	Laira Shops
4/2/45-28/2/45**R**	Laira Shops
25/6/45-20/7/45**R**	Laira Shops
27/7/45-10/8/45**R**	Old Oak Common Shops
28/8/45-10/10/45**G**	Swindon Factory
14/2/46-2/3/46**R**	Laira Shops
8/7/46-3/8/46**R**	Laira Shops
30/8/46-18/10/46**L**	Taunton Shops
28/10/46-11/11/46**R**	Laira Shops
29/11/46-8/1/47**I**	Swindon Factory
30/1/47-6/2/47**L**	Swindon Factory
26/5/47-3/7/47**R**	Laira Shops
2/6/47-10/6/47**Tender**	Newton Abbot Factory
15/7/47-30/7/47**R**	Laira Shops
8/8/47-16/8/47**R**	Laira Shops
8/10/47-29/10/47**R**	Laira Shops
8/12/47-23/12/47**L**	Swindon Factory
30/12/47-13/1/48**R**	Laira Shops
28/2/48-14/3/48**R**	Laira Shops
20/5/48-17/6/48**L**	Swindon Factory
18/10/48-5/11/48**R**	Laira Shops
26/1/49-28/2/49**HG**	Swindon Factory
27/6/49-23/7/49**U**	Laira Shops
25/10/49-9/11/49**U**	Laira Shops
4/12/49-26/1/50**U**	Laira Shops
29/1/50-17/2/50**U**	Old Oak Common Shops
7/3/50-30/3/50**U**	Old Oak Common Shops
28/4/50-17/5/50**U**	Laira Shops
2/6/50-29/6/50**LC**	Swindon Factory
10/9/50-10/10/50**U**	Laira Shops
10/11/50-22/12/50**HG**	Swindon Factory
4/6/51-19/6/51**U**	Laira Shops
16/10/51-29/10/51**U**	Swindon Factory
23/12/51-7/1/52**U**	Laira Shops
5/3/52-23/3/52**U**	Laira Shops
31/3/52-19/5/52**HI**	Swindon Factory
5/11/52-26/11/52**U**	Laira Shops
23/1/53-5/3/53**LC**	Swindon Factory
6/7/53-18/7/53**U**	Laira Shops
5/8/53-6/10/53**HG**	Swindon Factory
1/1/54-27/1/54**U**	Taunton Shops
17/5/54-21/5/54**LC**	Newton Abbot Shops
26/6/54-15/7/54**U**	Taunton Shops
23/7/54-6/8/54**U**	Reading Shops
19/8/54-28/9/54**LC**	Bath Road Shops
12/10/54-12/11/54**U**	Old Oak Common Shops
26/11/54-6/12/54**U**	Laira Shops
23/2/55-3/3/55**U**	Laira Shops
20/4/55-27/5/55**HI**	Swindon Factory
31/10/55-16/11/55**U**	Laira Shops
27/1/56-11/2/56**LC**	Bath Road Shops
8/3/56-22/3/56**U**	Laira Shops
6/4/56-25/4/56**U**	Bath Road Shops
19/5/56-21/5/56**U**	Laira Shops
16/8/56-1/10/56**HI**	Swindon Factory
21/3/57-15/4/57**U**	Bath Road Shops
12/6/57-21/6/57**U**	Laira Shops
8/11/57-18/12/57**HG**	Swindon Factory
3/2/58-14/2/58**LC**	Newton Abbot Shops
9/7/58-22/7/58**U**	Laira Shops
3/10/58-11/10/58**U**	Laira Shops
26/11/58-12/12/58**U**	Newton Abbot Factory
20/12/58-9/1/59**U**	Swindon Factory
6/2/59-21/5/59**HI**	Swindon Factory
30/12/59-30/12/59**U**	Newton Abbot Factory
13/5/60-14/6/60**U**	Old Oak Common Shops
14/10/60-1/11/60**U**	Old Oak Common Shops
14/1/61-29/3/61**HG**	Swindon Factory
16/4/62-2/5/62**U**	Old Oak Common Shops

Boilers and mileages

Date	Boiler	Mileage
First	4692*	
14/4/32		97,026
1/12/33	4691	199,738
22/1/35		268,559
25/4/36	4677	346,427
23/6/37		427,954
4/8/38	4672	504,968
30/6/39		566,617
27/6/40		639,108
10/11/41	4686	732,110
8/5/43		823,725
10/10/45	4666	952,568
8/1/47	4665	1,017,522
28/2/49	4668	1,115,790
22/12/50	4675	1,200,487
19/5/52	4667	1,277,155
6/10/53	8613	1,353,813
27/5/55	4696	1,449,091
1/10/56		1,537,135
18/12/57	8604	1,624,250
21/5/59		1,708,338
29/3/61	8611	1,789,263
Final mileage		1,859,278

Tenders

Date	Tender
First	2413
29/7/33	2388
1/12/33	2392
30/6/39	2606
10/11/41	2716
17/6/48	2776
27/5/55	2723
1/10/56	2772
9/1/59	2904
21/5/59	2865
3/12/60	2740
29/3/61	2580

Below. 6029 KING STEPHEN on the turntable at the LMS Agecroft shed in September 1930 before being exhibited at the Liverpool & Manchester Railway Centenary. It was renamed KING EDWARD VIII on 14 May 1936, several months after the death of King George V in January of that year. Eric Mason/Rail Archive Stephenson.

Bottom. 6029 KING EDWARD VIII at Exeter St David's with a Down express on 22 May 1954. It had regained green livery in May 1952 and had been fitted with a 'WB' higher superheat boiler in October 1953. Initial Photographics.

An immaculate 6029 KING EDWARD VIII awaiting the arrival at Plymouth North Road of the Up 'Cornish Riviera Limited', the 10.00am from Penzance, which it will work forward non-stop to Paddington. 6029 had received a Heavy Intermediate Overhaul that was completed on 1 October 1956 and the photograph was probably taken the same month. The notice visible on the railings asks enginemen to keep noise and smoke to a minimum whilst waiting on these sidings for the comfort of patients in the Eye Infirmary, the red brick building seen in the background. P. Kerslake/www.rail-online.co.uk

Waiting at Westbury, 6029 KING EDWARD VIII is at the head of the 8.30am from Plymouth to Paddington on 21 October 1956. It was a Laira engine at this period, before a transfer to Old Oak Common in May of 1959. 6029 was one of the sixteen Kings which did not receive replacement front frames and new inside cylinders in the late 1950s. www.rail-online.co.uk

6029 KING EDWARD VIII at West Bromwich with the 11.40am Birkenhead-Paddington. It had been fitted with a double chimney in December 1957. It was in its second spell at Old Oak Common, the first lasting from new in 1930 until the outbreak of the Second World War. M.Mensing.

Following twenty years at Laira, from 1939 to May 1959, 6029 KING EDWARD VIII spent its final four years at Old Oak Common. At Princes Risborough in 1962, it has steam to spare working the 'Inter City' from Wolverhampton to Paddington. www.rail-online.co.uk

Endpiece

6021 KING RICHARD II passes Westbourne Park on the approach to Paddington with the 7.15am from Plymouth in August 1948. Colling Turner, Rail Archive Stephenson.